92                 $31.95
SCH   Schulze, Tilli Horn

Tilli's story: my thoughts are free
        38656000043563

DATE DUE

92                 $31.95
SCH   Schulze, Tilli Horn

Tilli's story: my thoughts are free
        38656000043563

DATE DUE	BORROWER'S NAME

Tilli's Story

Tilli's Story

✦

My Thoughts Are Free

By Lorna Collier and Tilli Schulze

iUniverse, Inc.
New York Lincoln Shanghai

Tilli's Story
My Thoughts Are Free

iUniverse, Inc.

For information address:
iUniverse, Inc.
2021 Pine Lake Road, Suite 100
Lincoln, NE 68512
www.iuniverse.com

ISBN: 0-595-32270-0 (pbk)
ISBN: 0-595-66504-7 (cloth)

Printed in the United States of America

To Herbert, Barbara, Erich, Regina, Kirsten and Monika.
This is for you.

Contents

Part II

Part III

Part IV

Author's Note

I am not a hero.

I did not suffer more than other German children did during World War II and the Russian takeover of East Germany. In fact, I'm sure I suffered less than some. There were certainly quite a few children who underwent even more horrible ordeals than I did.

I didn't save anybody's life; I didn't perform any dramatic rescues, other than my own. Nobody in my family died.

Why, then, should you read my story?

Because what I went through is typical not only of what many German children experienced during World War II and its aftermath, but also of what all children endure during any war—a suffering that is unforgivable but also, unfortunately, often overlooked and shrugged aside as an unavoidable cost of war.

I first began this project in 1991, two years after the Berlin Wall came down. Once that happened—once Germany ceased to be split into West and East, free and not free—I was able to go home again.

For the first time in 40 years, I saw the small farming village where I grew up. I saw old friends and neighbors and relatives who had not been able to escape, as I had. I visited my brother's grave. I stepped inside my old house. I walked through the park, which had been such a refuge for me as a child.

And I remembered.

I remembered what was done to my family and to countless innocent families throughout my country. We suffered under both Hitler and Stalin. Neither of these rulers believed we should have the right to think freely, to act freely, to travel and work and write and worship and live as we wished.

I remembered also what was done to me. My innocence was taken. My childhood was taken. My life was almost taken.

I never shared with my children and with even my closest friends much of what happened to me during the war and the Russian takeover. I kept it buried. I moved on with my life. I tried to forget.

But the memories wouldn't die—and I've realized I can't let them.

I want my family to know the truth. I want the world to know. Maybe it's naive to think that telling stories like mine will make a difference, but I hope this will be the case.

We need to never forget the importance of freedom, which is sometimes taken for granted in America. We need to realize that war makes everyone its victim, that real people on both sides, including innocent children, suffer the battles their leaders plan.

I didn't want to write a political book. I am not out to defend all Germans for their actions during World War II, nor to castigate all Russians for the inhumane behavior some Russian soldiers displayed towards me. I most certainly am not trying to downplay or diminish in any way the appalling sufferings of the Jews and other Holocaust victims.

I simply want to tell my story, my personal story: to relay to you what I saw as a child in Germany, as a child of war, and to try to convey the lessons, the truths, that I learned through that experience.

Although this story contains a lot of sad and terrible things, I don't want this to be a depressing book. I see my story as being about survival and the triumph of the human spirit, about the way we can overcome anything if we keep fighting, even if our battles can only be waged within our thoughts.

That's the way my mother fought. This book is named for her, for her softly humming resistance to those who would try to take control of her mind.

In writing this book, I tried to reconstruct what happened to me from the war's beginning in 1939 through the first five years of the Russian occupation. As best as I could, I tried to remember conversations and feelings that I had. Some of these conversations, of necessity, have been recreated. I could not always remember word for word what people said, but I could remember the gist of an encounter, the mood of a moment, the force of a meeting. All of the major events in this book happened, and they happened to me.

This is my story.

—Tilli Horn Schulze

My Thoughts Are Free

My thoughts are free, who can guess them?
They fly by, like nightly shadows.
No one can guess them, no hunter can shoot them.
It's a fact, my thoughts are free.
I think what I want and what makes me happy,
But orderly and quietly to myself.
Because my thoughts tear down fortresses and walls,
My thoughts are free.
—German folk song, author unknown

PART I

Prologue

It is night and they are back. Enemy planes, growling in the distance: thunder that does not stop, but grows closer, closer, until it invades my sleep, until I jump up in bed, my dreams crashing away into broken bits of terror.

My mother stirs next to me. She pats my arm; she is awake, too, but we don't say anything. I struggle to breathe normally. She is silent.

I curl into a ball, my comforter tight to my chin in the blackness. The thunder booms louder, louder, and there is nothing to do but wait for whatever is going to happen next.

Now the window glass is rattling. The floor is vibrating. The roar is so near—I can hear it, feel it, all around me; I just can't see it. I wish I could scream and I wish I could cry but I've done that before and I know it's no use.

I shut my eyes, put my hands to my ears, trying to silence the sounds, trying to find a peaceful place in the darkness of my mind, and somehow the minutes pass and then finally the grinding and rumbling and roaring begins to fade. I let out a breath and start to relax. Maybe I will be able to get back to sleep before dawn, before my chores, before the two-mile walk to school.

Bang! Crash!

The house shakes, the sounds blast—above me, behind me, below me. Again, again, again. Horrible thuds like giants falling, the earth opening, splitting, dear Lord please help me help me help me.

Bombs. These are the sounds of bombs falling, exploding. I have heard these sounds before, but always they have been quieter, from a greater distance. Now they sound like they are right next to us, and moving closer.

Again I try to block from my ears, my mind, this terrible noise, try not to think where the bombs are falling—on empty fields or deserted businesses or vacant school buildings? Or on homes, where people are sleeping, where children—children like me—are hiding in their beds, perhaps still shaking off the fragments of their dreams?

I am ten years old. I have been living with this war since I was five. When the airplanes started flying over us, everyone said they would never bomb us, that our little farm village in northeastern Germany was too small for them to care about. We would be safe, everybody said. Even my mother said it, holding me against her, telling me to hush and not worry.

Now she lies still in bed, frozen just as I am frozen. We have no bomb shelter to protect us, like the people in the cities have. We don't even have a basement. We have nowhere to hide.

On the wall beside me is a picture of Jesus hanging on the cross. I can barely make it out in the darkness. Because of the war, we have to keep black shades on the windows at night and aren't allowed to use electricity or candles. But my eyes are used to darkness by now and besides, I know this picture so well. I have stared at it so often during the past few years, ever since I began sleeping downstairs with my mother in her bedroom.

I've always been unsettled by this picture—by the blood dripping down Jesus' wrists, but mostly by the sorrow in His eyes. I used to wonder what it would feel like to be nailed to a cross, trapped and helpless for the world to see.

"I am sweet and pure and my heart belongs to Jesus alone," I whisper, repeating the prayer I have been saying every night, for as long as I can remember.

I hope it will help; that Jesus, somewhere, is listening.

And still the bombs fall. Over and over, on and on, death free-falling from the sky. I start to shake, my teeth to chatter, and I know that I can't stay here, in this moment. I force myself to stop listening, stop thinking, worrying, picturing what is happening outside. Instead, I create places in my mind, beautiful safe places where I can laugh and play until the bombs stop and I can go home again.

Sometimes I visit a house made entirely of the sweetest candy, a house I can eat my way through. Other times, I am in the meadow, riding Max, one of our two horses, the other horse, Moritz, running free beside me, all muscles and mane and joy. I take the horses into the pond for a glorious cooling splash, then lie in the long grass, surrounded by weeds and wildflowers, trying to taste the warm breeze with my tongue, as happy as it is possible to be.

My dreams mix with memories—of the days before war came, of the early days of the war when my life was still more or less normal—and I wonder if will ever be safe and happy again.

1

The first time I heard about the war, I was making sand castles in the schoolyard. It was a bright fall day, sunshine left over from summer warming the top of my head as I mounded the damp brown sand beside me into a grand palace. A princess lived inside, a gentle, golden-haired princess in an emerald gown. All around the castle lurked evil, fire-breathing dragons, but my princess was safe, because the walls of my fortress were so strong.

Hans ran up to me, panting.

"Guess what, Tilli!" he yelled. "Germany is at war!"

I stared at him. I didn't know exactly what a war was, though I had an idea it had something to do with soldiers and guns.

"Really?" I said, not sure whether to believe Hans, who liked to tell stories.

"My cousin might go fight in it," Hans said. "My aunt is home now crying."

That scared me. I'd never seen an adult cry before.

Hans ran off to tell the others. I went back to pouring sand on my castle, making it taller, wider, stronger, until it was perfect. Soon I'd forgotten what Hans had said.

After kindergarten, I ran home through the meadow to my street, then turned onto the road and walked the rest of the way under the cool canopy of the linden trees, which arched across the road like a lacy green rainbow, their leaves like hundreds of tiny hearts. I hurried down the path past our gate, skipped through my mother's flower garden, which filled our front yard, and went inside to the kitchen.

At this time of day, my mother usually would be getting dinner ready. When she'd see me, she'd give me a hug and kiss and sometimes had a special snack ready for me. But that afternoon, she wasn't there. The great stove was cold and silent. The long wooden table stood empty and bare.

I ran outside to the barnyard. "Mami! Mami!" I called.

A yellow barn cat streaked across the yard and shot up at tree. We had so many barn cats I never bothered to name them. Bello, our big outdoor dog, ran

5

up to me, his tongue hanging out and his tail wagging. I patted his thick, solid head. There was no sign of my mother or father anywhere.

I walked back into the kitchen. "Mami?" I called again into the stillness.

Then I heard my mother's footsteps, coming from the living room in the back of the house, which we never used during the daytime. Following close behind were the clicking toenails of Fanni, Mami's pet dog, who was always nearby.

"Hello, Tilli, did you have a good day?" Mami said, holding out her arms to me.

"Where were you?" I asked, hugging her, then reaching down to pet Fanni.

"Just listening to the radio."

I noticed, then, the very faint scratchy sounds of crackling men's voices. My parents kept a big radio in the living room, which we only listened to at night, when music came on.

"That idiot Hitler!" my father shouted from the living room. That was also odd, that my father should be home this early and not at work in the fields. I was used to him yelling about Hitler, who had been ruling Germany ever since I could remember. My father hated Hitler, and often said so, which seemed to terrify my mother. "Hush now!" she would hiss at him, looking over her shoulder as though she expected Hitler himself to come bursting through our door to punish my father for his words.

I began helping my mother set the table for supper, putting out plates for my parents; Wilhelm, our farmhand, who lived with us; my brothers, Heinz and Helmut, who were eleven and twelve and still in school—the elementary school, not the kindergarten that I went to; Paula, my older sister, who was fifteen and finished with school; and for myself, Tilli, age five, youngest child in the Horn family.

As my mother handed me the dishes, she began singing softly. It was a song she had been singing a lot lately. *"My thoughts are free, who can guess them? They fly by, like nightly shadows."*

Sunlight filtered through the delicate lace curtains at the window and glinted off the silverware, casting prisms of fiery color—orange and yellow and red—about the room, onto my mother's face. I suddenly remembered what Hans had told me in the sandbox.

"Mami, Hans said that Germany is in a war."

My mother stopped singing. She set down her spatula, then lowered herself beside me, frowning deeply. "Tilli, some people have crazy ideas. They think they can go to another country and take the land and make it theirs again."

I didn't understand.

My mother tried again. "Yes, Germany is in a war. We invaded Poland. But it will be over very soon."

"Hans says his cousin might go fight," I said. "Will Helmut and Heinz and Hugo go fight, too?"

My brother Hugo, who was thirteen, was deaf and didn't live with us, except for holidays and other breaks from his special school, which was in another city several hours away by train.

"No, we don't need to worry about the boys," my mother said. "They're much too young. The war will be over long before they would have to fight in it."

My mother went back to the stove. I wandered into the living room, where I was surprised to see not only my father but also Wilhelm in the room, both of them hunched next to the radio.

I tried to sit on my father's lap, but he pushed me away. "Not now!" he snapped, waving me away with his hand.

"We're busy listening to some very important news," whispered Wilhelm, more gently.

Besides being our field hand, Wilhelm was also my godfather. When I was two, he had given me a doll and stroller. They were the only toys I had ever had. The doll had porcelain skin, long brown hair the same color as mine, gold-and-brown flecked eyes with real human eyelashes, and a blue-and-white dirndl dress. I named her Doris. My mother said Doris and her brown leather stroller were much too fine to play with or even touch, so I kept her propped in the corner of my bedroom, which I shared with Paula. Sometimes I liked to lie on my stomach on the wooden floor and imagine what Doris might be thinking and whisper secrets to her. Paula laughed at me for that.

"Did you hear? Did you hear?" shouted Helmut, bursting into the living room, breathless and red-faced, his thick, dark hair wild and tousled. Heinz, as always, followed close behind him; though he was a year older than Helmut, he was at least a head shorter, and his legs didn't carry him as far. Heinz was adopted and, with his curly light brown hair and crooked grin, didn't look like anybody else in the family, but we didn't care. I never thought of it and neither did Helmut, who spent every minute he could with Heinz.

My brothers started talking rapidly to my father and Wilhelm. I only caught snatches of what they said, most of which I didn't understand.

"...going to take Poland..."

"...our land to begin with, after all..."

"...six weeks, tops..."

"That idiot Hitler!"

My father seemed angry, while Wilhelm and my brothers acted more excited than anything else. I didn't know how to feel. Nobody had been crying, which was good. But I didn't like the worried, tense expression on my mother's face. I felt like my life was somehow changing; shifting, like dry sand, beneath my feet.

2

I was right to feel uneasy and afraid, because after the war began, nothing in my life was ever the same again.

During the first few months of the war, everyone—my parents, my brothers, the neighbors—spent every free minute talking about the war, listening to news reports about the war on the radio, reading war stories in the newspaper. Our neighbor, Herr Pech, who was my friend Lori's grandfather, began coming over in the evenings to listen to the radio with my father. Both men hated Hitler and shouted back at the fuzzy voices bringing the news into our living room. "Hitler is an ass!" Herr Pech would yell. "He is an idiot!" my father would agree.

My mother would scowl at this and try to hush them and, when that wouldn't work, she would hum her free-thoughts song to herself as she swept the floor, keeping a nervous eye on the window as if she were expecting somebody to arrive at any moment, though I couldn't imagine who would be visiting us during those chill, wet fall evenings, when the sun set by four and the rains pounded and the wind sometimes blew so hard the stern radio voices disappeared into ghostly echoes.

While all this was going on, nobody paid much attention to me. It felt like a wall had been erected around everybody who was important to me. I was outside the wall, alone, not understanding what was happening on the other side and feeling powerless to break through its invisible barrier. I could feel the vibrations that the war-talk caused; it made me cold and nervous.

I tried to calm my uneasiness by thinking about other things, like the happy boys and girls in my picture books, or the soft, dusty feeling of Fanni's fur beneath my fingers as I stroked her. I thought that if I just kept quiet and waited for a little while longer, the war-talk would be over; then we could forget all about it and my parents would lose the tense, unhappy looks from their faces and quit arguing with each other, and we could be a peaceful family once again.

Out of all my family, only my sister Paula didn't seem terribly concerned about the war. When she wasn't busy with chores, she was off doing Hitler Youth activities. Hitler Youth was a group of organizations that Hitler had ordered everybody over age ten to join. The organizations were divided by age and sex. Paula liked her group a lot. She wore a fancy uniform with a tie; she and her friends would hike in the woods and sing songs and help old people clean their houses. I didn't talk to her about the war. I didn't talk to Paula much at all. Even though we shared a bedroom, she was more like an aunt than a sister to me. At fifteen, she was practically grown up. To her, I was just a silly, annoying child.

Even though the war was supposed to be over soon, my mother thought she'd better start stocking up on food, just in case. She and Paula began preserving more fruits and vegetables than ever before, producing jar upon jar of cherries and tomatoes and beets and rutabagas, rows of glistening glass lined up like soldiers on our table.

I didn't have a lot to do while all this was going on. I was considered too young to work in the fields and I didn't have regular chores yet. When I wasn't at kindergarten, I hid in the flower garden or chased the barn cats or visited our horses, Max and Moritz.

Sometimes I played with my best friend, Klara, who lived next door. Her house was attached to ours by a common wall. Her family, the Oleniczaks, were our best friends; her brothers spent a lot of time with my brothers, and Paula was good friends with Klara's older sisters, Trudy and Marie. My mother and Klara's mother also were very close. Klara and I shared the same birthday, but not birth year: she was two years older than me to the day. At that time, she had more responsibilities than I did, so she wasn't around as much as I would have liked. Still, when we could, we played hopscotch in the yard or picked the fall-crumpled flowers off their browning stems.

Sometimes I ate dinner at Klara's house. Because the Oleniczaks were from Poland, they ate different things than I was used to, like fruit soup with dumplings. I enjoyed my nights with Klara's family, and not only because the food was different. It was a welcome change of pace to be with gentle, calm, soft-spoken people. No one ever raised his or her voice in Klara's family, unlike at my house, where someone—usually my father—was always shouting.

One day, not long after the war began, an officer from the German Army came to our house and gave Wilhelm a draft notice. Wilhelm was ordered to report in two days to basic training in Rostock, a harbor town about thirty miles away. Wilhelm's parents, who lived in another part of the country, wouldn't be able to get here in time to say goodbye to him.

I didn't understand any of this. At first, I didn't know what "drafted" meant. When my brothers explained it to me, I didn't see how such a thing could be possible. It seemed so unfair: how could someone be forced to be a soldier, to shoot a gun at strangers who would be shooting back, when all he wanted to do was plant wheat and harvest potatoes?

My brothers laughed at me when I asked this.

The day Wilhelm left, our family and the Oleniczaks walked with him to the train station. As we made our way down the road, neighbors came to their windows or stood in their yards, calling to him as we passed. Several people came running out of their yards and hugged him and wished him good luck.

Wilhelm seemed surprised at the strength of the goodbye from the village. Several times he swiped at the corners of his eyes with his shirtsleeve. He smiled a shadow smile at everybody and waved awkwardly, not quite the way I'd pictured princesses doing when they rode in their carriages past their adoring subjects.

About halfway to the station, I ran up beside Wilhelm and grabbed his rough, scratchy hand. I was surprised to feel how cold it was. Wilhelm looked down blankly at me, as if he didn't know who I was or where he was, and I felt for a second the depths of his fear.

Then he winked and was Wilhelm again. He hauled me up onto his hard, broad shoulders. I rested my cheek in his curly blond hair, which smelled vaguely of lye soap and straw, and rode like this the rest of the way to the station, where Wilhelm lifted me off him onto the platform.

The train was late. We stood with Wilhelm, pacing and craning our necks around the fields and trees to catch the first glimpse of smoke, to hear the first shriek of the whistle. Everybody was quiet.

"God will watch over you," my mother said softly to Wilhelm.

"I know, Frau Horn," he whispered back to her. "Thank you for everything."

He was really going away, I realized. He was saying goodbye as if we might never see him again.

I began to be very scared.

Suddenly the big dark train was there. It roared up to the metal stationhouse and squealed to a stop with a hiss of gray smoke. We surged around Wilhelm. He hugged us all goodbye, then tugged one of my braids and smiled at me.

"Don't forget your godfather, Tilli," he said.

I tried to memorize his face at that moment: his high, hard cheekbones, his blue eyes with the spots of green and brown, his wide, crooked teeth, white against his tan.

Then, before I knew it, before I could finish remembering him, he had turned and was climbing onto the train. His head reappeared a few seconds later from a window at the back. He waved.

The whistle screamed and then the train pulled away. We watched it for a few minutes, as it disappeared into the rows of fields. It looked like a dark branch floating down a silver-green river.

"Lord, please watch over Wilhelm," said my mother. "Please let him stay safe."

"Amen," said Klara's mother.

We walked home. The street was silent. The careful smiles, worn to protect Wilhelm, were gone from the adults' faces. I could see, then, how truly upset they all were. Especially my mother.

During the next few weeks, more of the village's young men were drafted. Klara's brothers, all three of them, left on the same terrible day. My mother's best friend, Anna Theis, who had fourteen children, also sent three sons.

With so many men leaving, the goings-away became almost routine. No longer did townspeople come rushing out to wave goodbye and shout their prayers as they had with Wilhelm. Everybody tried to be consoled by the thought that all the men who had been drafted should be home very soon and probably wouldn't be hurt. Germany was doing very well in the war, everybody knew that; the whole thing was going to be over with very quickly and our lives would get back to normal before we knew it.

3

Christmas has always been my favorite time of year, from Advent to St. Nicholas Day to Christmas Eve and then the day itself. But that first Christmas after the war began, things were not quite the same. Everywhere I turned, there was an undercurrent of sadness; I could sense the shadows of the men from the village who were not there. Especially Wilhelm.

We went through the rituals I had grown to expect and to love. For Advent, Paula and I gathered pine boughs outside and my mother shaped them into a wreath, which she tied with red ribbons and set in a special holder on the dining room table. My mother got the faded Advent calendar out of its box and put it on the wall in the kitchen. I was given the honor of opening the little paper doors to see which pictures were hiding behind them each day—a bell, a star, a Wise Man—as we counted down the days to Christmas.

St. Nicholas Day came next, on December 6. As soon as kindergarten was over, I hurried home and started scraping the mud off my boots in the front yard. This was difficult to do, since mud left by the heavy fall rains was everywhere: in the barnyard, up and down the road, all along the path to kindergarten. Finally my boots were clean, or as clean as I could get them. I set them carefully on the ground outside the kitchen door, hoping it wouldn't rain, hoping that St. Nicholas would find me worthy of reward.

According to the legend, if children had been good and had cleaned their shoes well enough, St. Nicholas would leave treats in their shoes when he flew by. If they had been bad, they would receive only coal or, as happened to my brothers once, dried branches, a sign that they needed to receive a switching on the backs of their legs.

I tried to stay awake that night, to listen for St. Nicholas. But somehow I fell asleep and then it was the next morning already. I ran downstairs and, still in my nightgown, opened the door to a blast of frosty air and pulled in my boots. Inside their cold leather pockets I found cookies, still warm, shaped like birds, their wings outstretched. I couldn't stop smiling. St. Nicholas knew that I was a good girl.

At kindergarten, we made Christmas presents for our mothers. I stitched yellow thread around the edges of a plain white handkerchief. I wanted my thread to look like gold edging, but unfortunately it came out as tangled snarls, looking like oily smears of butter against the white linen. I wished my present had turned out better. My mother deserved so much more than what I could give her.

The Army let some soldiers come home for Christmas, but not Wilhelm or the Oleniczak brothers. My brother Hugo arrived about a week before Christmas, having spent hours on the train from Ludwigslust, where he lived with another family and attended a school for the deaf. I liked Hugo a lot and wished he could be with us more. He was tall and handsome, with wavy dark hair and a wide smile and blue eyes that looked intently at me when I talked to him. Hugo could tell what we were saying by reading our lips. He'd even learned to talk, but his voice had an odd sound to it and I had trouble making out his words. My father said that Hugo should be learning sign language, but Hitler had forbidden its use. My father said this was because Hitler hated people who had anything at all wrong with them.

With Hugo home, my mother seemed happier than she had been since the war started. She sang Christmas carols and didn't talk about the war at all, making me wonder whether she had truly forgotten about it or was just pretending it no longer existed.

A few days before Christmas, several of my mother's friends came over with their children for my mother's annual cookie bake. This was another of my favorite Christmas traditions: the kitchen would be so crowded there was barely room for us all and the big oven would burn all day long, toasting the house and flavoring the air with sweet scents of yeast and sugar and cinnamon and ginger. The women talked and laughed. None of them mentioned the war, even Anna Theis, who surely must have been aching for her three sons. Sometimes the women burst into Christmas carols and pretended not to notice as we children snitched bits of hot, just-baked cookies.

Amid all the happiness, it was disappointing to be having Christmas without Wilhelm. He had always been part of our celebrations, loudly singing carols and playing hide-and-seek and other games with me. I missed him now more than ever. It seemed so long ago that he left. We hadn't heard from him at all, not one postcard.

Finally Christmas Eve came. I put on my good navy-blue church dress and walked with my brothers and Paula to our church in Boddin, about a half-hour from our house in Doelitz, which we went to every Sunday. Our church was over one thousand years old and was cold inside during the winter, but it was beautiful, with its carved wood and huge stained-glass windows and spire reaching way above the tops of even the tallest pines. I usually felt so peaceful when I was there. But on Christmas Eve, it was hard to sit still in the pew, knowing what was waiting for us at home.

Paula glared at me as I wriggled. Herr Pastor Scharnweber talked longer than usual. Beside me, my brothers—Heinz and Helmut on either side of Hugo, all dressed in their good shirts and pants—were having trouble keeping their legs from swinging, their hands from punching and poking each other.

My parents weren't with us. My mother was busy at home, getting our Christmas dinner and Christmas Eve supper together. My father was home, too; he never went to our church. Sometimes he went to another church in Gnoien, a bigger town a half-hour's walk away. That church, which was Seventh Day Adventist, met on Saturdays instead of Sundays.

Just when I thought the service was finally over, the pastor read a special prayer for "our sons who are serving Our Fatherland." He recited a long list of boys from Doelitz and other nearby villages. Some people sighed or cleared their throats, and I heard a few women crying.

At last the pastor set us free. We hurried along the path back home. Light flakes of snow were falling, dusting the ground, but we didn't notice them. We rushed through the gate, then burst into the kitchen and there it was at last: the aroma of my mother's Christmas dinner. Deep strong scents of goose and onions and apples and fresh-baked bread, hitting us with a warm blast as we came in from the damp outdoors, flecks of snow swirled in our hair.

My mother was waiting to greet us, rubbing her hands on her food-smeared apron and smoothing the tendrils of brown hair that had escaped the headscarf she always wore. "Merry Christmas," she said, her round face shining with love.

She turned and walked into the living room. We followed her, eager to see The Tree.

Before church, my brothers and father had gone into the woods and chopped down a spruce tree, hauled it home and propped it up, naked and crooked and ugly, in the corner. Now the tree was transformed. Flames from candles, which rested in holders tied to every other branch, glistened beside sparkling walnuts—some painted gold, others silver—and red and yellow apples. A huge star glowed on top. Underneath I could glimpse things, but I couldn't tell what they were. These must be gifts from the Christ Kindl, I thought excitedly.

The Christ Kindl, or Christ Child, was the spirit of Christmas. She was golden-haired, wore white robes, and looked like an angel. On Christmas Eve, she flew from house to house, leaving gifts. I always imagined her amid the stars, her wings flapping, her halo close over her head, smiling with pure love in her eyes as she gazed down at all the tiny villages and bigger towns and cities below, which somehow she managed to visit all in one night.

I started to run to the tree, but my mother caught me, shaking her finger. "Not yet," she said. "It's supper time. Aren't you hungry?"

We sat at the dining room table, where my father was waiting. The candles in the Advent wreath were all lit and my mother had placed an embroidered table-cloth on the table. The good china would be used the next day, for Christmas dinner, so my mother had set out our everyday dishes. But with the candlelight reflecting off them, they, too, had been transformed, as had everything in our lit-tle old house, into something elegant, something magical. Even though we were a poor family by most standards, that night and the next day we ate grandly. I stuffed myself with my mother's soft yeast rolls, filled with apples and onions and covered with hot stew made from goose giblets and potatoes, everything sweet and spicy and wonderful.

After dinner, we didn't do dishes or wash the walls or the floors, like we would on an ordinary day. Instead, we gathered around my mother as she sat in a rock-ing chair beside the Christmas tree, her old black Bible in her lap. She opened it and read out loud to us, as she did every Christmas, the story of Mary and the birth of the baby Jesus. Then she turned her attention to those somethings under the tree.

"Oh my. It looks like the Christ Kindl has been here," she said, reaching down and coming up with a pair of cream-colored socks. "And look what she left for Tilli!" she exclaimed, handing me the socks with an amazed smile. She contin-ued, giving gifts to everyone except herself. New writing books for my brothers, an apron for Paula, a jar of currant jelly for my father—gifts that might have been considered modest by richer families in the big cities, but which, to us, were per-fect.

After the presents were given, Helmut brought out his accordion. It was time for singing: Christmas carols, hymns, folk songs, whatever was in our hearts.

On and on we sang, all of us together into the night, the magical Christmas Eve night. The painful, disturbing war was a distant, faded thing, far away and, for these few hours, forgotten. The candlelight glowed on the tree, joyous music swelled around me and I felt enveloped in a cocoon of love and security and pure sweet happiness.

◆   ◆   ◆

Three weeks after Christmas, I came home from kindergarten to find a strange man leaving our house. He passed me on the way out, without noticing me, without a smile, his face long and stern.

When I walked into the kitchen, I was shocked to see my mother sitting at the table, her hands clasped together, her head bowed.

She looked up when she heard me. Her eyes were brimming with tears. Her chin was crumpled, her cheeks red.

I had never seen my mother cry before.

"Oh Tilli," she half-whispered, half-gasped. "Go get your father. Find your brothers. Find Paula."

I raced into the slippery cold barnyard, calling, calling.

They all came, finally. And then my mother pulled me onto her lap and told us the news, the horrible news.

I went upstairs after that, after we had all held each other. I picked up Doris from her stroller, even though I was not supposed to touch her. I curled up with her on my bed and stroked her silky hair.

Then I told her what my mother had told us.

My godfather Wilhelm would not be coming back to Doelitz. Not ever again. He had been killed in Poland.

4

Before the war began, winters meant time with my family. The rest of the year, everybody was busy with farm work. Our fields were a couple of miles away from our house; in spring and summer and fall, my parents and brothers and Paula were making constant trips back and forth to tend the crops, and were hardly ever around. But when winter came, all that stopped. My brothers and I could spend hours together, sliding on the frozen pond in the park or riding sleds or just talking. My mother, too, slowed down; she didn't have to walk to the meadow to milk the cows, because they stayed in the barn. Her vegetable and flower gardens didn't require anything from her—they were dead until spring. My mother spent her time indoors, catching up on her sewing and knitting. It was at these moments, when she was sitting in the kitchen or living room, that I could be with her and tell her how my life was going.

But now, even though it was winter, I couldn't get her or anyone else's attention. With the Christmas holidays finished, the war was all everybody thought about. Other families had also started receiving terrible notices from grim Army officials. Wilhelm wasn't the only man from Doelitz to be killed, just the first. Other men were wounded and came home missing arms or legs, their faces thin and pale, their eyes shocked and staring.

I felt as though the war invaded our lives more and more each day, like a vine wrapping itself around a tree, curling tighter, tighter.

My mother began going to special Nazi Party meetings, held for the women of Doelitz at the big villa-house in the center of the park. The villa had once been a rich man's home. He'd been so rich he'd owned all the land in Doelitz. Then he died and his widow divided it into seventy-eight farmsteads, one of which my parents bought and began farming a couple of years before I was born. The villa—with its gleaming parquet floors and glittering chandelier—remained standing and was now used by the people of Doelitz for town meetings and weddings and other special occasions. I liked to peek in the windows when I played in the park and imagine myself living in such an elegant place someday.

My father didn't approve of my mother going to these meetings. "It's all for Hitler, isn't it?" he said. "You're going to become one of Them now, aren't you?"

My mother shrugged, trying to ignore him. My parents had been yelling at each other more than ever lately, as if the war, with all its tensions and hatreds, was infecting them somehow, making them angrier and angrier. Not that they had ever been exactly loving with each other. But now it was painful to watch them together.

"Heinrich, you know I have to do this," she answered. "Think of your family, your children."

I couldn't understand why my father was so upset with my mother for going to the meetings. Often she would bring home plates of leftover cookies and other treats, which she let us eat the next day. My mother said she learned recipes at the meetings, ways to make food stretch to serve more people, and that the group was planning a used clothing drive for needy people in nearby villages. These seemed like good things to me.

Not long after she began attending the meetings, my mother came home wearing a dull silver cross on a chain around her neck.

"Why are you wearing that necklace?" I asked, reaching over to touch it. It was soft and heavy.

"Oh this," said my mother, making a face. "It's a mother's cross. It comes from Hitler. It means I am a good mother because I have a lot of children." My mother laughed and took off the necklace, then put it in her apron pocket. The only times she ever wore it after that were when she went to the women's Party meetings.

One night she came back from her meeting with a large package wrapped in newspaper.

"What's that, Mami?" I asked.

"You'll see," she said, setting the package on the table and ripping off the newspaper.

My father came in from the living room and looked over my mother's shoulder.

"Ach!" he cried, as if he had been struck.

My mother ignored him. "See?" she said to us, holding up a framed picture. It showed a blue-eyed girl, a little older than me, with blond hair wrapped in a thick braid on top of her head, like a halo. She wore a flowered dirndl dress and was smiling shyly at a man standing just behind her. The man, who looked familiar, had a small black mustache, was wearing a uniform, and seemed very stern.

"How dare you bring that here!" my father shouted.

My mother pretended not to hear him. She kept talking to my brothers and Paula and me. "We need to have this here, now," she said.

"Hitler?" Paula breathed, her eyes darting from the picture to my father's reddening face. "Here?"

"I'm afraid so," said my mother. "We have to put his picture up in our house. It's the law."

So this was Hitler. He didn't look very nice. He didn't look particularly evil, either. Just sort of average. The little girl was pretty, though.

My father paced in front of the stove. I watched him nervously. Finally he banged his coffee mug on the table and took his coat off the hook. "That thing had better be gone before I get back," he shouted to my mother, waving his finger at the painting.

"Don't you realize we have no choice?" she said in a low voice. She reached out to him, trying to grab his arm. He ignored her and pushed out the door. We stood in silence staring at the picture on the table.

"Helmut, get a nail and hammer," my mother said. Then, to the rest of us, she added: "I tried to get the nicest one. Your father doesn't understand. They're making the villages follow the same laws as the cities, now, and they say we have to have a picture or else—Well, anyway. Isn't that girl lovely?"

She and Helmut hung the picture in the living room. Then we all went to bed.

Later that night, I awoke to the sound of shouting below. I heard my father and mother's voices, but I couldn't make out what they were saying.

"Paula?" I whispered.

My sister was lying beside me, in her half of the bed. Faint moonlight streamed through the window. I could see her face but I couldn't tell if her eyes were open and I couldn't hear her breathing.

The yelling continued. I wrapped myself tightly in a ball, my goosedown comforter pulled close around me, shivering.

Somehow I fell back asleep. The next morning, the picture was gone. All that remained was a tiny black hole in the wall where the nail had been.

When it came time for the next women's group meeting, my mother stayed home.

"I decided I didn't really like that group," she said. "It was not for me."

I felt a little sad about this, partly because going to the meetings seemed to make my mother happy, and also because I liked eating the leftover cookies.

My mother missed two more meetings. Then, one afternoon, I came home from kindergarten to the sound of pounding in the living room. I found Mami stepping off a chair, her face grim, holding a hammer in her hand. The Hitler picture was back on the wall.

Mami didn't see or hear me. She looked at the picture for a moment, shook her head, then sighed and began singing that song again. *"My thoughts are free, who can guess them?"*

That night, there was more arguing between my mother and father, even louder than before. I couldn't sleep. I got out of bed and sat at the top of the stairs to listen.

"They're just bluffing," my father was saying. "That's how they control weak people. With bluffs and lies."

"But what if they aren't?" said my mother. "They'll sterilize Hugo, castrate him—is that what you want? Well, I won't have it! I won't have him touched! No matter what I have to do. No matter what stupid picture we have to keep on our wall, no matter what silly group I have to join!"

My mother was crying. I hurried back to my bed and put my head under my pillow. I was so confused, so frightened. None of this made any sense to me. Why couldn't everything just go back to normal?

This time, the Hitler picture survived the night. As I walked past it the next morning, I could see it watching me—Hitler watching me, new evil in his stern eyes.

Later that day, Paula told me that the Nazi Party had threatened to have something terrible happen to Hugo because he was deaf. Hitler thought deafness was so bad that it should never be passed on to other children. The Nazis wanted Hugo to have an operation, one that would make him unable to ever have his own children. My mother tried to tell them that Hugo had not been born deaf. He became deaf from an ear infection he'd had when he was two months old. He couldn't pass his deafness on to his children if he tried. But they didn't care what she said. Their minds were made up. If my mother wanted to save Hugo, she had to become a Nazi.

So she did.

5

Despite the war, school went on as usual. I started first grade in March, when the new school term began, walking with Klara and her sisters to the windowless one-room building where all the other children in the village between the ages of five and fifteen went every day, Monday through Saturday.

Right away, I loved everything about school, unlike my brothers, who hated going. On the first day, my mother gave me my *Schultüte:* a cardboard tube covered with shiny paper and red ribbons, filled with little candies and sugar cookies and raisins. All the first-graders had them. I carried mine proudly into the room, where I met my teacher, Herr Schlorff, and was assigned my very own desk, in the front row where all the other first-graders sat. Its sagging wooden top was covered with the carved initials of the students who had gone before me. Beneath my desk I kept my tattered brown rucksack, which had once been Paula's, and my little chalkboard, also Paula's, which had an eraser attached by a long yellow string.

I liked Herr Schlorff, whom the older boys in the back rows called Herr Wart-ski because of the huge mushroom-shaped wart that grew out of the top of his nearly bald, egg-shaped head. I thought Herr Schlorff was kind and patient, though I was surprised that he didn't yell at the older boys, instead of meekly putting up with their hoots and name-calling and other nonsense.

Most of all, I loved learning. I loved reading: seeing how letters made sounds and sounds made words and words made stories—tales filled with exciting people and places and adventures. Each new thing I learned thrilled me, from writing my name to adding columns of numbers, but I took special joy in deciphering new words, because that meant I could understand even more of what was happening in the storybooks I borrowed from Herr Schlorff.

Before long, I was far ahead of the other new first-graders in our main work-book, which was called the *Fiebel.* I could even read from Klara's books, and she was in third grade.

At the end of the first semester in June, Herr Schlorff had my mother come meet him at school one day. He asked her to consider sending me to Gnoien for the rest of my schooling. He said that I was too smart to waste my time in his school.

My mother was proud of me, but other adults, such as my father, thought the idea of me going away to school was silly.

"She's just going to marry a farmer, right?" he said at dinner, waving his fork in my direction but not looking at me. "Why bother with all this trouble? She's just going to wind up thinking she's better than she is."

"She is better, at least better than you think she is," my mother snapped back. Then she looked at me and her eyes darkened, as if she had suddenly realized I was listening. "I'm sorry, Tillilein," she murmured. "Don't worry. Everything's going to be just fine."

I was scared, though. I didn't want to change schools. I was just getting used to this one. I didn't want to leave my friends, Herr Schlorff, everything I knew, and travel by myself every day all the way to Gnoien, which was about a three-mile walk. Gnoien was a bigger town and I hadn't been there very often. I barely knew how to get there and I didn't know any children my age who lived there. And what if Herr Schlorff was wrong about me—what if I was really stupid and couldn't keep up with the city kids? What if I failed at the city school?

"I don't want to go to Gnoien for school next year, Mami," I told my mother one afternoon, when I had her alone in the kitchen.

She stopped pounding the bread dough and looked at me in surprise, flour settling into the ridges on her forehead.

"What? Why not?"

I shrugged and didn't say anything.

"Why not?" she repeated.

"Well," I paused. "I don't know how to get there."

"Don't worry about that," she answered, pounding the dough again. "You're getting a new bicycle. I just got the ration ticket yesterday. It's all been approved by the burgermeister. We'll pick it up at the store in Gnoien next week and then we'll walk by the school and you'll see where it is and everything will be just fine. Okay?"

"But—" I said. "What about Klara? I'll miss her. And I won't have any friends."

My mother stopped pounding the dough and put her arm around me. "Is that what this is about? Don't worry. It's hard to imagine, I know, but soon you will have lots of new friends."

She looked at my long face and sighed.

"Tilli, this is such a wonderful opportunity for you. Don't you see?"

I shook my head, looking at my too-big feet straining against my old, cracked boots.

"Don't you see?" my mother repeated. "If you go to school in Gnoien you'll get to go on to high school. And if you finish high school you could maybe even go to university. You can learn so much, do so much. You can learn English there. You can't learn English here—there's no high school here in Doelitz, you know that."

English! I hadn't thought of that. English was the language of America, the place where Aunt Bertha had moved, the shining, amazing, beautiful place in the magazines she sent us, magazines I had looked at so many times the pages were falling apart. People in America had indoor bathrooms with real toilets, so different from our outhouse in the barn. The houses in the pictures were so big and clean and gleaming. Aunt Bertha sent us clothes and shoes from America, too—perfectly fine clothes that rich Americans sold for pennies at yard sales. From the magazines Aunt Bertha sent, it seemed like everybody was rich in America. I longed to go there someday.

The idea of school in Gnoien had just become easier to bear.

◆   ◆   ◆

Before I knew it, it was March already, and I was standing in front of a huge stucco building, surrounded by leafless maple trees and about a million other children, all staring at me. At least that's how it felt to me.

"Do you want me to walk in with you?" my mother asked. She had ridden with me to school that morning, through the damp, chill streets with the breath of rain in the air.

I shivered. "No," I whispered. I gave her a quick hug, then turned and started slowly up those endless stairs, noticing, with a shamed feeling settling in the back of my throat, the flecks of mud and dirt on my legs and boots. Try as I might, I couldn't avoid the dirt of daily living, even on the first day of a new school. To get to the bathroom, I had to walk through the barnyard and the horse barn. To get my bike, I also had to walk through the yard. Mud and manure and hay and animal smells clung to everything, including me.

I also wished I had better clothes. We hadn't received anything from Aunt Bertha in more than a year—she had been the one to give us most of our new clothes in the past, but now because of the war we were forbidden to have contact with her. All I had to wear was my everyday dress. My mother wouldn't let me wear my church dress to school, even though I begged her. As I walked up the stairs, noticing my dirty legs and my dingy dress, I shot quick glances at the crowds of wrestling, laughing children in the schoolyard, and it seemed to me that everybody else's clothes looked newer, nicer, cleaner.

As I got to the door, the sound of horse hooves clattering on the cobblestone street stopped me from going in to the building. I turned to see a horse-drawn carriage pull up, a man in a black uniform jump down, and then a girl, about my age, emerge from the carriage. She had long, wavy, golden hair, tied with a green silky-looking bow, and was wearing a dark green coat and white stockings and shiny black shoes that I was sure had not the slightest spot of dirt on them.

Feeling filthy, too frightened to breathe, I pushed through the heavy double doors and walked slowly down the busy halls to Room Two, my new classroom.

A plump, short, white-haired woman was standing outside the door. "Hello, dear. Your name?" she said, holding out her hand, a big smile on her crinkled face, her blue eyes bright and warm. She wasn't more than a few inches taller than me.

"I'm Tilli Horn," I managed to say. "From Doelitz."

"Hello, there, Tilli Horn From Doelitz," she said. "I'm Fraulein Brandt. I'm your teacher. I'm so glad to meet you."

She put her paper-smooth hand in mine and circled her arm around my shoulders and led me into the classroom, which was a sea of children, a jumbled mass of swirls and shapes: brown hair, black hair, blonde; pigtails, braids; boys, girls; smiles and frowns; freckles and missing teeth.

"You can sit here, by my desk." Fraulein Brandt pointed to a desk which looked a lot like my old one on Doelitz—how I wished for Herr Schlorff at that moment!—except this desk didn't sag and had no scratches and there was ink in the inkwell.

I slipped into my seat, which was attached to a row of four other desks. Next to me sat a thin, short girl with two limp brown braids. Next to her was a pudgy girl with curly blonde hair and glasses, who turned to stare at me.

Fraulein Brandt stepped to the front of the class, where there was a large swastika flag mounted to the wall, next to a picture of an unsmiling Hitler. His black eyes followed me everywhere, I thought, from home to school. This picture had no beautiful young girl in it, either. Just Hitler, glaring out at us.

The rustling and chattering quieted. "Heil Hitler!" barked Fraulein Brandt, the soft grandmotherly smile gone from her face. She raised and shot out her arm in one quick motion.

The previous summer I had learned about this, about the Hitler Salute. My Aunt Liesel had come for a visit during the rye harvest. Aunt Liesel was one of my mother's younger sisters; she lived in a big city called Kassel with her husband, my Uncle Paul, who worked in a cigarette factory. Aunt Liesel looked like my mother and Paula: round and short, with a wide smile and sharp blue eyes. She didn't wear a headscarf and apron like my mother did, though. She wore her hair curly. She also liked to wear jewelry and perfume and listen to music and dance.

Aunt Liesel didn't care to work in the fields harvesting rye. Instead, she spent time with me, drawing pictures of women with interesting hairdos and dresses; teaching me the foxtrot, and, one day, taking me on a shopping trip to Gnoien. We strolled slowly down the main street, staring in the windows. I was so happy: to have an adult pay attention to me was wonderful enough, not to mention the excitement of looking at all the things on display that some people apparently had money enough to actually buy.

A store that sold dresses and hats grabbed Aunt Liesel's eye. "Let's try this one," she said. We pushed open the glass door and went in. Aunt Liesel turned to the clerk and flashed her arm out. "Heil Hitler," she said, as if she were saying, "Good afternoon." The clerk said the same thing back to her.

In the next store and the next, Aunt Liesel did this. People in Doelitz never made these motions with their arms or said Heil Hitler, at least not that I had noticed. "Why are you doing that?" I finally asked Aunt Liesel, who seemed surprised at my question.

"In Kassel, we have to do this to everyone we meet, coming and going, no matter where we are," she said. "You don't, huh?"

I shook my head.

"Hmm. Well, I guess the Party doesn't care much about a little place like Doelitz, then. But in bigger places like Gnoien, people follow Hitler's orders."

"Why does Hitler tell people to do this?"

"I don't know. That's just the way it is. If you don't do it, they'll put you in jail. Or worse. So I do it."

"I don't want to go to jail. Should I do it, too?"

"I think you're going to have to, since you'll be in school here and coming every day."

So I started saluting in the stores that we visited. In a way, it was kind of fun, like saying a secret password. I held my arm out as straight as I could and said the words in a loud voice: "Heil Hitler!"

Some of the shopkeepers smiled at me when I did this, as if I were the cutest child imaginable. Others just looked at me with no expression.

Aunt Liesel came to a store with figurines and statues in the window. She paused at the door. "I wonder—" she murmured.

"What is it?"

"The stores that are approved have flags and Hitler pictures in the windows, but I don't see anything like that in this store window."

"So?" I didn't understand.

"The Party says only stores with Hitler pictures are approved. Stores without Hitler pictures are probably run by Jews."

"What are Jews?" I was getting very confused.

Aunt Liesel frowned down at me, her eyes far away. She seemed angry about something. "That's it," she muttered, almost to herself. "I don't care what they say."

We walked into the store, which had no other customers. The clerk was an elderly woman with gray hair. She gazed at us, no expression on her face, and didn't even welcome us to her store. Aunt Liesel looked frightened. She did the Hitler salute. I did, too. The clerk didn't salute back or say anything. She just stared at us with her sad stony eyes.

Aunt Liesel glanced out the window at the people passing by on the street outside. She picked up a small blue vase, turned it around in her hand, then set it back down.

"Thank-you," she said brightly to the clerk. Then she took my hand and we left the store without buying anything or saying Heil Hitler.

"That was just too much for me," she said quietly. "Money, I mean."

Later that night, Aunt Liesel told my mother she had taught me the Hitler salute. My mother sighed. My father wasn't there, which was a relief. I was worried what he would say to me about doing anything in obedience to the man he hated.

"I was going to talk to you about these things before school started," my mother said. "We don't need to do the Hitler salute here in Doelitz, unless an Army or Party official comes, but Liesel is right that you have to do it in Gnoien."

"What does it mean?" I asked, finishing the last of the sour milk dessert my mother had made in honor of Aunt Liesel's last night with us. We were sitting outside in the barnyard, eating special after-dinner treats and waiting for a storm that was threatening the evening. The air was hot and still, the sky greenish-black at the edges.

"What does what mean?" asked my mother, pouring me another cup of raspberry juice, chilled to ice cold perfection by the creek running through our yard.

"Heil Hitler. Why do we say it?"

"It means we will obey Hitler, that we honor him," my mother said, frowning.
"Do we? Honor him, I mean? Papa hates him."

"Tilli, Tilli. This is so hard. I don't want to teach you to lie. Lying is a sin. But we have to do things sometimes to keep our lives—to be safe. This is one of those things."

I told my mother I understood what she meant, but I really didn't. At least I was prepared, though, on that first day of school in Gnoien, when Fraulein Brandt snapped out her arm. I stood with all the other children in my new class and repeated the words: "Heil Hitler!"

Fraulein Brandt lowered her arm and smiled and she looked again like the nice old lady who had greeted me in the hall. "Welcome to second grade, boys and girls," she said.

"My name's Ilse," whispered the thin girl with the braids who sat next to me. "You can play with me at recess, if you want." I nodded and smiled in surprise.

Fraulein Brandt continued talking to us, going over rules and what was expected of us, such as homework every day. In Doelitz, so many children had to work on farms that Herr Schlorff knew not to expect any homework from them, but here it was different. Fraulein Brandt passed out textbooks and pens and paper. I couldn't believe so many books were assigned just to me, not to mention the stacks of interesting looking books on the shelves against the wall. When I looked at all those books, I felt like a starving person who has just found her way across the desert to a table piled high with food.

School in Gnoien turned out to be much easier than I had expected. The homework wasn't terribly difficult: just a little reading and writing and handwriting practice and math problems. I liked doing it, except for the math, and it gave me a good excuse to get out of helping with the dishes and other chores. My mother checked my work every night, so I got to spend an extra few minutes with her at the end of the day.

Most of the children in my class were friendly, though I never stopped feeling like an outsider. Only two other classmates were from farms and even they must have had more money than we did, because they didn't wear the same clothes to class every day like I did. Most everybody else was from Gnoien. Their parents worked in stores or factories. Some of the children were rich and talked about trips they had taken and their new toys and outings to the theater and dinners at restaurants. The richest person in my class was Margaret Timm, the girl who rode the carriage to school every day from her estate outside Gnoien. Margaret always looked perfect, with velvet bows in her hair and her shiny white fingernails glistening at the tips of her soft hands. At least Margaret didn't act like a princess:

she ran around and played like a normal girl and once even shoved Christian Giersdorf and got yelled at by Fraulein Brandt. Margaret talked to me sometimes at recess and once I played tag with her.

Ilse Nussman was my best friend in school. She was the smartest person in our class and always was assigned first chair, which meant she got the highest grades in every subject.

Bike riding back and forth to school worked out fairly well, except when it rained—which was often during spring and fall. I wished then that I could have someone riding beside me with an umbrella. Instead, I packed all my books and papers in my rucksack, tied it to my back, then put my raincoat on and sloshed through the puddles to school. What I hated most about these times was arriving at school soggy, my hair stringy, and my legs splattered with mud.

One thing I missed about my new school was being able to come home for dinner. In Doelitz, I went home every day at noon to a nice hot meal and sometimes even a nap before going back to school to finish the day. In Gnoien, we didn't have a proper dinner break. We got two short breaks during the day, one at ten, the other about noon, during which we could stretch our legs outside and eat quick snacks. Usually I ate a lard sandwich or an apple. School was done around two in the afternoon, when I would go home for a real meal.

Every week, Fraulein Brandt let us borrow two books from her library. I usually finished mine the first day I got them, though sometimes it took two or three days if the books were longer. I liked to pick out stories with colorful pictures: pirates and castles, monkeys and magic kites. The boys and girls in these stories had such interesting lives, with all sorts of adventures. They didn't stay on farms every day, peeling potatoes and cleaning out horse stalls.

◆   ◆   ◆

Hitler's birthday came on a Sunday that year. My birthday—April 17—was only three days before his. I thought that was odd, and perhaps even unlucky, but it didn't seem to bother Klara, who also had been born on April 17.

On Hitler's birthday, everybody was supposed to display a swastika flag outside their house to show their loyalty. My father couldn't stand this. But he had no choice. At least that's what my mother said, and I believed her. So, before we went to church, my mother dragged the red, white and black swastika flag out from a closet and hung it to a post attached to my bedroom window, where it flapped like a huge crow in the damp spring wind. After dinner, my mother turned on the radio, but the stations, all of them, were playing the same songs over and over again, songs that sounded like parades.

"Why are we all following like rabbits?" my father grumbled. "He is no hero. He is a stinking crazy bastard." My father jumped up and started spinning the dial on the radio so that a crazy screeching sound whistled around the room, followed by crackling, a marching song, crackling, screeching, more yelling from my father, then my mother too: "Stop it! Stop it!" and then they were screaming at each other, the room suddenly so full with their glares and hot faces that I couldn't stand it any more.

I slipped outside. All the houses on the street had the same flags flapping. I imagined thousands of houses throughout Germany, all covered with these flags, so many flags that if a strong enough wind came along and filled them, the houses would lift up and fly through the sky, an army of them, red and black wings fluttering as they moved through the clouds.

Max and Moritz were standing outside the barn, waiting for my brothers to finish cleaning their stable. The spring air was cool and misty and sweet. I rubbed my face against Max's silky chest and he leaned his head over to nuzzle me. I wished I had something to give him to eat.

Our horses were my favorite animals on the farm. Both were brown, with white stars on their foreheads, but Max had blond mane, while Moritz's was dark brown. I started braiding Moritz's mane. Paula had taught me how to braid before she left, late last fall, for a year's work in another farm in another part of Germany, a job she was required to take through her Hitler Youth group. *Over, under, one, two, three*, I counted to myself. *Over, under, let's forget about me.*

I had been trying to braid my own hair but couldn't manage that yet. My mother still had to braid it for me every morning. Max and Moritz were easier to do. Sometimes I tied ribbons at the ends of their braids, but I didn't have any with me and I didn't want to go back in the house to get some. I wished I could stay outside forever, away from the anger and hatred and ugliness. But I couldn't.

At least when I went back inside, my father was gone. He didn't come home until after I'd gone to bed and Helmut had taken in the flag, which my mother rolled up and put back in its box until next year.

The next morning at school Fraulein Brandt announced that we would be spending the day celebrating the Führer's birthday.

This was crazy. Why did Hitler need to have all these birthday parties? Why did a whole country have to come to a halt just because he had grown another year older?

We trooped single-file outside to the schoolyard, along with the rest of the school. Herr Principal Gross, a thin man my father's age with round glasses and a pale, stiff face, was standing on a wooden platform that must have been built just for this occasion. In chairs beside him were about ten boys in Hitler Youth uniforms.

"What's going on?" I whispered to Ilse.

"You'll see," she whispered back, keeping her eyes straight ahead as we marched.

Fraulein Brandt frowned at me and put her finger to her lips.

Finally everybody was in place, arranged by class in front of the platform, with the first graders in the very front. We stood, perfectly still and quiet, waiting in the soft April sunshine.

"Heil Hitler!" shouted Herr Principal Gross.

"Heil Hitler!" we shouted back, our arms on springs, rolling in, rolling out, snap, snap, snap.

Herr Principal Gross kept his arm out, so we kept our arms out, too. We were a sea of straight arms and chins, staring ahead, expressionless.

"Today is a glorious day because it is the day we celebrate Our Führer's birth," Herr Principal Gross recited. "In honor of this joyous occasion for Our Fatherland, let us first sing *Deutschland, Deutschland, über Alles.*"

We broke into the song, our voices high and clear. For a moment, I felt a thrill at the sound of everybody singing together, of our voices circling the schoolyard and lifting out into the streets beyond. I had never sung with this many people before, more even than the entire church choir. It sounded glorious.

My arm, though, was starting to hurt.

When we finished singing, I waited for Herr Principal Gross to release us from our salute. But he didn't. His arm stayed straight out, like a branch on a tree.

"As you know, Our Führer is leading Germany on a glorious quest to reclaim our rightful lands," Herr Principal Gross said.

He motioned to the boys on the platform next to him. They stood up, lifting two folded flags from their laps. Each flag was so big it rested across the laps of four boys.

The boys started singing another song, the *Horst Wessel Song*, about a man who was killed by bad men but who would live forever in our hearts. I thought that was supposed to be what Jesus was all about, but this song did not mention Jesus.

"*Raise high the flags! Stand high on rank together,*" sang the boys. "*Storm troopers march with steady, quiet tread.*"

Herr Principal Gross motioned for us to join in. I didn't know the words, so I moved my lips with no sound coming out and hoped he wouldn't notice.

The boys finished the last chorus and, still standing, started another song: *"Up Goes the Flag."* As we sang, they unrolled the flags and put them in flagpoles on the platform. By the time the song was over, the flags stood at attention.

The boys faced the flag, their arms raised. Herr Principal Gross kept talking and soon I stopped listening. He led us in more songs, our arms still up.

Forward, forward, are calling the trumpets
Forward, forward, youth knows no dangers.
Führer, we belong to you.
We, comrades we.

We continued singing:

Our flag leads us into eternity.
Our flag means more than death.

Another song, more slowly paced:

We feel our time is closer, the time for young soldiers.
Marching in front of us with torn flags.
The first heroes of this young nation
And above us the call of the heroes,
Germany, Fatherland, we hear your call.

My arm was throbbing, stiff pains shooting down my shoulder. I didn't know how much longer I could last.

After all the singing, I thought surely we would put our arms down. But no. The boys took turns giving speeches. In the very front row, two men in uniforms nodded in approval as they listened. I guessed that they must be leaders of the Hitler Youth in Gnoien, or maybe they were somehow part of the bigger Nazi Party. Maybe they were even some of Hitler's friends. Maybe these were the men my mother was afraid of, when she warned my father not to speak his true thoughts. I hoped they didn't see me and I especially hoped they couldn't tell what I was really thinking.

The boys recited their words in slow monotones. *We must cherish Our Führer. We must honor our beloved country. We have to be honest and truthful and work hard and be the best Germans we can be.*

I quit listening to them. I couldn't believe we were still standing, all of us. Some of the first-graders were beginning to put their shaking arms down. Two little girls were trying to hold back tears and a few were shifting their legs. Every time a child fell out of line, a teacher was right there to scold them.

My arm hurt even worse than it did the day I learned haymaking and had to hoist a pitchfork all morning.

Finally I hit upon a solution. I inched my feet forward a little, until I was close to the row in front of me. Because I was so tall for my age, I had been placed in the back row of my class. My friend Anni Friede was directly in front of me. I let my hand drop onto her shoulder, resting the weight of my arm on her, and instantly felt blessed relief.

Anni stiffened. I knew she could feel my arm, but she didn't dare turn her head. No one else noticed that I had rested my arm; because I was so tall, my arm was still raised as high as the other children's. For once in my life, I was glad for my height.

Finally, finally, Herr Gross dismissed us. We did a last Heil Hitler, then trooped back to our classrooms.

"Thanks," I whispered to Anni as we filed back to class. She grinned. "Next time, I hope it is me behind you," she said, even though we both knew that that wouldn't work, unless she grew quite a bit by next year.

It was time for our noon break already. We had been outside the entire morning. I rubbed my sore arm.

"Do you do this every year?" I asked Ilse. "How awful."

"It started last year, but I don't remember it going on for so long then," she said. "I thought I was going to fall over."

School was soon finished for the day. I rode my bike home. In the kitchen, my mother was gathering a snack—bread and barley coffee—for me to take to my brothers in the fields. She looked tired and was singing that song again: *My thoughts are free, who can guess them?*

She stopped singing when she saw me. I slipped onto the bench behind the table. "How did it go today?" she asked, as she always did. She came over and rubbed my sore shoulders.

I almost launched into my string of complaints about my bad day. My head hurt, my back hurt, my arm hurt. Why did we have to do these horrible things? I hated Hitler.

But something stopped me, something weary and sad in my mother's eyes. "Fine," I said. "Just fine."

6

April 1941

Two weeks after the school ceremony for Hitler's birthday, we were taking turns reading out loud from a story when suddenly:

Rroww-rroww-rroww!

The sound was horrible: screeching and wailing like nothing I'd ever heard before, blasting through the halls, the room, my ears. I screamed. The other children didn't seem particularly upset, though. They got out of their seats and started packing their books and papers in their knapsacks. Some half-ran from the room without even waiting to be dismissed.

Rroww-rroww-rroww. Rroww-rroww-rroww.

I pressed my hands over my throbbing ears. Wouldn't it ever stop?

"Tilli!" shouted Ilse, tugging at my sleeve.

"What's happening?" I cried, barely able to hear my own voice.

Fraulein Brandt came over to us. We were the last ones left in the room. "Tilli, we're having an air-raid drill!"

So this was an air-raid drill. Fraulein Brandt had announced earlier that week something about drills starting soon, but I hadn't known what she was talking about. We hadn't had air-raid drills in Doelitz.

"You've got to go!" yelled Fraulein Brandt. "Hurry! Go with Ilse!"

"Get your books!" Ilse shouted at me, pointing at my things, which I quickly shoved in my rucksack. Then I followed her out of the room.

Rroww rroww rroww. It was even louder in the halls, a wail of pain and urgency. I clapped my hands over my ears again and rushed after Ilse, who was rapidly being swallowed by the crowd of boys and girls and teachers, all pushing toward the big doors.

Finally we were outside, where I expected the sound to lessen. But it didn't. It was also coming from speakers in the schoolyard. The sound was blaring throughout Gnoien. Up and down the streets, around the nearby houses, past the shops, through the yards and parks, around and around, an endless wailing in the air.

35

I could see men and women rushing around the streets. In front of us, a crowd of boys and girls were pouring away from the school like lava from an erupting volcano.

Ilse tugged at me again. "Come on!" She started jogging. I followed along. "Where are we going?" I shouted, but she didn't answer. I kept following her, through the schoolyard, across the street, onto a side road that led away from the school. The road, called School Street, was lined with tiny, one-story houses, no more than two feet from each other, and was badly cobbled. Many of the stones were missing or broken, so that I had to pick my way as I ran.

Silence. It was so sudden, I stopped running. The siren was gone.

Ilse shot me a look of panic and started running even faster. "Hurry!" she called over her shoulder. "We're supposed to be off the streets before the siren stops!"

We ran for another block before Ilse stopped in front of a tiny, crumbling building. She unlocked the door and we pushed inside. Ilse quickly pulled down black shades over the windows. Then we sat on the sofa, panting.

"Ilse, what's happening? What is the siren for?"

"The siren is to warn us a bomb is coming," she said.

"A bomb? It's coming?" My mouth dropped open and I looked to the ceiling, not knowing what to expect.

"No, not really a bomb. I'm sorry—don't be so scared. It's just a test, just practice, in case of a real bomb. We have to pretend there's a bomb coming so we can hurry inside. Then when they want us to come out again, they play the all-clear and we go back to school."

"What's the all-clear?"

"Just another sound, like the siren, but not as bad."

"Why do we have to leave school?"

"The school isn't safe, they said. It doesn't have a basement. Or a bomb shelter."

I was confused. "But why are we here, then? Shouldn't we be in a basement somewhere? Or a bomb shelter?"

"We don't have a basement. I don't know why we're here, Tilli, but they said we should just go to our houses."

"Could a bomb really hit us, for real, I mean?" My hands were cold and I felt like I couldn't swallow.

Ilse looked away. "I don't know," she whispered.

I shivered. I'd always felt safe from the war, far away from it, somehow. The only people who were hurt in the war, besides the soldiers in other countries, were people in big cities, like Aunt Liesel. Or so I'd thought.

"Don't be afraid," Ilse said, taking my hand.

I opened my mouth to tell her that I couldn't help it. That I kept thinking about the crashing sounds and screams I heard on the radio one day, when the announcer spoke from the scene of a bombing. And that I was not safe any more. Those screams could be mine. No one was safe.

But I couldn't say any of those things. I smiled at Ilse. "So, this is your house? Where do you sleep?"

Ilse showed me around her house, which consisted of a kitchen half the size of ours and a living room with a bed pushed up against the wall. She lived here with her mother and her brother, Günter. Ilse's mother worked in the jam factory in Gnoien. Her father had been drafted and they didn't know where he was. Her brother went to high school.

We ate sandwiches and worked on our spelling and math until a sudden lilting noise broke the silence.

"There it is—the all-clear. Time to go back," said Ilse.

We gathered our things and walked slowly back to school, to the big brick building that only that morning had seemed so strong and secure.

The drills occurred about once a week after that, never at the same time. I never knew when to expect them, so I was always on edge, half-waiting.

On the day of the first drill, I told my mother what had happened.

"We could hear the siren, too," she said, wrapping me in her arms. I laid my head on her chest and listened for the thump of her heart.

"Were you scared?" she asked, kissing my forehead.

"A little," I said. I didn't want her to know how much. "Is my school going to get bombed? Are we really in the war now?"

My mother sighed. "You know how if there is a bad storm in the summer we sometimes go down in the cellar?" she said. I nodded. "And when we come up, everything's always okay? Well, that's how it is with the drills. The chance that a plane is going to bomb your school is very unlikely, but they have to plan for it just the same. But it's not ever going to happen. So please don't worry."

After that, I tried not to let the drills frighten me. No airplanes ever appeared in the sky and I repeated to myself what my mother said, about the chances of anyone ever coming for us being so very small.

But sometimes all I could hear inside my head were the wails of sirens and sharp explosions and then scream after scream. And all I could see when I closed my eyes was fire and smoke and broken buildings, like the pictures in the newspapers of cities that had been bombed, cities for whom the sirens had been no drill, no practice; cities where the men and women and children—children like me—had seen, had heard, had felt real bombs tearing apart the sky, ripping apart their lives.

7

Despite the war and the threat of bombs, we went on living our lives as normally as possible. We kept up with our regular routines, which were dictated by the rhythms of the farm: planting, tending, harvesting; seasonal rituals which busied and, in a way, comforted us, providing certainty in these uncertain and fearful times.

As I grew older, I was given more chores to do. I didn't like most of them, but I was glad to feel useful. Without Wilhelm, my brothers and my mother had to work harder than ever in the fields and barnyard. At least Hugo came home in the summer to help with the harvest. My father was spending less and less time at home or on the farm. He spent hours at the blacksmith shop, where men from the village liked to gather. Other times, I didn't know where he was.

With Paula living and working at another farm far away, my mother had even more to do. I tried to help as best I could, but I was pretty useless when it came to household and farm chores. I couldn't even manage to milk the cows. My fingers just didn't work. The cows would stand there, mooing impatiently and staring at me with what I imagined to be annoyed expressions; my mother soon gave up trying to teach me to milk. My jobs were to peel and chop potatoes in the morning, buckets and buckets of them, sitting in the barn next to the washkitchen stove, and to help in the fields, either thinning or planting crops or harvesting them when the time came.

Even with all my chores and homework, I found time some days for play. In the fall, when the rains poured so relentlessly, day after day, turning the barnyard and the roads into mud pits, my friends—Lori and Klara and Henni—and I would make mud hills and delight in sliding down them. When the weather was nice enough, I would take the geese to the pond and watch as they splashed in the water. Sometimes I got wet, too, but I never went in very deeply. I was afraid of the water and didn't know how to swim. Once a little boy drowned in the pond behind our house and after that I saw water as sinister and not to be toyed with.

As the winter of 1941 worsened, we heard more about the fighting going on in Russia. Germany had invaded Russia earlier that year, infuriating my father. Now the German soldiers were freezing to death, trapped by heavy snows and icy temperatures. We didn't know which soldiers were there: was Ilse's father one of them? Klara's brothers? Lori's father?

Christmas that year was more somber than in the past. When my mother's friends came to bake Christmas cookies, it was different than before. The women no longer chattered and sang; they were muted and downcast. The younger children ran upstairs to play tag with Heinz and Helmut, but I stayed in the kitchen, standing at the edge of their circle, catching their talk if I could and helping when they would let me.

"I don't know how much longer they can last," Anna Theis suddenly said, her voice loud and sharp and terrified. She started to cry, rubbing her face with flour-drenched hands. My mother grabbed her. Anna Theis was her oldest and best friend. My mother cradled her head against her shoulder, as if she were a child. Then all the women started talking, rapid and frustrated and angry, their words hissing and spitting like bacon on the stove.

"What can our boys do?"

"—leave, just desert..."

"Hitler should try to survive in that ice hole himself, if he were any kind of man.."

"Sshhh! Watch out for the S.S.—"

I tried to follow the conversation, but my mother noticed me and sent me out of the room, off to play with the other children, though I didn't feel like playing. Sometimes I barely felt like a child any more.

A few days later, my mother gave us some sad news: Heinrich Häde, who used to live across the street from us before he got drafted, and who was a good friend of my brothers', was missing in Russia. His mother, Frau Häde, had asked us to pray for him.

When we said grace that day, and for many days after that, we included a new request to God, in addition to all the other men we prayed for. Now we asked Him to also please bring Heinrich Häde safely home.

In March, I began third grade with a new teacher, Frau Zell, who was quite a change from gentle Fraulein Brandt, with her violet perfume and kind eyes and wrinkled-soft hands holding mine. Frau Zell had dark hair pulled tight in a bun and wore thick, black-framed glasses, along with a stern expression.

At recess the first morning of third grade, I sat with Ilse and Eleanor, whose father owned the Gnoien hardware store.

"Well, what do you think of Frau Zell?" Eleanor asked.

"She seems kind of mean," I said, unwrapping my sandwich.

"Oh, I like her," said Ilse, who never disliked anybody. "I think she's just shy."

"Well, you can't expect her to be very happy. I mean, after what happened to her," said Eleanor.

"What do you mean?" I asked.

"You know. What happened to her husband."

Ilse and I stared blankly at Eleanor.

"You haven't heard? My mother said her husband was a minister and he got sent away last year because of being disloyal."

"Sent away?" I said. "What do you mean? Who sent him away?"

"You know." Eleanor dropped her voice to a whisper and drew us close to her. "The S.S. You can't say bad things about the Party, about Hitler. Herr Pastor Zell wouldn't even put a flag out on Hitler's birthday and he wouldn't say Heil Hitler. That's what my mother told me. So one day they came and took him away."

"Where is he now?" I asked.

"The K.Z., I guess. If he got that far."

KZ was the abbreviation for concentration camp. I had been hearing a lot about these horrible places. They were like jails, only worse, and the people who were sent to them never came back.

After break, I looked at Frau Zell with new eyes. I began to see Ilse's point about her being shy rather than stern. Only I didn't think it was shyness that kept her from smiling at us; it was sadness. I noticed her eyes, the weary, worried look in them, and I thought that rather than being mean, Frau Zell was simply miserable.

During religion class, Frau Zell took out a soft-looking, cracked black leather Bible. As she held it, almost caressing it, I wondered if it had been her husband's Bible. Did they read it together sometimes? How she must miss him. Yet it seemed to give her strength of a sort. She became more relaxed and even smiled gently as she read us a passage about passing safely through the Valley of the Shadow of Death.

After religion class, Frau Zell moved on to other subjects and once again became distant. At the end of the day, when we said Heil Hitler as part of dismissal, I watched her closely. She held her arm out almost limply and her eyes were far off as she mouthed the words. We, on the other hand, almost shouted it—"Heil Hitler!"—unthinkingly. We had been trained to say it so often that I no longer thought anything of it. It had become a matter of habit, done as automatically as buttoning my coat to go outside.

Two weeks later, when it was time for religion class to begin, Frau Zell didn't pull her black Bible out of her drawer as usual. Instead she reached to the top of her desk and picked up a thick brown textbook, one I hadn't seen before.

"Boys and girls, we are not going to be studying religion any more. We have a new social studies program to learn," she said, her voice flat and even.

"But why?" blurted Eleanor.

Frau Zell ignored her. "Here are your new workbooks. Please pass them down the rows."

The question of why religion class had been stopped was not answered. Instead, we started learning more about Germany and how lucky we were to be part of such a wise and great land, to have such a strong, forward-thinking leader, and how we must work our hardest to improve ourselves and succeed against our enemies.

That afternoon, I told my mother we had stopped learning religion.

"I wondered when that would happen," she said, shaking her head.

"What do you mean?"

"Hitler has forbidden religion in schools. He lets our church, the Lutheran Church, hold services. And the Catholics, too. But he doesn't want to. He doesn't like religion."

"Doesn't Hitler believe in God?"

"I don't think so. Hitler thinks that he is God."

My mother stopped and raised her hand to her mouth. She looked out the window to make sure no spies were standing outside. Then she went back to washing dishes, the steam coming up from the boiling water, which must have been the reason her cheeks were so red.

◆   ◆   ◆

One Saturday in early May, in the middle of war fears and the beginnings of food and fuel shortages, a carnival came to town. It was a gypsy carnival, with a real carousel, and it was supposed to be in Gnoien for the afternoon. There had been big ads in the newspaper about it and everybody at school had been talking about it all week.

I had never seen a carnival before, at least not that I could remember. My mother had taken me to one when I was little; she said I loved grabbing the heart-shaped gingerbread cookies hanging from the booths, but I didn't remember anything about it. I wanted to go to this carnival desperately.

"Please, please," I begged. At first my mother said no; this was a busy time of year and there were so many chores to do and we had so little money. But I didn't often ask for things and at last she relented. She gave me two pfennigs and told me to have a good time.

After school that afternoon, I walked with Eleanor and Ilse downtown, streaming along with a group of children and adults, all of us drawn by the wild, different-sounding music: tinkling, happy, irresistible sounds. We walked faster, nearly running, until we reached the spot where the carousel had been set up. It was enormous, with six sets of jewel-bedecked wooden horses, painted silver and gold, all with gleaming bridles and eyes of dazzling green and red and amber.

A ticket booth was set off to the side of the carousel. A crowd was lined up in front of it, handing money to an old woman, who wore her white hair swept back with a purple and green scarf. The woman had dark skin, darker than anybody I'd ever seen, and wore huge silver hoop earrings.

I held out my pfennigs. The old woman took my money with gnarled, bony fingers and handed me a purple piece of paper, which was my ticket for the carousel. Eleanor and Ilse wanted to go to the other booths, but the carousel was all that I cared about.

Around and around, dipping up and down in time with the music, sailed the teams of horses, looking for all the world like the magical steeds of my storybooks. A young woman with dark hair and bright red lips was running the ride. When the music would wind down and the horses would slow to a standstill, she would turn a big crank over and over until it started up again. A long line of people stood behind the woman, waiting to get on the ride.

I slipped to the back of the line and waited.

A few minutes later, the music stopped. A little girl got off her horse. The carnival woman let a little boy at the head of the line take her place. I waited for everybody else to get off, too, but they didn't. Grown-ups and children, couples, families, mothers holding babies—they all clung to their horses and ignored the rows of people waiting. The carnival woman didn't make them get off; she just took more tickets from them and cranked the music up again, starting the horses once more.

That's not fair, I wanted to yell. People should take one turn at a time. The carnival will only be here for a little while.

I didn't say anything, though. I was too young to be listened to.

Some women ahead of me started grumbling but said nothing to the carnival woman. The ride stopped again, and the same thing happened, and again nobody complained. We all just stood there, waiting patiently.

The people on the carousel laughed, clutching their golden bridles. A woman that I recognized from the place where we bought our fruit trees was riding a horse next to her teenage children. She looked like she was having more fun than they were, spinning around with the breeze tossing her long blonde hair, a big smile on her round face. Her name was Lotti Kreitz. Her husband had been drafted a long time ago, at the beginning of the war. Her father ran the Seventh Day Adventist Church, which my father attended.

Now Frau Kreitz perched on her painted horse as if she were a princess on her way to her castle, not bothering to acknowledge the common folk waiting at the side of the road.

Around and around again, over and over, no one willing to leave the magic circle of horses.

Finally, I gave up. I put my ticket in my pocket, collected my bike from the schoolyard, and rode home.

"How was the carnival?" asked my mother, who was weeding the flower garden.

"Not so great." I knelt down beside her.

"Why?" My mother continued snatching weeds.

"I wanted to go on the carousel but nobody would get off when their turn was over."

My mother sat back on her heels and looked at me. "What do you mean they wouldn't get off? Weren't their parents there to make them get off?"

"But it wasn't the children who wouldn't get off. Mostly it was grown-ups."

"What? Grown-ups don't know any better than that?" my mother shook her head. "Who were they?"

"Well, one was Frau Kreitz. She was riding a horse with her children the whole time and never got off once."

My mother jumped up, her face suddenly a deep red. "What?" she thundered. She grabbed me, yanking me to my feet. "That's terrible! Come on!"

Before I knew what was happening, my mother was marching down the road to Gnoien, still pulling me by the arm, garden dirt smeared on her face and hands.

"Wait. I don't care any more," I said, frightened.

But my mother wouldn't listen. She was muttering, half under her breath, and tossing her head, and walking so fast I had to do little hops to keep up with her all the way to Gnoien.

When we got there, the first thing I noticed was the quiet. Then I realized that the crowds had disappeared. We went to the spot where the carousel had been. It was gone. A big covered wagon with the words *Ziegeuner Baron* painted on the side was standing in the spot. An old, dark-skinned man and the carousel woman and the ticket lady were struggling to lift a few big pieces of metal into the wagon and were yelling at each other in a language I didn't understand. Apparently the carousel came apart in sections. Just like that: one minute it was a wondrous circle of prancing stallions, the next minute it was hunks of metal and wood in a box.

I fingered my ticket in my pocket. My worthless ticket.

"I guess we're too late," I said to my mother. My disappointment was over; I was more worried about my mother, who was acting so strangely, as if she were feeling my pain for me. My mother couldn't seem to accept that the carnival was finished. She walked the block, as if looking for another carousel somewhere. Then she came back to me, her cheeks still a dangerous brick-red color, her eyes blazing, her lips set in a thin straight line.

"Let's go," she said.

We walked home. I tried to talk to her on the way. I felt guilty about wasting our precious money on nothing and I felt even guiltier about bringing such terrible anger to my mother. But she wouldn't talk to me.

"It's okay, I don't mind," I said. "I got to see the carousel, even if I didn't ride it. It's okay."

My mother threw me a keep-quiet look, so I shut up.

When we got back, she resumed her gardening without saying a word to me, shoving at the poor helpless weeds with her spiked tools, ripping and tearing at the earth.

I sought out Heinz, who always helped me when I was confused about things. He was brushing Max in the barnyard. I told him what had happened.

"I can't figure out why Mami walked me back to the carnival and why she is so mad," I said. "Why does it matter so much to her that I didn't get to ride it?"

"Don't you know?" said Heinz. He set his brush down. He had a funny, guarded look on his face. "Tilli, don't you know who Lotti Kreitz is?"

"She lives on the other side of the park," I said uneasily. "She has two children. Her husband's in the war. Her father runs the nursery and the Seventh Day Adventist Church."

"No, no, that's not what I mean." Heinz paused. Then he decided to tell me. "Tilli, Frau Kreitz is Father's girlfriend."

After that, things made sense, a terrible sense.

Ever since the war began, my father had been going to the Seventh Day Adventist Church, which had a small following, compared with the Lutheran Church that my mother, brothers, Paula, and I attended. The Adventists believed in a lot of different and, to me, strange things. They worshipped on Saturdays and worked on Sundays, so for the past two years, my father hadn't lifted a finger around the house or farm on Saturdays, although on Sunday mornings, as we got ready to go to our church in Boddin, he sometimes would start some of the farm machinery, which would drive my mother—who believed in not working on the Sabbath—crazy. Adventists didn't eat meat, so my mother couldn't feed him the same food she fed us, though she did fry his potatoes in lard, rendered from our pigs, since there was no other kind of fat to fry them in. My father pretended not to notice this.

My mother had been angry with my father for a long time for joining the Adventists. Not only was she upset that he didn't believe the same things she believed, but Hitler forbid this church and punished people who went there. My father said he didn't care what Hitler said and refused to stop going. Now I wondered what was really the attraction for my father—the Adventist beliefs or Lotti Kreitz?

How long had my mother known? What would happen to my family? How could my mother put up with this? It was so unfair. I had rarely seen my father during the past few years; he was not a large part of my life. But now I hated him. I loved my mother more than anything in this world, and my father had hurt her. I spent the next few days after I learned the truth looking at him with cold eyes, trying to make him feel the punishment of my vanished love.

He never noticed.

And then it didn't matter any more. Not long after the carnival, my father was drafted.

"What?" shouted Helmut, when my parents announced the news. It was at breakfast. I knew something was wrong before they said anything—my mother's eyes were red and puffy, with deep circles under them, and my father wouldn't look at anybody, just scowled.

"I have no choice," my father muttered, staring into his coffee cup.

"But farmers don't get drafted," said Helmut. "They don't. Everybody knows that."

"Oh really?" said my father, glaring at Helmut. "Well, this one has been."

"Great!" shouted Helmut, rising to his feet. "Oh thanks a lot! Look what you've done to us. You and your big mouth, all your talk, Hitler this, Hitler that and then making a big show of going to that woman's church like you really cared about it when we all know why you have really been going there."

Helmut stalked from the kitchen, slamming the door behind him. Then Heinz got up and rushed after him.

We sat in silence, my parents and I. My mother poured more coffee. Her fingers were white. My father sipped it, his face in the steam, his hand trembling so that some of the coffee sloshed over the side of the mug onto the table.

I got up, went to my father, and put my arms around his neck, like I used to when I was a little girl and he loved us and there was no war and everything was so different. I felt his scratchy whiskered cheek against mine, smelled his warm coffee breath. I hadn't been this close to him in so long that I had forgotten what he smelled like.

"I'm sorry you have to go," I whispered.

He didn't look at me. He didn't answer. He just sat there, so still. Then he pushed me back. He stood up and looked around the kitchen, blinking.

"Goodbye," he said. Then he picked up his suitcase from a corner of the kitchen and went out the door.

My mother walked to the window and watched as he left, saying nothing.

8

With my father gone, my brothers had even more work to do. They trudged home at night so dirty and tired that they hardly seemed like themselves. They didn't tell jokes or chase each other, just collapsed on the bench in the kitchen, ate, washed, and fell asleep, only to begin the same routine early the next morning.

My mother became thinner and quieter, working feverishly from before dawn until well after I went to sleep at night. I don't know when, or if, she herself slept.

The summer dragged on, my brothers growing more and more exhausted, until one day help arrived, in the form of a French prisoner of war named Jan.

The Nazis had begun bringing groups of prisoners from other countries to work in the factories and on the farms throughout Germany, to replace the men who had been drafted. Doelitz was assigned a bedraggled group of Frenchmen, who were marched by soldiers to an abandoned farm outside of town that became their barracks.

I met Jan two days after the Frenchmen arrived in Doelitz. I was finished with school for the day and was bringing my brothers their afternoon snack in the sugar beet fields. Heinz and Helmut trotted up to greet me as I rode up on my bike, balancing a warm loaf of yeast bread on the rack attached to the back wheel.

"He's here," murmured Heinz, who looked sweaty and exhausted as he reached for the water pitcher. Heinz gestured behind him and I saw a tall, burly stranger stepping out from the rows of beets. He was almost as old as my father, with a mass of bristly black hair, bushy eyebrows, and deep-set dark eyes; his sleeves were rolled up, showing muscular arms covered with dirt and sweat.

"I am Jan," he said to me in a thick accent. "Who you are?"

"Tilli."

Jan looked me over skeptically. "How old you are?"

"Eight."

"Why you not working?"

I couldn't answer. I was too surprised at Jan, who wasn't acting like a beaten-down prisoner, but instead like someone who was used to running things.

"Sometimes she helps," said Heinz. "She brings our food to us and she helps at home and she has a lot of homework because she's very smart in school."

"My daughter in fields since this tall," said Jan, motioning to my shoulders and looking at me with scorn. He tore some bread off the loaf, then strode away and sat down with his back to us, staring at the acres of green waving before him in the light summer breeze.

"So what do you think of our prisoner?" Heinz said softly, grinning.

"Why is he so mean?"

"I don't know," said Helmut. "But he scares me."

My brothers chewed their bread and watched Jan, who was still intently examining our fields.

"He's a good worker," offered Heinz. "Best I've ever seen—better even than Wilhelm. I'm sure he was a farmer in France. He's strong, too. Look at those muscles."

"Yeah, no goofing off with him around," said Helmut. "Though I don't know how after one day he's all of a sudden our boss."

"It must be terrible to be kept away from your family and your own land," I said, thinking of Jan's daughter. "It must be horrible to be someone's prisoner."

Jan got up abruptly, as if he had heard me. He turned to us with such rage on his face that I shivered.

"Time to go!" Jan barked, then stomped back to the fields.

My brothers shrugged. "At your service, master," muttered Helmut.

Jan took over our household like a sudden, fierce storm. Even my mother, to my surprise, let him run things. Jan decided when to harvest and in what order; he rearranged the hay barn; he moved the manure pile from behind our house to behind the barn, where the smells were more hidden. He spent hours fixing and cleaning up everything: nailing back loose boards, sweeping the barnyard, making our farm look better than it ever had before.

Although Jan slept every night in the barracks with the other Frenchmen, he ate all his meals at the kitchen table with us, as if he were a member of our family. This was against the rules: we were supposed to feed our prisoners but were forbidden to have unnecessary contact with them. They weren't supposed to sit with us and we weren't supposed to speak to them except to give orders. But my mother didn't believe in these rules. She gave Jan a seat at the end of the table, near the window. That way, if anyone we didn't trust made a surprise visit, Jan could quickly move his seat to the windowsill, his back to us, so that it would look like we had kept him at the proper prisoner's distance.

Jan rarely talked to us, unless it was about the farm and what we were doing wrong and what should be done to improve it. Sometimes he complained about Hitler. "He's a monster and a fool. He will drive your country down. You'll see," Jan said once, which scared my mother. "Be quiet, for God's sake!" she said. "Don't say that. They will lock you up for good." Jan only laughed, a hard, bitter sound.

Even though Jan's German improved the longer he lived with us, he never talked about his life in France. We never found out about his farm or how many children he had. All I knew was that he cared fiercely about farming. He drove Heinz and Helmut and—when he was home during the summer—Hugo very hard, expecting them to do the work of grown men, even though they were only thirteen, fourteen, and sixteen. Sometimes he made them do chores, such as cleaning the barn, over and over again until everything had been done his way, which seemed to be the only right way to do things.

"Why do we have to obey Jan?" Helmut complained to my mother once after Jan had gone back to the barracks for the night. "He's our prisoner. He's not supposed to be our boss."

"Don't talk that way," my mother snapped. "Jan is not our prisoner. He is the Army's prisoner, maybe, but we certainly don't own him. He's not our property. He's a man who is helping us a lot and you show him the proper respect! I know he isn't always pleasant, but remember he is far away from his family, being held against his will. I don't want to hear any more talk about this."

Jan seemed particularly annoyed with me. Maybe I reminded him of his daughter; when he saw me, he remembered all that he was missing back home, and that made him angrier than ever. I never knew why he didn't like me, but I did know that my chores were never done thoroughly enough for him, nor did I do enough around the house, even though it seemed to me that I was always working: washing dishes and floors and walls, feeding the animals, helping my mother weed the garden, peeling fifteen pounds of potatoes each day, sitting in the barn before breakfast, my hands red and cold and scratched from the paring knife.

Jan tried to get me to help with the milking. He said that, at eight years of age, I should be milking, that his own daughter had been doing it since she was six. I tried to tell Jan that I didn't have the touch for it, but he made me try anyway. I sat miserably on the milk stool with my pail, tugging and twisting away, but nothing came out of the cows except for a few little drips and some angry mooing. Finally the cows moved away from me, their tails switching in disdain. Jan shook his head at me in total disgust.

"I tried, I really tried," I said. "I just can't do it."

"Girl your age can't milk. My God," he said, staring at me with contempt.

Other chores I liked much better. I loved taking the geese to the pond in the meadow every few days for drinks and a swim. They followed me in a honking, clamoring crowd, with Bello beside them to keep them in line. Once at the pond, the geese splashed and fluffed their wings, which I stretched out under a tree, reading or daydreaming.

Another job I liked was rinsing off Max and Moritz at the end of the day in the little pond behind Henni's house. I took turns riding first one horse, then the other, into the greenish-brown water, getting my legs wet and feeling the cool spray on my face.

When I could, I helped my mother with the honey harvest, which she did during the brightest, hottest days of the summer, when the bees were sleepy and wouldn't cause her much trouble. She would close the kitchen windows and draw the shades, then put on her bee suit and take the honeycombs from the beehouse behind the barn and bring them into the kitchen. Stray bees would buzz about as she put the trays in a spinning machine and then sat there, turning the crank to spin out the golden glaze. I helped her with this, but I couldn't spin for long because my wrists were weak and would soon start to hurt. We would take turns, in the hot dark kitchen, spinning for hours, winding up drenched in sweat and exhausted. I didn't even like the honey that resulted from all this trouble, though my mother and brothers did. We kept a small container of it for ourselves and poured the rest in glass jars, which my mother sold in Gnoien.

Once summer was over and school started up again, I had an excuse to get out of my chores. I would tell Jan and my mother that I had homework, lots of homework, which was true, except that I usually finished it sooner than Jan or my mother realized. Then, if nobody spotted me, I would turn to my books—not my textbooks, but the novels I had borrowed, with their delicious tales of adventures in faraway places.

Sometimes during meals I would sneak a book to the kitchen table. I usually sat at the far end of the bench. When neighbors and other people were eating with us, which happened often, the adults at the other end of the table, such as Jan, couldn't see me very well. Lost in the crowd, I would slip my book out of my skirt pocket and open it in my lap, then peer down at it and become lost in its world, which was always so much better than my own. Heinz, who sat next to me, acted as my lookout. If he spotted Jan watching me, he would nudge me or put his elbows up on the table to hide me.

Even so, on a couple of occasions, Jan spotted me. He stood, pointed, and yelled at me, right there at the table, right in front of everyone. My cheeks burning, I would hand over my book to my mother, who would return it later that night, with a lecture about how I needed to follow Jan's rules and focus on our family, not a make-believe world.

I also liked to read in other parts of the house, especially the old chaise lounge in the living room. Once Jan caught me. I had begged out of my chores, saying I had a terrible load of homework. Actually, I was in the middle of a novel about a girl my age and a boy hunting for treasure on a deserted island and I couldn't wait to finish it.

"You are such a lazy girl!" Jan shouted when he saw me.

I hadn't heard him coming. I jumped up, dropping the book on the floor.

"Think what you could be doing!" Jan thundered. "Think how hard we work and what do you do? Lay around and waste time reading your stupid books!"

Despite Jan's disapproval, though, I continued reading whenever I could. The lives I could live through books, the people I met and the places I visited and even the person I could pretend to be, were too precious to me to relinquish, no matter what Jan or even my mother, her face so puzzled and concerned, said to discourage me. My mother only read the Bible; I knew she couldn't understand why it was so important for me to go to places where no one worried about bombs or starvation or missing fathers, where wars were short-lived affairs between giants and dragons, and where, no matter what, there was always a happy ending.

9

One day at recess, Margaret Timm, the richest girl in school, asked me to her birthday party.

I had never been to a birthday party before. I'd never had one, either.

"Well? Can you come?" she asked.

I was sitting with Margaret and a group of her best friends under a half-bare maple tree at recess. Every once in awhile, Margaret invited me to play with her, and I always accepted. Margaret was so beautiful that I had a hard time thinking of her as just another girl. She always wore elegant, new-looking clothes and tied her shining blonde hair with different ribbons every day. I wished my mother would let me wear my hair in a ponytail like Margaret's, but she insisted I wear braids, two little-girl, boring braids. My mother believed girls should wear braids until they were fourteen, even though I told her that most of the other girls didn't wear braids and some even had short hair, which I thought looked so sophisticated.

"Well?" said Margaret impatiently.

"Sure! Of course! Yes, I can come to your party," I said, then immediately was struck by the thought that I had nothing to wear to such an occasion. The only clothes I had were my everyday dress and my Sunday dress and I was sure my mother wouldn't think a birthday party was fine enough for my Sunday dress.

"Wait until you see the cake my mother is having made," Margaret said. "And we're going to do different games, not the ordinary ones, and I've got presents for you guys, too."

"What are they? What presents? What games?" Those of us gathered around Margaret pressed for details, but she shook her head and laughed. "You'll just have to wait until you get there."

Margaret invited ten other girls in the class. She didn't invite Ilse. She and Ilse had never been friendly with each other, for some reason.

That night I told my mother I had been invited to a party. She was sitting in the living room, mending a basket of socks. "That's nice," she said absently.

The next morning when I got to school Margaret was already sitting in her seat in the row behind mine.

"Good morning," I said, turning to face her as I settled in.

Margaret didn't look at me or say anything.

"Margaret?"

She finally looked up at me, but she didn't meet my eyes.

"Margaret, my mother said I can come to your party," I said, smiling.

"Oh. Tilli, about the party," said Margaret, looking down at her silver charm bracelet and fiddling with the dogs and ponies encircling her thin wrist.

"Yes?"

"I shouldn't have asked you."

"What?"

More kids were coming in, sitting at their desks and pulling out papers and making noise, which must have been why I thought she said she shouldn't have asked me, but that couldn't be right, that didn't make sense.

"Tilli, um…Look. My mother says you can't come. That's all."

"What?" I repeated. I didn't know Margaret's mother, though once I saw a woman riding beside her in the carriage, a thin woman with silver-blonde hair swept high up off her long, elegant neck.

"She says you can't come," Margaret repeated, still playing with her charms.

"Why not?"

"Because you're—you're—well, from a farm. You know. It just wouldn't work. We're too—different. That's what Mother says. I want you to come, you know that. But she said no."

Margaret readjusted her bracelet and began poring over her perfect white fingernails, examining them for specks of dirt. I turned away from her and faced the front of the classroom, blinking rapidly to keep the tears from springing down my cheeks. The rest of the kids sat down, the bell rang and then we stood: "Heil Hitler!"

At recess, the girls that Margaret had chosen followed her, like bees surrounding their queen. I sat under a different tree, this time with Ilse, and watched the other girls, trying to see how they were better than me. *You're from a farm. We're too different.* The other girls, the ones Margaret had picked, all had nice clothes, lots of clothes, dress after dress. They didn't look like me, with my little-girl braids, wearing the same worn-out dark-blue flowered dress day after day, often coming to school with dirt on my cracked boots.

Then I noticed Frieda, at the edge of Margaret's cluster of friends. Frieda, I knew, had also been invited to the party, yet she wore faded old dresses—she had two of them that she rotated—and Frieda lived near Ilse, so she certainly was not rich.

As we were walking back from recess, I pushed my way to Margaret's side, then whispered angrily: "What about Frieda?"

I hadn't planned on ever talking to Margaret again. I'd also vowed not to show her how hurt I was. But I had to know.

"What do you mean?" said Margaret, trying to shy away from me.

"Frieda. Why Frieda? You never play with her. Why did you invite her?"

"Her mother's a doctor, Tilli. My mother said to ask her because she was right for the party, because of her mother. And you weren't. Right, I mean."

We're too different. You're from a farm. You're not right.

After that, I never played with Margaret again or smiled at her jokes and I tried not to admire her golden ponytail swinging like sunshine down her back.

I didn't tell my mother what happened and she never asked. She had forgotten all about the party. I wished that I could, too.

◆   ◆   ◆

Rroww-rroww-rroww. The air-raid siren never failed to make me jump, no matter how often it went off. It was an early November morning, clear but cold, and I hunched my shoulders against the wind until Ilse and I made it to her house. Once inside, Ilse pulled the shades and we sat in the semi-darkness doing our schoolwork and sharing the lard sandwich I'd brought from home.

Then, just as we finished eating, the house started to shake. A bowl clattered on the table and the kitchen window began to vibrate.

"Ilse?"

She was as confused as I was. We sat closer to each other and listened to what sounded like thunder, like a very bad storm coming. But how could it be a storm like this, a summer storm, when the sky had been blue and cloudless?

"Ilse, what's happening?"

The thunder grew louder.

Then I heard it: a whirring sound. Whirring just like the airplanes we'd spotted last summer, foreign airplanes flying high over the fields. Heinz had said not to worry and I never did see those planes again, or any others for that matter, but I did remember them, what they looked like and how they sounded, and now I could hear that sound again.

I went to the window and pulled back the shade to take a peek, but I couldn't see anything, only the empty courtyard.

"Get away from the window!" Ilse shouted.

I went back to the sofa and sat next to Ilse and, as the noise grew louder and I felt my stomach pinch and twist, I grabbed Ilse's cold hand in mine and then we waited.

"Ilse, what if the bombs are coming? What do we do?" I said.

"I don't know."

We sat for hours, or maybe only minutes, as the planes flew over our heads. We sat and waited for blasts and crashes and fire and darkness and whatever came after that.

But nothing happened. The plane sounds faded away until there was silence once more.

My teeth were clattering against each other; I couldn't stop them. Ilse looked pale and sick.

When the all-clear sounded and we walked back to school, we found shiny strips of silver paper scattered along the street and around the schoolyard. I picked up one of the strips and took it with me. Was this part of a bomb? Had we been hit with silent bombs? Was anything destroyed?

Frau Zell looked deadly serious as we filed back into the classroom.

"Boys and girls," she began, when we were all sitting down. "As you know, some planes flew over Gnoien today."

We all started talking at once. Frau Zell held up her hand for silence.

"Gnoien is not a bombing target. Please don't be scared. Our enemies are beginning to attack cities not so far away, which is why that plane was here, to fly past us to get to its target."

Christian Giersdorf raised one of the silver strips, just like the one I had found. "What's this?"

"A camouflage strip," said Frau Zell. "You will find them when the planes go over during the daytime. The pilots dump them so that the sun will reflect off them and nobody will be able to see the plane until it is too late."

I imagined a cascade of glittering silver raining down from the sky, while only the sounds of engines and propellers gave any hint that there were deadly airplanes overhead. It sounded pretty, in a way, and I almost wished that I could see it some time.

I rode my bike home that day searching for silver glimmers in the clouds.

10

The day after the airplanes appeared in the skies over Gnoien, Jan didn't go to the fields as usual but spent his time in the living room, taking apart the radio. When I got home from school, he had the back off; fragments of metal and big silver tubes were scattered all over the floor and Jan was muttering to himself in French.

Just before supper, he summoned us into the room. The radio was back together again and Jan had—could it possibly be?—a small smile on his face. "*Et voila*," he said, turning a knob on the radio. I heard a British-sounding voice speaking, sometimes in German, sometimes in English. "Germany calling! Germany calling!" the voice said.

My mother turned pale and put her hands over her mouth. She ran back to the kitchen and I heard her locking the door and pulling the window shades down, even though it wasn't dark yet.

That night, my mother and my brother sat with the radio on for hours. My mother wouldn't let me listen to the new station that Jan had found; she wouldn't even allow me in the room when it was playing. I had to stay in the kitchen to do my homework.

"I want you to promise me that you will never tell anyone that we listen to 'Germany Calling,'" she said. "Do you hear me? Don't tell anyone, especially people in Gnoien, even your friends at school."

"Why not?" I asked.

"Very bad things can happen to us if anybody finds out we listen to it. It's forbidden. We could be—well, taken away, I think. Or worse."

"If it's forbidden, why are you listening to it?" This was Jan's doing; we were going to get in trouble now, because of him. I wished he had never come here.

My mother sighed. "It's hard to explain. I want you to do the right thing and obey the law. But sometimes the laws are wrong. We have to protect ourselves first and the best way to do that is with information, with the truth. So Jan has helped us, once again."

I supposed that my mother was right—that listening to American or other foreign radio programs would help us by making us less likely to be tricked. But what I couldn't understand was how we were supposed to know who was telling the truth: our government or our enemies? Because that's what the Americans and the English and the French were: our enemies. And if we decided the government was lying to us, then what? What were we supposed to do about it? I thought of what had happened to Frau Zell's husband and to my father. People who didn't do what the government said didn't seem to stay around very long.

The air-raid drills took on new terror in the weeks that followed the appearance of the planes. Now that I knew that we could indeed be targets, each time the warning siren screamed, I was struck with a paralyzing fear. Could this be it? I would think, my heart pounding painfully. Is this finally it?

Before the planes had come, somehow the war hadn't seemed completely real to me. I had been living with the war almost since the beginning of my memories. But it had always been a distant thing, on the horizon somehow, a shadow trailing my life, making people sad, sometimes snatching men away from us, but never truly touching me.

That innocence was over. The planes were indeed here, after all, actually and truly here, flying in our sky, carrying real bombs. Could real soldiers, enemy soldiers with bullets and bayonets, be far behind?

Sometimes I couldn't sleep at night. Just as I started to slip off, panic would rise, chilling me. I hugged my pillow, trying to imagine happier places, lovely peaceful worlds with no wars in them. And then, just as I drifted off into the gardens of my safe city, I would hear a drone, a vibration from far away, and I would jump wide-awake, unable to relax for the rest of the night.

"Aren't you scared?" I asked Ilse one morning. She looked terrible: pale, with circles under her eyes, her hair dull and lifeless.

"My mother keeps saying no one will ever bomb us," she said. "They don't want to waste their bombs on a tiny place like Gnoien, on little people like us. They're just passing us by on the way to the cities."

"But what if something falls out by accident?"

"It won't. We can't think that way, Tilli."

◆   ◆   ◆

Every few days, during morning announcements, Frau Zell would read an official paper, telling us about the successes the German Army was having. One day in late November, she read to us about a huge fight in Russia, near Stalin-

grad, that Germany was sure to win. Our Führer was more confident now than
ever before in Germany's speedy victory, said Frau Zell. We were all to rejoice in
how well the war was going.

I told this to my family at supper. Heinz and Helmut burst out laughing.
Even Jan looked amused.

"That's what they want us to think," Heinz said, sounding like my father.

"It isn't true?"

"Not according to the radio, to Germany Calling. We aren't winning at all."

"Shush," said my mother. "That's enough of that."

Then she passed a bowl of sauerkraut and asked Jan if the hay barn needed fixing before winter.

Because the war had dragged on for more than three years, food in Gnoien
was growing scarce. Stores were running out of even the most basic foods: flour
and sugar, eggs and milk. Since Ilse's mother worked during the day, Ilse had to
go after school to stand in line for food. Many times, the store's supply was gone
before she reached the front of the line and she had to go home empty-handed.
Some days for lunch she brought only a brown roll, hard as stone. She wasn't the
only one; many of the poorer children never seemed to have food any more and
were growing weak and listless.

"Boys and girls," Frau Zell said to us one morning. "I have a plan to help those
of you who aren't getting enough to eat."

She told us that she would like the farm students to adopt as special "godchildren" those in the class who had been going hungry. Besides me, there were four
other children who lived on farms. When Frau Zell asked if we would try her
plan, we all said yes. Then she assigned us our godchildren. I got Ilse, Eva, and
Ingeborg.

Starting the next day, I asked my mother to pack me an extra sandwich. "I'm
feeling so hungry lately," I told her. "I think I'm growing."

I was afraid to tell her about Frau Zell's plan, in case she said we couldn't give
our food away. I didn't want to disappoint my godchildren.

Every day after that, I gave away my entire lunch, which usually consisted of
rye sandwiches spread with lard, sometimes laced with apples and onions. My
stomach growled as I handed over my sandwiches to Eva, Ingeborg, and Ilse, but
my heart was happy to know that I was helping them. After I got home from
school, I would eat and eat, amazing my mother. "You eat more than your brothers," she would tease. "You're going to grow a foot this year."

I liked helping my godchildren so much that I started to give them even more
than my lunch. Twice I sneaked into the storeroom at the back of the attic where

the big bags of sugar were stored—sugar from our sugar beet harvest. I filled two handkerchiefs with the grayish-white crystals, then traded them to a shopkeeper in Gnoien for ice cream treats for my friends. I took not only Ilse, Eva and Ingeborg but also a few other girls from school to the shop and gave them all bowls of ice cream with strawberry sauce on top. It wasn't real ice cream, since there was no more cream any more due to the war; it was more like ice with red sauce. But it tasted wonderful anyway, though after two of these trips, my conscience got the best of me and I quit stealing sugar.

In return for the food I gave them, Eva, Ingeborg, and Ilse gave me their brown rolls.

"No, that's okay, you can keep them," I protested. "You need them."

"We can't take something for nothing," Ilse said firmly.

So I took the rolls, which were hard as bones, and pretended to chew them, even though I couldn't get my teeth into them. Sometimes I snuck them in my rucksack and, when I got home, tossed them to the chickens, who couldn't seem to peck them apart; the rolls stayed for days in the dirt before finally disintegrating.

One day during recess, Eva asked me to go for a treat with her after school.

"What kind of treat?" I was picturing more of the hard rolls, which were the only food I'd ever seen Eva bring to school.

"Look." Eva pulled two ration coupons, marked Bakery, from her pocket. She flashed them just long enough for me to see what they were. Then she put them back in her pocket, looking around to make sure nobody had seen them.

"Where did you get those?" I asked.

"I found them in the store, on the floor, the last time we went to get bread. I didn't tell anybody. Nobody knows I have them. I put them in my pocket when nobody was looking."

"I don't know—" I hesitated. This seemed like something that could get Eva in trouble.

"Please, Tilli, please," Eva begged. "I really want to pay you back for the food and ice cream and everything."

"Well—" I didn't want to get caught with illegal ration coupons. On the other hand, it would make Eva happy to be able to give me something in return. And I was very hungry. "Okay."

Right after school, we went to the bakery. My mouth watered as I stood with her at the counter, looking down through the glass at the freshly made cakes and rolls and pastries. I hadn't eaten since breakfast.

"How about these?" said Eva, pointing to two glazed doughnuts. I nodded. Eva gave her coupons to the store clerk, who took them without comment, then handed us the doughnuts, wrapped in paper. We ran to the park to eat them.

I tried to savor mine, but I was too hungry and gobbled it in three bites. Eva took longer, chewing hers with her eyes closed. When she was done, she gazed dreamily at the sky and I could see how dark the shadows under her eyes were compared to the white of her skin.

The next day at school, the principal came to our room and, right in the middle of math, took Eva away. She didn't return at recess or at lunch.

Right after lunch, Herr Principal Gross came into our classroom again. He whispered something to Frau Zell, then left the room. Her head turned and her eyes, full of surprise and fear, met mine.

"Tilli, report to Herr Principal Gross in his office immediately. Take your things."

I stood, my heart tripping over itself, and put my books and papers in my rucksack. Feeling everybody's eyes on me, I opened the door and began walking down the long hall toward the office. Herr Principal Gross was way ahead of me, his heels clicking on the floor, his back stiff and straight. I had never been called to his office before. Everybody said he kept a big wooden paddle in his desk and that he liked to hit bad children with it. My legs were quivering and my stomach was twisting strangely, but I forced myself to follow him into his office.

Eva was sitting in a chair in the corner, her face red and puffy. Herr Gross motioned me to sit down beside her.

"Do you know why you are here?" he asked.

I glanced at Eva, who stared desperately at me, trying to tell me something with her eyes.

"No sir."

"Where were you yesterday after school?"

I didn't know what to say. What did he know? I couldn't betray Eva. But I knew that the principal worked closely with Party officials, and the Party knew everything.

I said nothing.

"Tilli, answer me," said Herr Gross.

"With Eva, sir," I mumbled. I had to tell the truth. He must know already, or else why would Eva look as though she had been crying?

"You were at the bakery, weren't you? Using stolen ration coupons to buy doughnuts. Right?"

Herr Gross stared at me, his eyes dark, his face somber. I shivered. "Yes," I whispered.

Herr Gross sighed. He shook his head. "Don't you girls realize what you did? Don't you see that because you used those ration coupons, the person who was supposed to get them had to go hungry, had to go without bread while you ate doughnuts?"

Fresh tears were streaming down Eva's face, which was turned to the wall.

"I'm sorry, girls," said Herr Principal Gross, in his thin, empty-sounding voice, the one he used when he recited all the Hitler poems and speeches at school assemblies. He sighed. "You will have to be punished. Eva, you will receive extra homework every day for a month. Also, I want you to report to the Party office for a community service assignment. Notices about what you did will be added to your school records and your parents will be notified. Have I made myself clear? Do you understand that what you did was very wrong?"

We nodded. "I'm sorry," Eva said. I added my apology as well, and then we were dismissed.

We walked into the hall together. "Oh, Tilli, I didn't mean to get you in trouble," said Eva, clutching my arm. "I'm so sorry!"

After school, I didn't want to go home and face my mother, so I rode my bike to the park. Many of the flowers had dropped in preparation for winter, but some late marigolds still showed their purple and gold faces. I looked at them for a while, then wandered down the path, wondering what was to become of me.

I came to my rock, my dreaming rock. I curled up on it, using my rucksack as a pillow, and stared at the sky and watched the birds fly between the trees. It looked like their wings could touch the clouds. Why couldn't that be me, free and above all this, never having to land again if I didn't want to?

But I did have to land. I forced myself to ride my bike home and tell my mother what I had done.

"How could you use such poor judgment?" she said.

I dropped my head. I hated having her so disappointed in me. I still hadn't told her about giving Eva and the others my lunch. To her, I knew, I looked like nothing but a greedy foolish girl.

"I'm so sorry," I said.

"Go to your room," said my mother, and the tone in her voice was the worst punishment she could have given me.

I went upstairs and curled up on my bed and let the tears come. Doris watched me from the corner. I could tell from her eyes that she understood. I wanted to pick her up and cradle her in my arms, but I had been forbidden to play with her, and I didn't want to make any more mistakes today, or ever again.

11

When I turned nine, I had the first birthday party of my life. I shared it with Klara, who was eleven on the same day. She, too, had never had a birthday party before.

Neither one of us could figure out why our mothers had decided to throw us a party now, in the middle of airplanes roaring overhead and bad news on the radio and so many shortages of food and supplies. I couldn't remember my brothers ever having birthday parties. Why me? Why now? I wondered whether somehow my mother had found out about Margaret's party and how I'd been uninvited. Maybe she wanted to make it up to me.

Or maybe she was afraid that the way things were going, there might not be any more birthdays for Klara and me.

Both Klara's mother and my mother were cheerful as they baked our two cakes in our kitchen. My mother also made cookies and picked some lilacs for the dining room table. We ate in the dining room, then played games outside in Klara's yard. It was warm enough to go outside without a coat. Henni and Lori Pech came over, plus Klara's sisters, and we played hopscotch and tag, giddy with the idea of having an actual party. Herr Pech took our picture, lined up smiling at the side of my house, early spring flowers blooming around me like caressing hands.

I doubted Margaret Timm could have had a better time at her party than I had at mine.

Three days later, it was once again Hitler's birthday. The flags came out and the officials gave speeches in the schoolyard and we stood for hours in the cold rain with our arms stiff in front of us. Afterward, we marched back into the building. I lagged behind, shaking my arm to try to get some of the feeling back. Frau Ohlerich and Frau Zell were just behind me, talking. Their voices were low and bitter.

"Such a spectacle," said Frau Ohlerich.

"These poor children," said Frau Zell. "It's insane."

"He's insane," said Frau Ohlerich. "But what can we do?"

Then they noticed me, dragging my heels to try to hear them.

"Move along, Tilli, hurry up," said Frau Ohlerich.

She and Frau Zell joined me as we trooped briskly into the building, our arms swinging in unison.

◆   ◆   ◆

At the start of the summer, my mother announced that we would soon be getting a visitor: a teenage girl from Berlin, who would be staying with us for a few weeks, until her family could find a safer place for her to stay. We were not the only family in Doelitz being asked to provide homes for older children from Berlin. The State was sending older children from all the big cities to the countryside for the summer, until safe havens could be found for them.

"What work will she do?" asked Jan.

"Oh, I don't know if she will work at all," said my mother. "She's not from a farm, so she probably wouldn't know how to do anything. Besides, she's mainly here to rest and recuperate."

"Recuperate from what?" I asked.

"From Berlin," said my mother. "Many people have been killed there. It's been bombed terribly. Many people have no homes—practically all the buildings have been damaged and aren't safe to stay in. There's hardly any food. We need to let her rest and eat."

We met our visitor at the train platform the next day. Franziska was tall and bone-thin, with wisps of red, curly hair. She stood by herself on the platform, her eyes flickering nervously as people got on and off the train.

"Hello," my mother said, stretching out her hand. "You must be Franziska."

She nodded timidly. My mother introduced my brothers and me, but Franziska didn't say a word, just nodded. Helmut grabbed her battered suitcase and we started up the road to our house. My mother chatted all the way, filling in Franziska on who we were and how we lived, trying to make her more comfortable, but still Franziska did not speak.

When we got to our house, my mother had Helmut put Franziska's suitcase in my bedroom and told me to move my clothes to a tiny spare room off the entryway that we once used as a pantry. I was dying to talk to Franziska—to learn about Berlin, about what the war was like in the big cities. I also wanted to have a girl close to my age to do things with and tell secrets to. I had hoped we could share my bedroom, but my mother shook her head and said Franziska needed her privacy.

It was just as well, because Franziska never talked to me and barely spoke to anybody else in the family, either. She ate a lot but otherwise didn't do chores or play games with us. All she did was stay in my bedroom, huddled quietly with her pictures of her family and with the thoughts that lay dark and deep in her eyes. A few weeks later, she returned to Berlin. We never heard from her again.

◆   ◆   ◆

One fall afternoon, just as school was letting out, Frau Ohlerich handed me an envelope to give to my mother. "This is very important, Tilli," she said sternly. "It concerns your promotion exam."

Our class was scheduled to take our promotion exams right before Christmas. These tests would determine whether we would be allowed to attend high school. Those who failed the test would have to stay in elementary school for the rest of their education.

Going to high school was so important to me. English was not taught in elementary school, only in high school. If I wanted to get to America some day, I would have to learn English, which meant I would have to go to high school. I had to pass the exam.

The envelope was thin. On my way home, I held it up to the sun, trying to make out the words, but I couldn't. I found my mother outside, singing as she hung clothes on the line. She greeted me with a big hug and smile.

"Frau Ohlerich gave me this to give to you. She said it's about my exam."

My mother slid open the envelope with her thumb and took out a sheet of paper. As she read it, her smile dropped into a look of shock, followed by fury.

"What!" she cried, shaking the letter in front of her as if she were scolding it.

"Mami, what's wrong?"

"I can't believe it. These people are crazy."

"Mami, please tell me."

My mother sighed. "Tilli, don't worry about this. There's been a little misunderstanding, that's all."

"A misunderstanding? About what?"

"It's complicated," my mother paused. "You see, in order to take the high school exam, the Party says you have to be a true German."

"What do you mean, a true German? Aren't we true Germans?"

"Of course we are. But our name, Horn, has made somebody in the Party suspicious. They think we might have some Jewish blood in us somewhere."

I remembered the shop in Gnoien that Aunt Liesel and I had visited two years before. She had said that it was run by a Jew and that she was afraid to shop there. That shop changed hands soon after our visit; now it was a dress shop and there were Hitler pictures in the windows. I don't know what happened to the Jews who owned it. Sometimes in the newspaper or on the radio or in speeches at school the teachers or the principal talked about Jews, about how they couldn't be trusted and were going to destroy our country if they weren't stopped. Jewish people weren't supposed to walk on the sidewalks with us—they were supposed to stand in the road. They couldn't have regular jobs and they had to wear badges to identify themselves. At least, these were the laws that I'd heard about. There didn't seem to be any Jewish people in Doelitz. I'd never seen any in Gnoien, either, except for the shopkeeper who was no longer there.

"Are we really Jewish?"

"No." My mother looked around to make sure nobody was nearby to hear her. "No, we're not. But there's nothing wrong with being a Jew, do you hear me? Jewish people have a different religion, that's all. That's it. That's the only difference. They are just like anybody else and what is said about them, what the Party is doing to them is wrong, wrong, wrong."

The next morning, my mother went with me to Gnoien. While I went to school, she visited the Party offices, to talk to the officials in charge of our area. She didn't get home until late afternoon.

"I had to wait in that office all day," she fumed, slamming the pan on the stove and chopping the sausage with furious whacks of her knife.

"Well, what did they say? Can I take the exam?"

"I don't know. They kept saying they were just following procedure for someone with a name like ours. That Corporal Ring—he was enjoying himself. I asked him to please look into this but he wouldn't even get up from his desk. He just said it was my problem now."

I was afraid. What if I couldn't take the exam? It was only two months away. "What are we going to do?" I asked.

"Don't worry, don't worry. There's got to be a way to prove our heritage."

We talked about the problem at supper. Helmut asked my mother if maybe the Party was still angry with my father for what he used to say about Hitler and for becoming a Seventh Day Adventist, and was now taking it out on me. This scared me, to think that the Party might act this way, that they might hold a grudge. But my mother said she didn't think this had anything to do with my father.

"It's just the way the Party is," she said. "It's just little people who want to feel like they have big power."

The next day, my mother wrote to her relatives and my father's relatives, who lived in Hessen, to see if somebody could send us records about our family.

For the next few weeks, I couldn't stop worrying. My friends at school kept talking about the upcoming exam, about what they should be studying and how hard it was going to be. I couldn't tell them I might not be able to take the test at all.

Finally our records arrived from Hessen. My mother spent the next few days working whenever she could on the pile of papers, creating another, bigger paper, covered with names and dates, written carefully in her tiny script.

"This is our family tree," she told me, showing where she had put our names and where my ancestors' names were written. "I've gone back as far as the fifteenth century: no Jews anywhere. That's as far as I can go with the records we've got. We'll just have to hope that satisfies them."

The next day, my mother took our family tree to the Party officials. They made her wait for three hours before somebody took it from her, without looking at it, without giving her an answer or telling her when one could be expected.

One week before the exam, Frau Ohlerich had another letter for me. "This came from the principal's office," she said, putting her hand on my shoulder. "Good luck, dear."

I took the envelope and rode home as fast as I could, my face burning in the bitter December wind. I found my mother in the washkitchen.

"It came, it came," I said, trying to catch my breath. I thrust the letter at her. She dropped what she was doing and tore the envelope open and then she burst into a huge smile. "Yes. Oh yes. Tilli, you have been approved to take the exam!"

After that, I didn't mind the extra studying or the two days spent hunched over my desk taking the test. It was such a relief to know that I had this chance. The test didn't even seem that hard to me.

We wouldn't get the results until January or February. I had two months to wait until I found out whether I would be going to high school.

12

One night shortly before Christmas, as we were cleaning up the kitchen after supper, there was a loud pounding on the door.

"Army! Open up!"

My mother's face went white. Jan had already gone back to his barracks for the night; my mother, brothers, and I were the only ones in the house. It was dark already, a bad time for visitors, especially from the Army. "What do they want?" said Helmut. My mother shook her head, wiped her hands on her apron, and opened the door.

Corporal Ring pushed past her into the kitchen, leaving the door open behind him, frosty air invading the room.

"Heil Hitler!" he said.

"Heil Hitler," we all responded, standing beside the table.

"Frau Horn, we have something for you," Corporal Ring said.

Before we knew it, two more Army officers were standing in our kitchen. Between them, their arms on hers, was a woman. I couldn't tell how old she was; she had a scarf wrapped around her head and face. All I could see between its folds were wide, frightened brown eyes. She had thin hands and ankles, but otherwise seemed rather plump, with bulky arms and back and a wide waist. Bits of branches clung to her muddy dress, which was torn and scattered with brownish-red spots that looked like blood. Her shoes had gaping holes, so that I could see her bare feet. She was shaking.

"What—?" My mother looked stunned.

"She's all yours now, Frau Horn. She's a prisoner—use her however you like. Heil Hitler!" said Corporal Ring. Then he turned and walked out the door. I could hear him just outside, laughing loudly with his men, their boots crunching on the icy ground.

The woman stood before us, trembling. I didn't know whether she was trembling from fear or the cold, or both.

"Where is she from?" asked Heinz.

"I think Russia—the women wear babushkas like that in Russia," said my mother softly. "Tilli, get the poor thing some coffee. Helmut, go get her a blanket."

In a few minutes, the woman was sitting on our kitchen bench, at the end closest to the hot stove, wrapped in a blanket and holding a mug of hot barley coffee in her cold-reddened hands. When she lowered her scarf from her nose and mouth to drink the coffee, I could see that she was young, maybe Paula's age.

My mother gave her some bread. After she'd eaten—slowly at first, then gobbling it as if she'd been starving—my mother tried talking to her. She smiled broadly, pointed to herself, then said: "Frau Horn." She pointed to the girl and raised her face into a question.

"Maria," whispered the girl.

My mother smiled. "Maria?" The girl nodded. "Now at least we know what to call her," she said to us, then gave Maria more bread.

After Maria was done eating, my mother sent my brothers upstairs to fix up a bed for Maria in the spare room in the attic. "Tomorrow we'll figure out what we're going to do with her," she said. "For now, we're all tired and need to get to sleep."

My mother led Maria upstairs. I followed. Maria walked gingerly, as if she were hurt in some way. My mother showed her to her bed and made sleeping motions with her head and hands. Maria nodded. Then we all went to bed.

The next morning, I woke up before the roosters, remembering right away that a new person was in our house—another girl. I got dressed just in time to hear my mother moving across the attic to the spare room. She rapped on the door. "Maria?" she called softly.

The door opened and there was Maria, just as she had been last night, fully clothed, her head still wrapped in a scarf.

"Goodness, she didn't even get undressed for bed," said my mother.

Maria stared wide-eyed at us and it looked like she was trembling again. I wished I could speak Russian, so I could tell her that we wouldn't hurt her. I wondered what other people had done to her, to make her so afraid.

Maria followed us downstairs. "I'm going to take her milking with me," my mother said. "But first we've got to get her cleaned up."

We walked Maria across the frozen barnyard to the washkitchen. I didn't see how Maria could stand it in this icy weather with no socks and torn shoes. At least the washkitchen was warm. The pot of water on the stove was steaming, already boiling for the potatoes. Beside the oven was a pail of water with several cups beside it. My mother pointed to the water and handed Maria a towel and a piece of lye soap.

Maria looked blankly at the towel and soap, then set them down and slowly pulled her scarf away from her face, so that again I could see her fine small nose and mouth. She scooped a cupful of cold water out of the pail, sipped it, swished it around in her mouth, then spit the water into her cupped hands and began washing her face with it, water spilling down her chin, the front of her scarf, her dress.

"No, no, no," said my mother. She took the cup from Maria, who looked scared again.

"We need to wash all of you," said my mother loudly, as if speaking loudly would somehow make a difference in Maria's understanding.

My mother made scrubbing motions with her hands and the piece of soap. Maria stared blankly at her. My mother sighed.

"I'm sorry to have to do this," she said, reaching over and tugging at Maria's soiled scarf.

"*Nyet, nyet,*" Maria cried. She held her hands on her scarf to prevent my mother from removing it.

Mami gave up on the babushka and began undoing the buttons on the back of Maria's dress. Maria shrieked and folded her arms over herself, struggling to get away.

"Tilli, take her arms."

I went to Maria and held her arms, marveling at how squishy-soft they were, compared with her bony hands. I smiled at her with what I hoped was a reassuring expression. "It's okay," I said, crooning as I would to an injured animal. "It's okay. We just need you to wash. Don't be afraid."

Maria's eyes flashed from my mother to me; she looked like a trapped bird. We lifted Maria's arms and my mother eased her dress over her head, only to find, underneath it, another dress, this one cleaner looking.

As we undressed Maria, we found four layers of clothing, including a sweater. "The poor thing probably is wearing every stitch of clothing she owns," Mami said.

Maria had given up. She stood with her eyes closed, tears running down her cheeks, her hands limp at her sides.

"Mami, do we have to do this? She really doesn't like it."

"Yes, we do. I hate to say this, but she could have lice. We have to do this."

Moving more quickly, my mother set the last of Maria's dresses in a pile on the ground. Maria was wearing only a bra and underpants. She was very thin and pale, except for the bruises, lots of bruises, scattered all over her body in purple and green blotches, especially on her back and legs. Her bones jutted out like spikes. I could see her every breath and feel her every shiver.

My mother tried again to untie the babushka. This time Maria didn't resist. My mother pulled it off as gently as she could; it was wrapped around and around Maria's head like bandages on a mummy, but at last it came off.

I gasped. I knew that I shouldn't have made a sound, but I couldn't stop myself. The sight was too shocking.

Maria was bald.

Not completely shining-skull bald. There were tufts of brown hair sticking up here and there, little unruly weeds amid the pink, scabbed, scratched scalp. But she was bald nonetheless.

Maria started sobbing, her hands on her head, her face, her eyes, trying to cover herself.

"There, there. There, there," whispered my mother. She took a rag and some soap and tenderly, with the softest of motions, wiped Maria's arms, neck, head.

Her eyes downcast, Maria reached for the cloth and finished cleaning the rest of her body. My mother gave Maria a bundle of clean clothes—a dark blue dress that used to be Paula's, a sweater of her own, an old jacket of Helmut's, socks and scuffed boots.

"Let's leave her alone now," my mother said. We stepped outside into the barnyard, which was still dark, although the sun was beginning to cast pink shadows along the horizon.

"What happened to her hair, Mami?"

"Oh, Tilli," sighed my mother. Her voice was as sorrowful as I had ever heard it. "Maria is a prisoner and sometimes, especially with women, the Army shaves their heads. They say it is because of lice—those bugs that live on people's heads, in their hair. The prisoners live in bad, dirty conditions and the Army wants to make sure they don't have lice spreading around. Though I don't think that's the real reason they shave them. I think it is to make them feel like prisoners instead of people."

"But why is Maria a prisoner?" I asked. "She's not a soldier, is she?"

"No, I'm sure she's a perfectly ordinary girl," said my mother. "But when the Army takes over countries, they figure they own the people, too, and they decide to take some of them to be workers over here."

"So they can just take them? Just like that? Away from their families, even when they're children? Even when they're girls?"

I was stunned. Maria wasn't much older than Trudy or Klara, or me for that matter. If my country did this to our enemies, I thought, what would our enemies do to us—to me—if we lost the war? Could I be taken away, like Maria, and given to strangers in another land, to be their property, as if I were a dog or a horse?

Maria stepped out of the barn. Her babushka was back on her head. Our clothes hung large on her, but still she looked much thinner than she had with all her clothes layered one on top of the other.

"You'd better get busy with the potatoes," my mother said to me. Then she and Maria headed off to milk the cows.

At breakfast, Maria seemed slightly more relaxed. She left the scarf covering her mouth pulled down the whole time, not just when she was taking bites of food.

"Maria knows how to milk," my mother said. "She must be from a farm."

Jan walked in then, looking for his breakfast. He stared at Maria. She took one look at Jan, with his fierce, glaring eyes, and quickly pulled her scarf back over her face.

"Jan, this is Maria," said my mother. "She's from Russia. She is staying with us now."

"In the house?" said Jan, eyeing Maria warily. She shrank back in her seat.

"Yes, in the house."

"Not in barracks?"

"No, no barracks."

Jan scowled at Maria. "What work can she do?"

"She milked the cows with me this morning. She did a good job. I think she's going to be a big help to us."

"Hmmph." Jan glared at Maria again. I didn't know why he was being so hostile towards her; he was frightening her. Perhaps it was because he was French and she was Russian and their two countries didn't get along. Or perhaps he was just mean to everybody.

Little by little, over the next few days, Maria began to trust us. She learned German quickly; soon we were able to figure out that she was indeed from Russia, had been raised on a farm, and was sixteen years old.

One morning not long after her arrival, Maria came into the kitchen as my mother was braiding my hair. She touched my hair and said a word in Russian that my mother had determined meant: "What do you call this in German?"

"Braids," my mother said.

Maria pointed to her own head, covered as always by the babushka. "Braids." She made long motions with her hand, coming down the front of her chest, as if to show where her hair had been. Then her eyes filled with tears. "Braids." She sat down and started to cry, resting her scarf-covered head in her arms on the table.

I didn't know what to do for Maria. My mother put her arms around her and stroked her back. I wished I could tell Maria that hair didn't matter, but I somehow didn't think her lost hair was really what she was crying about.

On Christmas Eve, while we were at church, Maria helped my mother with dinner and the tree. I wished Maria could have seen what our tree looked like in the past, when we were able to decorate it with lit candles and painted walnuts, things that weren't available any longer because of the war. Still, my mother had been able to cook our traditional dinner of bread and stew and cookies, and the house smelled wonderful as always. I felt deeply thankful, knowing how very many families throughout Germany—and in other countries destroyed by this terrible war—were making do with much less. We hadn't heard from our relatives in different parts of Germany, in cities being destroyed by bombs. We could only pray that they were still alive.

Both Jan and Maria shared Christmas Eve supper with us. Afterward, they sat at opposite ends of the sofa. Jan had not warmed to Maria at all. He pulled himself in whenever she was around and shot her dark, hate-filled looks.

My mother reached under the tree and discovered that the Christ Kindl had given Maria a pair of socks—socks which my mother had made out of brown wool that she had unraveled from an old, ruined sweater of Helmut's.

I no longer believed in the Christ Kindl. I knew now that instead of being an angel it had been my mother all along. Even though my mother knew that I knew the truth, she still pretended it was the Christ Kindl. "Oh, look what she left for Tilli!" she exclaimed. "Oh, what did she leave for Maria?"

I really didn't mind losing the Christ Kindl, even though I used to daydream about someday meeting her. I knew that, in a way, I hadn't lost her at all. She was right in front of me.

Maria's eyes filled with tears as my mother handed her the socks. "Thank you, thank you," she said in her broken German.

Jan, too, received socks. He said a curt thanks, without smiling, and shoved them in his pocket.

Then it was time for singing. The lights were all off, the black shades drawn; we opened the door of the stove just a little, to capture the glow, which danced around the room. Then, sitting close beside each other in the golden shadows, we sang our familiar carols.

Maria hummed along. We paused after *O Holy Night*, trying to decide what to sing next. Suddenly, Maria started singing in her own language, her voice high and clear and beautiful, the song slow and haunting. I had no idea what the words to her song meant. But I could see as the stove light flickered over Maria's face that her cheeks were wet with tears. When she was done, she covered her face with her hands.

Once again, I didn't know what I could do to take away Maria's sorrow. There was nothing to do, nothing any of us could do.

13

As we settled into 1944, Maria adjusted to life in our household and even seemed to find some small measure of happiness with us. She began singing as she worked and no longer wore her babushka over her face, although she still kept it on her head; I could only assume her hair was growing in. My brothers liked Maria a great deal. Helmut sometimes brought out his accordion and tried to accompany her songs, while Heinz taught her German, which she learned rapidly.

We discovered that Maria possessed an important skill: she knew how to spin yarn. We had a spinning wheel that my mother's great-aunt had given her as a wedding present, but we had never used it as anything other than a decoration. Maria sheared the wool off one of our lambs and showed us how to push the wool through the wheel, then wash it and hang it to dry. My mother, who liked to knit, was overjoyed at suddenly having her own supply of yarn.

Jan still had little patience for Maria, though. He particularly hated her habit of carrying everything on her head. Laundry, eggs, milk—no matter what, no matter how heavy, she hoisted it atop her babushka and, with one hand for support, walked on, barely leaning.

"No, no, it will fall," Jan would yell, trying to get her to do it his way, although I couldn't see what difference it should make to him as long as she didn't drop anything.

Maria was still very fragile and after one of Jan's scoldings, her eyes would well with tears and she would seek out my mother for comfort. My mother would yell at Jan for this. "Don't be so harsh with her. She's only a young girl!"

Jan pouted at my mother's reprimands. He couldn't stand it when my mother opposed him; I got the feeling he wasn't used to having his actions questioned, and I wondered what his wife was like.

"How about I say I'm sick?" he would yell. "How about I sleep all day? You see how you do without me! How about that?"

Or else he would sulk and say, "I'm just a prisoner. Just a prisoner. So I work like prisoner!" Then he would work more furiously than ever, doing even more than he usually did, as if that were supposed to make us—to make my mother—feel guilty. Instead, my mother laughed. She wasn't bothered by Jan's outbursts; they only amused her.

"Why is Jan so mad at Maria all the time?" I asked her one day, as we were hanging laundry in the barn to dry. It was too cold and wet to hang outside, so we pinned everything to a line strung over bales of hay. If we were lucky, the clothes and sheets and towels would dry before they froze into stiff, ghostly boards.

"I think Jan is jealous of Maria," said my mother, clipping a pair of long underwear to the line.

"Jealous? Of what?"

"She gets to live here and Jan only comes during the day. That's probably one reason. And Jan liked being our only worker, so that he could be our savior. Maria takes too much of my attention away from him."

"That's silly," I said.

"Maybe so, but war does funny things to people." My mother stopped what she was doing. "Just remember: Jan is a good man. He doesn't need to be working so hard for us. We are his enemies and he is helping us so much. Try to be patient with him."

I tried, but it was hard, especially during the winter, when Jan was around so much more, instead of being out in the fields, where I could happily ignore him.

◆   ◆   ◆

Just when I thought it would never happen, Frau Ohlerich revealed the results of our high school exam.

I passed.

In fact, I came in sixth in my class. My future still had a light in it; there was an open pathway, leading who knew where. I would be able to study English. Maybe I would be able to go to college! Then I could do all sorts of things and some day, somehow, wind up in America.

In March, I reported to the high school, a big redbrick building about six blocks from the elementary school. It was newer and nicer than the elementary school and had a basement and an attic. The desks were arranged the same way: benches in rows, an aisle down the middle and the boys on the other side of the room. All of us were seated according to class rank.

In high school we had different teachers for different subjects. My favorite teacher was Fraulein Meyer, who reminded me of my mother. She was short and brisk, with lively eyes and a deep laugh. She took no nonsense from anyone, and sometimes even hit the wilder boys with a stick she kept beside her desk. But there was an essential kindness about her that made me wish I could have her for every class, not just English and music. Fraulein Meyer played the violin and also led the school choir, which I joined; it met after school two afternoons a week.

Fraulein Meyer had lived in America for four years as a governess for a wealthy family. She liked America and would have stayed there if her mother back in Germany had not become very ill just before the war began. Fraulein Meyer came home to be with her. After her death, Fraulein Meyer wanted to return to America, but by then the war was in full swing and the borders were closed. Someday, she said. Someday she would return.

I hoped I could be in America myself to greet her when she came.

◆   ◆   ◆

Not long after I started high school, Paula came home. She just showed up in the kitchen, her clothes rumpled and worn, carrying a suitcase. Her face was dirty and she looked exhausted and upset.

"Paula!" my mother cried, rushing to embrace her. I hung back, barely able to believe this was my sister, whom I hadn't seen in more than a year.

After my mother had given her something to eat and drink, Paula told us why she had come home: The farmer she had been working for in East Prussia had heard rumors that the Russians were about to invade. He was afraid for Paula and the other servants and sent everybody away to whatever safer places they could find.

"Thank God for that," my mother said, squeezing Paula to her again. "It's so good to have you back where you belong."

That's when Paula broke the news to my mother that she would not be staying with us for very long. She had lined up another job, this time as a secretary for a wealthy count who lived on an estate about fifteen miles away.

My mother's face fell, but she understood why Paula had to leave, and at least she would be fairly close to us.

Later that week, my mother found another reason to be glad that Paula had a job. The Army tried to draft Paula, as they were doing to many unemployed young women. They wanted women to go to other countries and help the soldiers in various support jobs.

But because Paula had a job and her new employer was a rich and influential man, the draft notice was rescinded. Paula would be safe on the count's estate, at least until the war was over.

◆　　　◆　　　◆

A couple of weeks after Paula left, I was riding home from school when I saw a man in a soldier's uniform on the road ahead of me, carrying a familiar-looking suitcase.

Could it be?

He turned and I saw then that the man was, indeed, my father.

"Tilli?" he said, shielding his eyes from the sun.

My father, who had always been so dark and handsome, had grown old. His eyes were drooping, his shoulders sagged, and the whiskers across his cheeks and chin were gray.

"Why are you home?" I asked, wondering if maybe the Army had released him because he was too old to fight.

"Just a furlough, that's all. I'm here for two weeks. Then I have to head back. It's a soldier's life I lead now, you know." My father laughed bitterly. "Heinrich Horn, a soldier in Herr Hitler's army."

My father pushed open the gate to our yard. I set down my bike and followed him inside the house.

My mother was spinning wool. With the clatter and whir of the machine, she didn't hear us come in.

"Well, there's a greeting for you," said my father.

"Heinrich!" My mother looked stunned. Her foot stopped pumping, but the spinning wheel kept turning on its own, whistling in the otherwise quiet room.

My parents stared at each other. "Hello, Regina," my father said stiffly, formally. He set down his suitcase. "I'm home."

The door opened and Jan walked in. "Frau Horn, there's a problem with—" He stopped talking when he saw my father.

"Who the hell are you?" my father demanded.

My mother stepped between the two men, her hand on my father's sleeve. "This is Jan, our helper. Jan, this is my husband, Herr Horn."

"A Frenchman, are you?" said my father, glaring at Jan.

Jan nodded, saying nothing, his eyes stony.

My father nodded curtly. "Well, then, take my bag to my bedroom."

"Yes sir," Jan said, spitting out the words. He picked up my father's suitcase and carried it to my mother's bedroom.

"Heinrich, please," said my mother. "Jan has been very good to us."

My father brushed off her hand and stared after Jan. "He certainly knows the way to your bedroom, doesn't he? What has he been doing for you while I've been gone?"

"Heinrich, don't be a fool."

Jan came back into the kitchen. "I'm going to the horse barn," he said, then turned and left the house.

My mother sat back down at the spinning wheel and gathered the strands of new yarn. "Are you home for good or is this a visit?" she asked my father, not looking at him, concentrating on the yarn.

"It's just a visit. Two weeks. Don't I get some coffee?"

"Of course." My mother got up and poured my father a cup of coffee. That's when she noticed me standing in the corner, watching them.

"Oh, Tilli, I didn't know you were home from school," she said. Then, turning to my father, she smiled brightly. "Tilli has been doing so well in school. She is in high school now! She passed the fifth grade exam, sixth in her class."

My father stared into his coffee cup as if he hadn't heard her. Then he set it down and got up. "I said it before and I'll say it again. What does a farm girl need with more school anyway?" Then he walked to the door.

"Where are you going? You just got home," said my mother.

"I've got to see what that stinking no-good Frenchman has been doing to my farm," he said, pushing his way out the door.

My mother sighed. "I'm sorry, Tilli," she said, sinking down onto the spinning wheel stool. "He's been through a horrible ordeal, you know."

"Don't worry, Mami," I said awkwardly. "It's all right."

But it wasn't.

Whenever my father and Jan were in the same room, I could barely breathe. I only hoped that they would be able to get through my father's two-week furlough without hitting each other. Jan tried to stay out of my father's way, but there were times, such as during meals, when they had to be together. My father glowered at Jan and made cutting, cruel remarks. Jan didn't respond, but I could see the bone pulsing at his jaw and temples as he ate.

Maria was frightened of my father. She wouldn't sit at the table with us, just scurried about the kitchen, serving us when needed and otherwise trying to stay hidden.

"Why does she wear that babushka all the time?" he asked my mother at supper one night. Maria could hear and understand him, but he acted as if she couldn't speak on her own.

"It's her custom. It's not hurting anyone," said my mother.

"Maria's wonderful," I piped in. "She's even taught us to spin wool."

"Good. I need new socks."

About a week after my father came home, I found him with a shovel and wheelbarrow, digging up the manure pile behind the barn.

"What's he doing?" I asked my mother.

She shrugged helplessly. "For some reason, he thinks he has to move the manure pile back to where it was before Jan moved it."

My father spent two days digging up the manure pile, which he said belonged next to our house. I thought Jan's idea had been better—it looked neater and certainly smelled more pleasant to have it hidden behind the barn instead of next to our house. But my father was insistent and after he had finally moved it, he strutted as if he had won a major battle.

"See," he said to Jan later that day. "That's the right place for a manure pile on a German farm. And that's where it's going to stay."

Jan sipped his soup without saying a word.

"It's going to stay there, you hear me?" my father shouted.

Jan raised his eyes from his bowl. He shot my father a gaze of pure contempt. Then he pushed his chair back from the table and stalked out of the room.

My father leaned back in his chair, grinning broadly. "See that, boys," he said to my brothers. "You don't have to listen to him or obey him. This farm is mine—yours—not his. Always remember that. He's just a prisoner."

"Heinrich, please," said my mother.

My father wiped his mouth with the back of his hand, then strode briskly, almost merrily, to the door.

"It's almost dark," said my mother. "Where are you going?"

"There's a friend I haven't seen in a long time. You don't mind if I go visiting, do you?"

He came back two days later, changed into his soldier's uniform, packed his suitcase and left. His furlough was over and, even though it seemed wrong to feel this way, I was glad. Life was easier without my father around.

14

Spring 1944

Shortly before my tenth birthday, Paula came for a visit. She brought with her a young man in a soldier's uniform.

"Mami, Tilli, this is Erich," she said proudly.

Erich was short, not much taller than Paula, with a round, soft-looking face and pale blue eyes. We said hello to him.

"Erich is on furlough. He's on his way to Teterow, and dropped by to see me before he left," said Paula. "Then he's back to the war."

"That's too bad," said my mother.

"Can Tilli show Erich the living room?" Paula said. "We need to talk."

My mother looked surprised. "Tilli, do as your sister asked."

Erich followed me into the living room. I stood awkwardly with him, trying to figure out what to say. "So, you have to be in Teterow," I said.

"Yes, by tomorrow," Erich said. He looked around the room, as uncomfortable as I was.

I didn't know what else to say, so I turned on the radio, hoping to find something besides the war voices. I should have known better. It had been a long time since there had been music on the radio.

"Do you want to listen to this instead?" I asked, tuning in one of the many war bulletins.

"No." Erich turned his pale eyes to mine. His face grew so sad it frightened me. "No. What good would it do me to know?"

"Know what?"

"What's happening. I can't change it, can I? I just have to accept what they say."

Erich was so dismal that I couldn't take it any more. "I'm going to see if they need any help in the kitchen," I said, leaving him sitting on the sofa.

I walked in on an argument.

"—absolutely the worst mistake you could make!" my mother was saying fiercely.

Paula's arms were crossed and her eyes were narrowed. "How dare you say that!"

They both saw me and stopped talking. My mother set a cake on the table. "I'm going out." She brushed past me and out the door, which banged loudly behind her.

Paula rubbed her eyes with the back of her hand. "I don't care what she says. Tilli, help me get the china down."

"The good china?" We only used these dishes for the most special of occasions.

"I'm not having him think we are peasants," she said.

I went to the dining room hutch and carefully took out two delicate, flower-patterned china plates and cups. I held them against my body as I walked back to the kitchen.

Erich came back to the kitchen and sat at the table. "Won't you have some cake?" she asked him. He nodded and Paula set a wedge of my mother's cake on his plate, then poured him some coffee. She served herself next, then sat beside him. They ate in silence.

"Tilli, how about you?" Paula suddenly remembered to ask.

"No, that's okay, I'm not hungry."

"Well, then." Paula looked at Erich. "I guess it's time to leave."

"I guess so," said Erich, looking glum.

"Tilli, I'm going to walk Erich to the train station," Paula said. "I'll stop back in a little while." She and Erich moved toward the kitchen door.

"Aren't you going to say good-bye to Mami?"

"I can't believe what she said," said Paula. "I thought she would be happy for me."

"Happy for what?"

"Erich and I are engaged. On his next furlough, we're going to be married."

After Paula left, I carried the pan of dishwater to the table and gathered the china plates and cups to wash. Normally, I did whatever I could to avoid washing dishes, but I loved looking at and holding these beautiful, delicate pieces of china.

My mother came in, her hands dirty from the garden. "Where's Paula?"

"She took Erich to the train station."

"I see." My mother frowned. Then she noticed what I was doing. "Why is the good china out?"

"They used it."

"What?" my mother shrieked. "How could she? Don't you even think of washing those. She's going to do it herself."

"Mami, Paula said she's getting married."

"No, she's not."

"That's what she said, that she and Erich—"

"And I said they're not!"

I went outside. Klara was in her yard, sweeping. I chatted with her until I saw Paula coming back from the train station, her head down, her shoulders sagging.

"I've got to go," I told Klara.

When I approached the kitchen door, I again heard yelling, though I couldn't make out the words. I stopped outside the door. I didn't want to see my mother and Paula fighting again.

The door flung open. Paula stood in the doorway, screaming at my mother. "I don't care what you say!"

"I'm still your mother! Don't talk to me that way!"

"I'm leaving!"

Paula burst past me and stormed down the road towards the count's estate. I went into the kitchen, where my mother was washing the good china.

After that, and for the rest of the day, my mother was unusually silent. That night, the sirens screamed their warning, waking me, but no planes came, and I fell back to a restless sleep.

The next morning, my mother had a job for me. "You need to take these things to Paula for me."

"You mean to the count's estate?"

"It's not that far. You can do it."

My mother gave me some sandwiches wrapped in newspaper and a large bundle, which was for Paula, then told me how to get to the count's estate. I took a jacket, since it looked like it might rain. Despite the gray sky and the tension I could see on my mother's face, my heart was light. I'd never been this far from home by myself, and I was looking forward to the adventure.

I packed my mother's bundles on the back of my bike and rode off, quickly at first, then more slowly as I came upon roads I'd never seen before. I passed farm after farm, some of which had barns and houses under the same roofs. There were farms like this in Doelitz, too, where the cows and pigs shared the same air as the people. I had never liked that kind of farm.

Gradually, the road grew bumpy and steep. I went up and down the hills, catching glimpses of huge houses set behind copses of trees. These were the estates of the wealthy landowners. The count's house would be like this, but I wasn't there yet.

I rode until I came to a turn-off my mother had told me about. It was a winding, uphill path full of muddy ruts from the spring rains. I would have to push my bike, but first I wanted to take a break.

I sat against a tree, my bike at my side, and unwrapped my sandwiches, reading the newspaper as I ate, the pages rustling softly as a cool breeze began to pick up. When I was done, I crumpled the newspaper into my bike basket, along with the bundle for Paula, and started up the path, pushing my bike along the narrow trail. Numerous branches forked off; I tried to remember my mother's directions. She had said to turn by the stream. There was a trickle of water running down some rocks: was that considered a stream? Or was there a bigger stream up ahead?

I followed the trickle for awhile, but didn't come to an apple orchard, which was the next landmark, so I reversed course, alternately pushing and dragging my bike over the bumps and rocks until I thought I had found the path I'd been on before. But after walking for a while it, too, looked different, horribly different. I tried another path, twisting and turning over unfamiliar ground, a cold fear settling in my stomach.

I was lost.

Already it was afternoon; the clouds were darker, more threatening. A few drops of rain hit my face. I pulled on my jacket and plodded miserably along. My feet hurt from the rocks; my arms and shoulders ached from pushing my bicycle, which had never seemed heavier.

Then, suddenly, I saw it. The apple orchard, with a path alongside it curving to the right, just as my mother had described.

I followed this path for what seemed like hours. The sky darkened further, the wind grew sharp, and the rain began pouring down. I shivered in my thin coat, turned a bend in the road, and then saw before me, surrounded by trees, a massive house, bigger than any house I had ever seen before. It had spires like a castle and walls of stone and a wrought-iron metal gate with spikes going all around it. Hanging from the gate was a metal plaque inscribed Count Graf von Bassowitz.

I pushed the gate open, then led my bike through, following the stone walkway past the gardens to the main door, a polished slab of dark wood that was twice the width of a regular door, with gleaming golden doorknobs and a huge golden doorknocker. Surrounding the doorway curved an ornately carved wooden trellis, covered with flowering ivy.

Before I had a chance to knock, the door swung open and Paula rushed out. "What are you doing here?"

Paula was wearing a new-looking dress, one I hadn't seen before, her hair was curled, and were those stockings she was wearing? She looked like somebody else.

"Mami sent me," I said, still breathing hard from my journey.

"What for?"

I reached into my bike basket and took out the large package wrapped in newspaper. It had gotten a little muddy from the times I tipped my bike over.

"She wanted me to give you this."

"Oh really?" Paula tore at the newspaper and looked inside. I smelled ham. A piece of paper fluttered out and fell to the ground. Paula picked it up, read it, then crumpled it.

She shoved the package and the wrinkled paper into my hands. "Take it back to her," she said. "Tell her I don't want it or anything else from her. Go on, go away. Take it back."

"What?"

"You heard me. Go home!" Paula's face was twisted with rage. She turned and started yanking on the doorknob, ready to slip back inside the mansion.

"Paula, wait! Wait!" Before I knew it, I was crying. "I can't go back now. I just got here. I'm so tired and cold. Please don't make me go back yet."

Paula sighed. "Oh, all right. Come on. You can stay here tonight."

I left my bike outside, along with my mother's rejected ham, and stepped through the giant doorway into the castle of my dreams.

Everywhere I turned my head, I encountered a new delight, from the polished floors with their thick, colorful rugs to the oil paintings, lit by tiny, gold-plated lamps, to the massive draperies of shiny, silvery fabric, to the towering stained glass windows.

"Oh, Paula," I breathed.

"Come on, come on," she said impatiently. "I've got to get back to work. Don't stand there staring like a bumpkin. It's just a house. You get used to it."

She took me up a long, curved stairway, with thick green carpeting running down the middle of the stairs and a gleaming wooden banister thicker than three of my hands.

"You can play with Victoria until supper," Paula said. "But you don't eat with us, you hear me? You eat in the kitchen, with the servants. Stay out of the way and don't embarrass me. You can go home in the morning."

I nodded, all of a sudden aware of how very hungry and thirsty I was.

Paula led me down a hallway longer than our house, with door after door on each side. Finally she came to a set of French doors; she opened them, then led me into a large room with walls that looked like brown leather. I caught a glimpse of a canopy bed at one end, with two large dressers and mirrors. At another end of the room were shelves of books and games and dolls, a child-sized sofa, two armchairs, and a fireplace.

"Hello? Who's this?" A girl about my age jumped off the bed and came over to us. She was dressed in green silk, with golden hair hanging from her head in tubes—banana curls, I thought they were called; I had seen them once in a magazine.

"Victoria, this is my little sister, Tilli, who has come for the night," said Paula.

"Wonderful!" said Victoria. "Hi, Tilli. Do you want to sit by the fire? You look frozen."

I found myself being led away by this magical girl, this real-life princess. She curled up on a fluffy white rug in front of the blazing fire. I sat down next to her and just about sighed at the feeling of warmth seeping through my chilled hands and feet.

"Tilli, remember, be good," warned Paula. Why did she have to say that? I was always good, but now maybe Victoria wouldn't think so.

Paula left. Victoria turned to me and smiled. "How old are you?"

"Nine. I'll be ten soon."

"I'm nine, too. Do you have any other sisters besides Paula?"

"No, but I have three brothers, but one doesn't live with us. Do you have any brothers or sisters?"

"I have two sisters, but they're grown up and they live far away, so it's just me here."

We listened for a minute to the sounds of the logs sizzling on the fire, which thankfully covered the sounds of my stomach growling.

"What's it like in Doelitz?" asked Victoria. "Do you have a lot of friends?"

"I guess so. I go to school in Gnoien—the high school—and I have friends there, too."

"You're so lucky. I don't have friends."

"None?" I found this hard to believe.

"Well, we don't live near anybody and with the war we haven't been traveling and haven't had any company and we have to be careful who we are friendly with, that's what Papa says."

"What about school?"

"I don't go to school. I have tutors and my governess. The servants live in their cottages and they don't bring their children here and Mother says I can't go visit them, it wouldn't be right."

"Why do you have leather walls?" I asked.

"That's to keep the noise out."

"What noise?"

"Well, if I ever make any noise, no one has to hear it. My parents put it on a long time ago, when my sisters were younger. Do you want to play with something?"

"Sure."

We got up and I looked through her toy collection, at the rag dolls and porcelain dolls and stuffed animals and stacks of board games. One of the games was Mill, which my brothers and I sometimes played with homemade cardboard game pieces. I got the box down and we set up the game on one of Victoria's child-sized wooden tables.

After awhile, the door opened and a young woman in a black and white uniform came in. "Victoria, time for—well, well, who is this?"

"Elsi, this is Tilli, Paula's sister," said Victoria. "She's staying overnight."

"I'm happy to meet you, Tilli," said Elsi. "Wouldn't you like to wash for dinner? You can use Victoria's bathroom."

Elsi pointed to a door next to Victoria's bed. I opened it and tried to keep from crying out. Victoria's bathroom was like nothing I'd ever seen outside the pages of a magazine. There was a shining pink porcelain sink, twice the size of an ordinary one, with a gold faucet. A real toilet, also made of pink porcelain. A massive pink porcelain bathtub with more gold faucets and claw feet. Gold-framed mirrors. Rose wallpaper, crystal bowls filled with different-colored soaps, golden towel-bars with soft-looking white and pink monogrammed towels.

I looked at myself in the mirror over the sink and could see why Elsi had wanted me to wash up. I looked terrible. I had mud on my forehead and my hair was coming out of its braids and my clothes were dirty and grass-stained. I wiped some water on my face and dried it with my sleeve. I was not about to soil any of Victoria's pure white towels.

A gong sounded and Victoria called to me through the door that it was time for dinner. I came out of the bathroom and we walked down the stairs to another hallway, through more rooms, so many I lost count. We neared the entry to what appeared to be a dining room. I saw a chandelier and a massive table and servants in black walking in and out carrying silver trays.

"I'm supposed to eat dinner with the cook," I said.

"Oh, no. That's too bad." Victoria looked hurt. "Will you come back and play with me after dinner?"

"I don't know. That's up to Paula."

Victoria's face fell. "Well, if I don't see you again, good-bye." She gave me a quick hug and I thought she smelled like my mother's flower garden in the spring. "The kitchen is over there. Good-bye."

"Good-bye."

I turned and walked to the door Victoria had pointed out and pushed my way through. Inside was a giant kitchen, larger than my whole house. There were at least three steel stoves and an enormous sink and mountains of dishes and pots and pans everywhere.

Paula came up. "There you are. What took you so long?" She took me to a table where a plump older woman wearing a white apron and headscarf was sitting. "Gretchen, this is Tilli, my sister that I told you about."

The cook smiled at me. "How skinny you are. Come here, dear, and have some roast beef."

Gretchen motioned me to sit at the table in front of her. She got up and started setting steaming plates in front of me.

"Remember now, be good," warned Paula, heading out the door toward the dining room.

I barely noticed Paula leaving. I was eating as fast as I could, devouring tender roast beef with thick brown gravy and buttery potatoes and cherries in a sauce and flaky white rolls. We never had food like this at home.

When Paula returned, I asked her if I could play with Victoria again, but she said no, it was time for bed. She took me to her bedroom upstairs. It was not as nice as Victoria's, but it was still much finer than anything in Doelitz. Paula had a large bed and a thick green comforter, grass-patterned wallpaper and a gold-trimmed lamp on a glass-topped nightstand.

I sank down on the bed, yawning already, so full and sleepy from my long day. Paula handed me a nightgown, which I slipped on. Then I climbed under the heavy covers and fell asleep instantly, dreamlessly, peacefully.

All the way home the next day, I thought about Victoria and her mansion and her life. Such an existence was so far removed from mine that it didn't seem real; it was almost as if I had dreamt the entire day. And Victoria, so pretty and friendly, and yet so lonely—I missed her, even though I barely knew her.

I also couldn't help thinking, even though I knew it was wrong to be greedy, how unfair life was. Why did someone like Victoria have so much, so many fine things, while others, like myself, had so little?

15

A week after my tenth birthday, and a few days after yet another interminable Hitler birthday ceremony at school, I received a notice from the district Party office. It was time for me to join Hitler Youth.

All girls who were ten and older were required to sign up for a branch of the Hitler Youth called the J.D.M., which stood for Young German Girls. There was another group for girls who were fourteen and older, called B.D.M., to which Paula belonged.

"Do you believe they're keeping this up?" said Henni, who was playing ball with Klara and Trudy and me. Henni was already ten and had been going to J.D.M. meetings for a few months; she said that there were no uniforms and all they did at meetings was learn songs and that it was boring and pointless.

"So what should I do?" I asked.

"Well, you'd still better register, just to be on the safe side. But I think it's pretty stupid. Everybody knows we're going to lose the war."

I went ahead and enrolled in the J.D.M. and it was just as Henni had described. We met in the villa every month, Henni and I and about twenty girls from Doelitz that I knew. Two sixteen-year-old B.D.M. members were in charge, although they seemed almost embarrassed about the whole thing. Sometimes we hiked in the woods, but mostly we sat there for an hour, singing songs about Germany and Hitler, the same songs we had to sing at school for Hitler's birthday, the same songs that made my mother snap off the radio in disgust.

Besides going to school, choir and J.D.M., my days were busy with farm chores, which always picked up in the spring, when it came time to plant and then thin the new seedlings. I didn't like any of these chores. Many of them, such as planting potatoes, were best done in the rain, and I hated getting muddy and chilled.

"Why do we have to grow so many crops?" I grumbled to my mother one night in the washkitchen, as I was pouring hot water on my arms and hands, trying to rinse off layers of caked-on dirt. "Why don't we grow just enough food for ourselves?"

"I guess I've never explained how all this works. You see, Tilli, the State orders us each year to grow certain quantities of all our crops, then turn them in. We only get to keep what's over and above our quota. And this year, the quotas are even higher. We will have just enough for ourselves—if the harvesting goes well."

"What happens if it doesn't?"

"There are punishments, but don't worry. We'll make it. We always have."

But I did worry. What if there was a run of bad weather—a drought or a bad storm or an early freeze? What would the State do to us if we didn't meet the quotas? What were the "punishments" that my mother had mentioned?

At least there was one farm task that I enjoyed: haymaking, which we did every year beginning on the first warm, dry, sunny day in June.

That year, when haymaking came, Maria, Jan, my mother, Heinz, Helmut, and I trooped out to the fields right after breakfast. Hugo hadn't been able to come home for the summer because of the war. The trains were so crowded and unreliable and in danger of being bombed that my mother and he had decided he should stay in Ludwigslust. Paula, too, wasn't there, because of her job with the count.

My mother, Maria, and I walked slowly behind the farm wagon, which Helmut drove. The wagon was loaded with pitchforks and food, and had a big gray machine roped to its back end. Max and Moritz trod carefully over the rutted, bumpy dirt roads as the machine rattled and squeaked. Jan strode on ahead, impatient with the slow pace of our procession.

The day brought memories of past haymakings, when all the neighbors would be out in their fields and we'd call to each other and share cake during breaks. Now almost all of the families had been broken up by the war; many of those in the fields were prisoners, like Jan, going through the motions of yet another task they were being forced to accomplish.

Still, even though the sense of communal joy was gone, I took pleasure in the dry, perfect weather, the bright blue of the sky with the sea of long yellow hay rippling in the breeze, the sounds of the birds singing to each other.

When we reached our land, Jan started up the gray machine, setting its teeth low to the ground and then driving it, with a loud roar, across the field. Stalks of fresh-cut hay shot out in rows on the ground behind it. Our job was to follow the machine and lift the fallen hay with our pitchforks, turning it over to dry in the sun. Two days later, we would come back and turn the hay again. If it was dry enough, we'd rake it into piles, then tie these piles with string, making bales of hay that we'd bring home and store in the barn.

Quickly we fell into rhythm with our pitchforks. My mother began singing the song we always sang during haymaking, a song all about a happy wandering miller. "*Wandering is the joy of the miller*," she sang. My brothers and I joined in and I remembered haymakings before the war got so bad, when my heart had been so light and this song would make me feel like soaring in the sky. "*It would not be a good miller, who never thinks of wandering, of wandering.*"

At mid-morning we took a break, sitting amid piles of hay to eat pieces of my mother's sweet yeast cake. Jan seemed impatient, tapping his foot, anxious to get back to the chore at hand. The rest of us, though, stretched and took our time with our snack. Straw was sticking in my boots, my dress, my hair. I felt pieces of it in my mouth, along with the cake, but I didn't mind. I liked being a scarecrow.

I lay back in a pile of hay, which was already warm from the sun. I looked up at the sky and wondered how far I was seeing, how many miles it was to the nearest cloud, how far away heaven was. The blue, the perfect innocent blue, looked as though it had no end, yet I knew from school that there were planets up there, spinning in darkness somewhere above us all. Heaven was up there, too, although I never understood where it was in relation to all those planets and galaxies and the deep dark outer space that my textbooks told about. Still, I liked to imagine angels flying around, watching over us; I wondered how we must appear to them at that moment. Specks in a golden field, that was us: busy giving the earth a haircut.

After our break, we worked until noon, walked home for lunch, then came back for more. My hands were red and sore from the pitchfork, but I felt curiously light, content, even—could it be?—happy.

It was one of the last happy moments I would have for a very long time.

PART II

16

"Hurry, Tilli! I can hear the whistle!"

Lori Pech and I are running down the road, our breath clouding in the crystal air. All around us are half-naked trees, their crimson leaves curled on the ground. The air is sharp with the smell of winter; the wind slaps our cheeks, but still we run, because the train is just pulling into the station.

Nearly every afternoon for the past two months, Lori and I have been coming here to look for her missing father. She is certain that someday he will be on the train. My mother says Lori is dreaming. "Herr Pech is dead," my mother told me one day, when Lori was not there. "Look how long he's been missing. Lori will have to face it, eventually."

Of course, I don't repeat this to Lori, who is only eight, young enough to believe in magic. Instead, I go with her as often as I can. Maybe when she finally realizes her father won't ever be on the train, I will be able to comfort her. So far, though, she is firm in her faith.

"Papa's coming home soon," she always says, her brown eyes blazing in her oval face, which is disfigured by a large red birthmark covering her forehead. Every day, after the train has emptied and her father is not on it and we are walking home, she repeats her belief: "Papa's coming home soon. And I'm going to be there for him."

We never know for sure when the train will show up. When it does, every car is jammed with people on top of people, some clinging to the outside walls, others hanging on the entryways where the doors have been taken off to provide more room.

Lori's father is never among the crowds of people who get off, most of whom are refugees who have fled their homes in other parts of Germany, who climb down hauling overstuffed satchels, their faces shocked and strangely empty-looking. They wander dazedly down the road, not appearing to know where to go next. Sometimes Army officials are there to intercept them, to direct them to the villa, where cots have been set up for these refugees until lodgings can be found for them among families in the village.

Sometimes soldiers get off the train—injured soldiers, horribly injured, with bloody rags wrapped around stumps where legs and arms had once been, men so pale they look ghostly, their eyes black as death.

The nearest hospital, which is in Gnoien, became so overrun with injured soldiers that officials had to open a second, emergency field hospital, which they set up in my old grade school, after moving the children to a nearby abandoned factory. Now there's a big red cross painted on the roof of my old school and the classrooms are filled with torn-apart men.

Today I notice with surprise that there are no refugees pouring off the train. In fact, nobody is getting off at all; it is idling at the platform.

"Papa! Papa!" cries Lori, running faster. We get closer and then we can see that the train is crammed full of soldiers—German soldiers, many of them wounded. They are bone-thin, frail, and many are bandaged: I see dozens of heads wrapped in gray, arms in slings, stumps of legs covered with blood-soaked cloths.

The conductor walks off, looking happy to stretch his legs.

"Papa! Papa!" Lori runs up to one of the boxcars. The soldiers look at her. "Hey," one of them yells. "We need food. We're starving."

A chorus rises from the cars. "Please, little girl. Please get food."

We rush back to my house. I burst in on my mother, who is in the kitchen, and tell her what's wrong. She fills two milk cans with the pea soup that we were going to have for supper. Lori and I each lug a heavy can back to the station, then pass them up to the soldiers, who take turns drinking right from the cans.

In a few short minutes, the cans are empty.

"Thank you," an ashen-faced soldier with a bloody eye patch says, his face twisting into a half-smile.

"Have you seen my father? Frederich Pech?" Lori asks.

The man shakes his head. The conductor is back; he shoos us away. We step down as the train whistle sounds, then watch the cars pull away from the platform, listening as the men call to us, their thin arms waving out the windows.

The next day, the train is back with its usual cargo of refugees and the occasional injured soldier. We keep coming, every afternoon, until one day, as the refugees stream off the platform and Lori makes her usual "Papa! Papa!" cry, a man calls back.

"Lori! My Lori!" cries Frederich Pech.

He walks up to us, a figure out of a dream. His right leg trails numbly behind him, swathed in dirty gray cloth. He is ashen, with yellow circles under his eyes, and has a scraggly beard falling to his chin.

But it is him.

Lori is beside herself, sobbing and repeating, over and over again, "I knew it, I knew it, I knew it." They hold each other tightly, wrapped in each other, not moving.

I hurry home by myself and find my mother in the living room, sewing. "Mami, guess what? You'll never believe it. Lori's father is back! He's here! I just saw him at the station."

"What?" my mother grins broadly. "Well, I'll be. I wouldn't have thought it possible."

That night, after supper, we bring the Pechs a cake and join in the family's celebration of their miracle.

After that, my trips to the train station become more infrequent. Sometimes Henni comes with me, just to see all the different types of people who are finding their way to our village. Lori never comes with us. She spends all her time with her father.

◆   ◆   ◆

One Saturday, while I am sweeping fallen leaves in the yard, Corporal Ring comes to the door, escorting a white-haired old woman, wrapped in a brown shawl and clutching an overstuffed green suitcase.

"Heil Hitler," I say, letting Corporal Ring and the woman into the kitchen. Maria, who is washing dishes, stiffens at the sight of the corporal. "Heil Hitler," he says, staring suspiciously at her as she repeats the gesture in a soft voice.

This fall, Maria finally quit wearing her babushka. Her hair is light brown with flecks of gold; it falls in soft waves around her face and past her ears, almost to her shoulders. It makes her look sophisticated and older than sixteen. I can tell that Corporal Ring does not recognize her as the starved, beaten girl in the babushka he left in our kitchen so many months ago, but he can tell she is not one of us.

The old woman, meanwhile, is looking our kitchen over with alert blue eyes. She grins at me, showing a mouth with no teeth.

Mami steps into the kitchen, brushing straw off her apron.

"Frau Horn, this is Frau Hoppe," says Corporal Ring. "She is a refugee from East Prussia and we have assigned her to your house."

"I see," says my mother.

"That's it, then," says Corporal Ring. More Heil Hitlers, and he is out the door.

"Won't you have a seat?" says my mother to the old woman.

Frau Hoppe sits down with a sigh. "Ah, this feels good, my dear. I've been walking for days, it seems like, trying to get away before the Russians come through. We've all been leaving, where I'm from. I wanted to get to my daughter in Berlin, but that's too far. I haven't heard from her in so long. I don't even know if she's alive. I hope I can get there soon. I won't be any trouble."

Frau Hoppe stops talking for a moment to drink some barley coffee and my mother starts to ask her a few questions, but before she can finish, Frau Hoppe is off and talking again, words bursting out of her as if she hasn't had anybody to speak to in weeks.

We settle Frau Hoppe in my room. I move my clothes and my doll, Doris, into my mother's room. My mother's bed has two mattresses, side by side, and I pick the one closest to the wall, right under the Jesus picture. I actually prefer sleeping in here with my mother instead of upstairs by myself, but other than this change, I don't really like having Frau Hoppe in our house, the main reason being that Frau Hoppe can't keep quiet. I had thought that after she told us the story of her life a few times she would keep her mouth shut, but she never does. She talks to anyone who will listen, on and on, with story after story about her children and her home and her sensitive stomach and her sciatica, which is worse in the fall.

One good thing about Frau Hoppe is that she loves to spin. She sits for hours every day, spinning yards of yarn, alternately singing and talking to herself. I learn to avoid her when I can. My ears can only take so much.

As November edges into December, with ice storms and cruel winds whipping over the hills, I expect the flood of refugees to dry up. Surely people won't leave their homes in this weather. But I am wrong. More arrive each day. Everybody I know has taken in at least one person or family.

One day near Christmastime, Henni and I discover another trainload of soldiers stopped at the station, with no one getting off. These soldiers are not wearing German uniforms. And they are in even worse shape than the German soldiers Lori and I had seen earlier that fall. They are so thin they are little more than skeletons, with just enough flesh pasted on to make them vaguely resemble human beings.

"Russians," says Henni. "See. The uniforms are yellow."

Some Army officials crowd around the train, talking in low voices to the conductor, the air freezing in clouds around their mouths. One of the Army men notices us. "Go on home, girls. The train is staying here for the night. There's nobody getting off. You can go on home."

When I tell my mother about the train, she gathers food together: loaves of bread and cans of hot soup and barley coffee. Then she and I and my brothers walk back to the station. It is late afternoon; the sky is nearly dark, the wind howling. The soldiers have no doors to protect them from the wind and cold, no blankets with which to cover themselves.

"Why don't they just shoot the poor bastards?" Helmut says.

"This is no way to treat anybody, no matter whose side they are on," says my mother angrily. "They are humans, people just like us."

The Army men standing guard look at us curiously, but don't try to stop us. I hoist loaves of bread up to the windows. A few of the almost-dead men stir enough to look at me, then take the bread and begin passing the loaves around. Helmut hands in the cans of soup. We wait and watch as about a third of the men in each car have enough life left in them to eat. We carry the cans from car to car. Soon the food is gone.

My mother stands near the platform, looking at the train cars and at the Army guards who seem oblivious to the intense misery seeping from the train, who don't seem to mind that dozens of men only a few feet from them are near death.

"Father, forgive them," she whispers. "For they know not what they do."

In the morning, the death train is gone.

Two weeks after that, Lori Pech walks to the station once again. Her father is with her, in uniform. He has recovered from his injuries and has been ordered back to his unit.

"What a joke," says Helmut. "The war's over, practically, and he's got to go back? What's the point?"

After Herr Pech leaves, Lori and I begin our vigil once more, trudging in the snow and ice to watch the daily parade of misery passing through Doelitz, hoping once again for a miracle.

But miracles never come twice, and Lori never sees her father again.

17

One morning after a bombing run that sounded especially close we look out the window to see thick black smoke curling on the horizon.

"Rostock," says Helmut grimly. "That's got to be what was hit."

Rostock is a medium-sized harbor town on the Baltic Sea, not more than thirty miles away. I've never been there, but still I shudder to think how the circle of bombings is tightening around us.

It is winter now. The days are short, with darkness falling as early as 4 p.m. We can't use electricity or kerosene or candles because of the war. So we sit in the darkness, barely able to see each other's faces. We sit for hours together after supper, usually in the kitchen, which is warm from the stove, listening to Helmut playing his accordion and telling each other stories.

My mother is the main storyteller, the one we clamor to hear. Over and over again she recounts to us our family's legends. How Heinz came to us is a favorite. My mother adopted him on the spur of the moment. She had gone with a friend to an orphanage. Her friend couldn't have any more children and wanted a baby girl to be a playmate for her daughter. The woman at the orphanage brought out a small, sickly looking little boy. There were no girls, she said, but how about this sweet boy? My mother's friend turned away, but my mother was so taken with the boy—with Heinz, then nine years old, though he looked five—that she adopted him right then and there, a decision no one has regretted for an instant.

Another story she tells is about the day, soon after I was born, when she left me in a potato field. She had been so busy and so exhausted from taking care of me and the rest of the family and working on the farm that she set me down beside her to sleep, right there between the rows of plants, and then forgot about me. She went back to the house to make dinner and only then realized she had abandoned her baby in a field. She ran back sobbing and found me sleeping peacefully.

My mother's stories fill the hours: How Paula let my baby carriage run into a tree. How hard it was for my mother to take Hugo to the special school for the first time, but how happy he soon became. How my brothers broke a neighbor's window with a rock and how angry my mother was at them.

We listen, over and over again, never tiring of them. But one night, my mother doesn't want to tell them any more.

"I'm so tired," she whispers. "Someone else tell something."

"No, Mami," I say. "I want to hear you."

"You always talk about our childhoods. Why don't you tell us something about your childhood for a change?" suggests Heinz.

My mother is quiet for a few minutes, then begins, her voice distant and already far away. "All right. I have been thinking a lot lately about my past. You know I was part of a large family—"

We huddle closer to her soft voice and for the first time I learn how my mother came to be who she is.

◆   ◆   ◆

Regina Louise Schneider was born in 1898, the fifth of nine children. Her family lived in Bottenhorn, near Marburg. Her father worked in a shale quarry—dark, dangerous work. The family also had a little land, on which they raised animals and farmed what they could. But the land was not good, and the family was very poor.

When Regina was fourteen, her parents sent her to live and work at a large farm in another part of town. She liked the family she worked for. The woman treated her like a daughter; for the first time in her life, Regina felt special, almost doted-upon, and she grew happy. She slept in the family's house and gradually came to love them.

The family had a son named Robert, who was two years older than Regina. Regina became fond of Robert. As she grew older, her feelings for Robert became more than just fondness. Regina fell in love with Robert, and he fell in love with her. When she was nineteen, Regina became pregnant.

She was afraid, but hopeful that maybe she and Robert could get married and raise their child together. But Robert's parents were furious. They—especially the mother, who had been so kind to Regina—felt that Regina had betrayed them, that she was trying to steal their son and worm her way into ownership of their property.

Regina's parents also were shocked. Her father slapped her across the face. Her mother refused to look at her. "We are respected people in this town," her mother said. "We raised you to be a good Christian girl. How could you do this to us?"

Robert didn't fight for Regina. He was sent to live with relatives. Regina packed her things and left, alone. Her parents wouldn't let her come home, so she moved in with an aunt and uncle until her baby was born, in a barn, with her aunt helping with the birth. The baby was a girl, a beautiful girl with a heart-shaped pink face. Regina loved her instantly, but her aunt pulled the baby out of her arms two days after she was born. "Go away, now," the aunt said to her. "We are raising this girl."

Regina begged and pleaded to keep the baby. The answer was no. She left, alone, and went to another farm in another village, where her parents had arranged a job for her. This farm wasn't as nice as the first, and the family didn't treat her as well. They knew her reputation.

Regina met a bricklayer named Heinrich Horn. He was darkly handsome, with nice white teeth. He loved to sing and dance. Regina by this time had given up hope that some day Robert would come and get her and reunite her with their baby. That only happened in fairy tales, she decided.

So, when Heinrich Horn came around, taking her to the harvest dance and singing to her in the moonlight, her heart opened to him. She never fell in love with him the way she had with Robert. But she was flattered that he admired her and she let herself be wooed.

And then she became pregnant again.

Heinrich wasn't happy about it. But he did the honorable thing. He married Regina and the couple moved in with his parents in a tiny, dark little house in a remote town called Ebersgoens. Heinrich was one of fourteen children, so the house was very crowded. Regina didn't feel well, partly from being pregnant but also from thinking, deep in her heart, that maybe she had made a mistake. Heinrich also was unhappy. The Depression had hit and it was hard for him to find work.

Their baby was born soon after their marriage. Another girl, another adorable baby girl; Regina named her Elisabeth. New joy blossomed in her heart with this baby, this second chance. She carried her everywhere, snuggled against her breast, and sometimes when she sang lullabies to Elisabeth, tears would run down her cheeks at the sight of her daughter's beauty, and her love would feel so sharp it would hurt.

When Elisabeth was nine months old, she became very sick. She coughed and wheezed and her skin grew sweaty and pale and gray and then, finally, blue. Regina did what she could. She held Elisabeth's tiny head over steaming water, over boiling chamomile leaves, trying to open her breathing passages. But there was nothing that could be done.

Elisabeth was buried in a tiny wooden coffin that Heinrich made. For a brief time after her death, Regina and Heinrich grew close again, and Regina had more children. Another girl: Paula, born in 1924. Then a son, Hugo, in 1926, and another son, Helmut, in 1928.

When Paula was two, one of Heinrich's brothers came down with tuberculosis. He had been a great favorite of Paula's; he was jovial and loved swinging Paula around in the air over his head. When he got sick, Paula asked for Uncle Leo. Regina, busy with her new baby boy, let Paula crawl into bed with her uncle, not realizing the danger until it was too late, until Paula, too, began coughing uncontrollably.

Paula had to go stay in a special tuberculosis hospital, a two-hour walk from Ebersgoens. Regina made the trip as often as she could, but she had a new problem at home. When Hugo was two months old, he became very ill from an ear infection. He screamed and screamed, but finally stopped. After that, he never moved when Regina called to him or sang to him. Gradually, she realized that Hugo was deaf.

Just after the doctors confirmed that there was nothing they could do to restore Hugo's hearing, Regina got a letter from her sister, Bertha, who was emigrating to America. Bertha invited Regina and her family to come with her. Regina and Heinrich talked it over. They decided maybe they would like a change. But when they inquired about getting permission to enter America, they found that they could not bring Hugo because of his deafness. Regina refused to leave Hugo behind, so they decided not to go to America after all.

Meanwhile, Paula, who stayed in the hospital for two years, had been operated upon. The doctors thought that a good way to treat tuberculosis was to drain the lymph glands near the face. After that, Paula had a big scar along one side of her face. But she was alive. Regina was able to bring her home, though she remained frail and prone to coughing fits that worried Regina constantly.

Then Heinrich heard about a wonderful opportunity in northeastern Germany. A rich landowner had died, and his widow had decided to turn his estate into seventy-eight homesteads for farmers. The government was helping with low-interest loans for anybody who wanted to make a new start.

With money borrowed from Aunt Bertha, who was already becoming rich in America, Regina and Heinrich joined the seventy-seven other new farmers moving in to stake their claims.

The first few years were incredibly hard, but also happy. Regina and Heinrich worked side by side establishing the farm, with Regina making most of the decisions since she had a farming background. Paula grew healthier in the fresh country air.

Then Regina got pregnant again. She kept working, even though being pregnant made her tired; she had no choice. She had a baby, a new little girl. Regina wanted to name her Marianna. She told Heinrich to file that name with the authorities, but when he came back from the courthouse with the baby's birth certificate, Regina discovered that he had named the girl Ottilie instead, keeping Marianna as the middle name.

"It's done, it's decided," Heinrich told her.

Regina decided not to fight. She was too tired to fight. The baby was named Ottilie, but called Tilli for short. Regina loved her very much, but it was difficult finding time to run the new farm and take care of another baby. Regina was under so much stress that, for the first time in her life, she had no milk for her baby. "What will I do?" she worried, as Tilli screamed in hunger.

Another woman in the village had also just had a baby. She was a large woman named Tilla. Tilla had no trouble making milk; she had more than enough. So Regina hired her as a wet-nurse for Tilli, who soon grew big and strong from Tilla's plentiful milk. Unlike Regina's other daughters, who were short like she was, Tilli grew and grew, soon becoming the tallest child her age in kindergarten.

Regina was happy, as happy as she had ever been. The farm was prospering; her children were healthy; she even began seeing her daughter again, her first daughter whom she hadn't seen in years, her daughter Dora, who by now had grown and had her own child, Regina's grandchild, the baby Ingrid.

And then the war began, and everything changed.

◆   ◆   ◆

My mother stops speaking. It has been hours since she started, since I have been transported back in time, into the life of this woman, this Regina. My mother. But I suddenly realize she is more than just that. So much more. She is a real woman, who has been young and has had a life completely apart from mine, a life with sorrows and joys and hopes and passions that I never knew the first thing about.

My mother has been in love with a different man—not my father—and lost him.

My mother has had an illegitimate baby.

And then it hits me. "You mean Dora is my sister?" I've only seen Dora a few times, when she came to visit us before the war became so bad that people couldn't travel any more. She'd seemed nice enough, though I couldn't really picture her.

"That's right."

"Didn't you know?" says Helmut. "I thought you knew."

"Then Ingrid is my niece?" Ingrid was Dora's little girl; I changed her diapers the last time they stayed with us.

"That's right."

"Really, Tilli," says Heinz. "We all knew that. Who did you think they were?"

I can't explain. I had seen Dora and Ingrid as simply a pair of my mother's many far-flung friends or distant relatives. They were nice to me; that's all I had ever really noticed.

I go to sleep that night thinking about my new big sister and my new niece. I wish I could see them again. It has been a long time. I hope they are all right, living in Kassel with bombs hurtling down on them. I would like a chance someday to get to know them better.

I also wonder about my sister, Elisabeth, the one who died when she was a baby, before I was born. She would be in her twenties now. Would she have looked like me? Maybe she would have had children—nieces and nephews that I could have helped care for.

I like to think that Elisabeth is my guardian angel in heaven. Everyone has to have a guardian angel, right? So why not my innocent baby sister?

On the other hand, I don't know what to think about God. My mother's faith never wavers: she prays several times a day, often sings hymns, recites long Bible verses from memory, and has never expressed a single doubt. But for me, even though I pray every night, it doesn't seem likely that God is there. I can't believe He is watching all these things happening in my country. If He were, surely He would stop them. He wouldn't let people kill each other like this. He would stop Hitler. He would protect us, if He were real. Wouldn't He?

18

As the icy darkness of winter settles around us, a new worry crops up in our household. Max, one of our horses, falls ill, his stomach puffed and bloated. My mother tries different herbal remedies, but nothing seems to help.

"I'm afraid we might lose him," my mother says to us one night at supper.

"Oh, no," I say. I can't explain how much our horses mean to me. I love them almost as much as my family. They are so gentle and kind and do whatever we ask.

I go to see Max, lying on his side in the straw, and rest my face against his sweaty neck. I pat him. He is quivering. "Max, please get better," I say softly. "Please, please. I love you."

Moritz stands worriedly nearby, letting out little whinnies of concern and shifting his feet.

I pet him. "Don't worry. Nothing will happen to Max. He'll get better."

In the middle of the crisis with Max, an Army official appears, one I haven't seen before. He brandishes a paper at my mother.

"No," she whispers.

"What was that, Frau Horn?" he says loudly.

"Please, our other horse is sick. We have to have horses to farm. If we can't farm, we can't meet our quotas, and then we can't give you food. Can't you reconsider?"

I am not used to hearing my mother beg.

"These are your orders, Frau Horn. Take me to your horse."

"Mami, what's happening?" I ask, tugging at her apron.

"Shhh, Tilli, stop it."

She puts on her coat. I follow. She takes the young Army man through the yard to the horse barn. We go in. Heinz and Helmut are kneeling at Max's side, rubbing him with a towel. They look up at us.

"Boys," says my mother. "This is Officer Schmidt."

They stand up. "Heil Hitler."

"Heil Hitler," says Officer Schmidt. He spots Moritz, goes over to him, pats his legs and hindquarters, and examines his mouth. "Yes, he'll do just fine."

"Mami?" says Helmut, his eyes blazing.

"Not now, boys," she says.

"Do you have a blanket for him?" says Officer Schmidt. "And a bridle, of course."

My mother hands the officer Moritz's blanket. She slips his bridle on gently, stroking the star on his forehead.

"Mami!" Heinz and Helmut are glaring at Officer Schmidt and are standing in front of Moritz, trying to protect him.

"Boys," says my mother, her voice impossibly weary. "Tilli. Moritz has—has been drafted. You need to say good-bye to him now."

"What!" shouts Helmut. Heinz and I are speechless. I feel my throat close, my eyes fill. I don't know how to say good-bye to such a dear friend. I rest my face against Moritz's cheek, rub his nose one last time, then, with a gasp, run out of the barn, run, run, my lungs burning in the cold, run to the back of the yard, where I slump in the fresh cold snow.

I don't watch as the Army officer takes Moritz away.

I hadn't known horses could get drafted, too, but my mother says it is happening all over Doelitz.

"Will he ever come back?" I ask.

"I don't think so, Tilli."

Max dies the next day. My brothers bury him in the barnyard, with Jan helping to dig the grave. They have to use picks to break apart the frozen earth. It takes most of a day. We say prayers over the hole after he is buried. Except for Jan, we are all crying, even my brothers, who are as shaken as I have ever seen them.

"Those stupid Nazi fools," he complains. "They've really crippled us. How do you run a farm with no horses? What will we do in the spring? Pull the machines ourselves?"

"We don't care about that!" I shout at Jan. I am amazed at myself, at the hot anger bursting through me. I have never spoken up to him before. "Don't you see? We love Max and Moritz. They are our family!"

Jan rolls his eyes and walks away.

My mother gives me a hug. She wipes my cheeks. "We have each other," she says. "Don't you ever forget that. So many families have been torn apart, but we are so very lucky. We have this greatest of gifts, to be with each other."

I try to take comfort in her words. But all I can think about is the empty horse barn and my two dear friends that are no more.

I should have listened to my mother. A week later, Officer Schmidt is back with another paper, although this time he hasn't come for an animal.

This time, he has come for my brother.

Helmut, at age sixteen, has been drafted.

◆   ◆   ◆

"It's not right, not right, not right!" my mother seethes, wrapping her arms around herself.

I have never seen her like this. Tears are pouring openly down her cheeks. Her headscarf is half off, so that her hair straggles out, but she doesn't seem to notice. She paces back and forth in the kitchen, her hands twisting nervously. They are coming for Helmut in an hour.

"We've got to do something," she says. "This can't be. He's only a baby. He's my baby."

Mami suddenly drops into a chair and cups her face in her hands, shaking and choking with tears. Maria and I put our arms around her. We don't know what to say or do. I am numb.

Heinz and Helmut come downstairs, ashen-faced, red-eyed. My strong, happy-go-lucky, high-spirited big brothers are gone, replaced by terrified children.

Fleetingly, I wonder why they didn't draft Heinz, too. He is, after all, a year older than Helmut, though he doesn't look it because he is so short, shorter than me now. Perhaps he is not in the Army's files because he was adopted.

My mother brushes quickly at her face, trying desperately to be in control, to be strong for Helmut, who is trembling.

"I'm going to be sick," Helmut says, then runs outside.

"Why are they taking him now?" says Heinz. "The war is over, damn it. Everybody knows that. Why are they taking him now?"

He's going to die, I think. What else can be expected, with the Russians and Americans so close at hand, so many of them, so powerful, overwhelming the German soldiers, winning all the battles? How can Helmut possibly survive?

Helmut comes back inside. We huddle on the bench, his head on my mother's shoulder. She strokes his hair, wipes his wet cheek.

The Army comes early. Slam! Slam! on the door, and then the words, those hated words: "Heil Hitler!"

Helmut marches off, as bravely as he can. He is not the only boy from the village to be taken. The Army has come through and cleaned out the houses, taking boys aged sixteen and up. Two Army men lead the parade along the icy roads, walking to Gnoien to join the other last-minute recruits; then my brother and the others will board a wagon and be taken God knows where.

My mother whispers a prayer as she stares after Helmut. "Dear God, dear God, dear God," is all I hear her say. Maybe that is all she needs to say.

We crowd outside the house, watching as Helmut and the other boys—the children's Army, I think bitterly—grow smaller in the distance.

"What madness this is," mutters Jan, his frown fiercer than ever. "What total madness."

◆   ◆   ◆

I don't know why school is still in session. We have no paper or ink or pencils, but even worse than the lack of supplies is the tense mood that makes it impossible to concentrate. Everybody in class is missing someone, worried about a father, a brother, a cousin. Rostock is being regularly hit with firebombs, so that the sky lights up a fantastic red and orange and yellow at night. We peek from behind the black shades to watch it and can only hope that there are no people caught in the inferno.

More refugees have been assigned to our house, which is so crowded that I can't walk through without bumping into someone. A girl named Ruth, about Paula's age, who fled Prussia with her family, has moved in with us, though her family is staying at the villa with other refugees. We also are home to the Pommerenkes: a father, mother, and two little boys. The Party brought them to our house one morning, dirty and exhausted.

"Come in, come in," my mother said, trying to be gracious. Then she drew the officer aside and asked him where she was supposed to put a whole family. The officer just shrugged. "You'll make do."

My mother moved the Pommerenkes into the living room. They use the sofa as a bed, all of them crowded together, and keep their suitcases covered with a blanket in the corner. They are polite and thankful for our generosity, but they are very quiet and rarely speak to us, although their boys, Fritz and Franz, follow Heinz around whenever they can. Frau and Herr Pommerenke spend a lot of time in the living room, staring at the walls.

Even though it is not yet spring and the ground is frozen, more and more I find myself escaping outside, searching for some kind of solace. It amazes me that everything looks the same outside as always. The sweeping sky; the bare, leafless trees; the neat rows of houses lining our road; the early flowers seeking the sun, their green shoots just breaking the surface of the ground. The geese, stroking powerfully in formation across the sky. The sparrows and robins, building nests for their babies, just as they always have, every spring; just as they always will. The animals are innocently going about the business of living, unaware of the danger on the horizon.

Don't you know? I want to scream at them. *How can you be happy when everything is so very wrong?*

I try to explain my feelings to Heinz. "If I were to go outside and see the ground in flames and the houses destroyed and a black hole where the sky should be, I don't think I would be surprised, because that's what it feels like inside."

"I know what you mean," says Heinz. "The world is upside down, even though it looks normal."

Poor Heinz. Without Helmut, he is lost. He wanders the barnyard, half-heartedly working on chores, with no spirit left in him. When Jan yells at him, he just nods.

For the first time since my parents started our farm, we are not planting any spring crops. "I just don't see how we can do it," my mother says. "Without horses, with all this uncertainty, I just don't see how we can."

"But what about our quotas?" Heinz asks.

"We're not the only ones who aren't going to be meeting our quotas," says my mother. "The State surely has more important things to worry about right now."

I begin to fear that we won't have enough food to feed ourselves or our animals, but Heinz tells me that we have extra food, hidden in a secret attic he and Jan built last summer when I thought they were working on our roof. It is a small space, accessible only through a tiny panel cut into the ceiling near my old bedroom, and runs along the length of the house, just below the roof.

"Why do we have to keep food hidden?" I ask.

"Because the State says we can only have so much of each kind of food per person," Heinz says. "Anything extra that we grow we are supposed to turn over."

"You mean we have been breaking the law?"

"Shhh," says my mother, looking around. "Tilli, I know I've taught you to obey the law. But sometimes you have to do things that are more important, that are for your family, and if the law is wrong, you have to disobey it. We need the food for us, in case the worst happens. The State probably won't be in power much longer anyway."

Heinz shows me the secret attic: it is dark and musty and filled with extra sacks of grain, flour, apples, sugar, and pickled meat from animals that my mother and Jan have slaughtered, also in disobedience of the law, late at night, with straw packed around the barn doors so that the animals' screams won't be heard.

◆   ◆   ◆

One day Officer Schmidt shows up again, this time leading a reddish-brown horse with blond mane.

"We've assigned you a horse, to compensate you for your sacrifice," he says. "Of course, we recognize that you need horses so that you can better fulfill your role in the Fatherland and help our country with your contributions. Which, of course, you will continue to make as scheduled."

My mother flushes at this, but pretends to be pleased at the gift of the horse. After he leaves, she and Jan inspect the new horse, which keeps shaking its head and rolling its eyes and shifting its feet.

"Maybe we can plant after all," my mother says, gently running her hands along the horse's powerful flanks. "It looks like they're expecting us to."

"Nah," says Jan. He holds the horse's mouth open; it jerks its head, its back legs stamping the ground. "Look—he's ruined. His tongue is ripped. He's no good."

My mother sighs. "I didn't see that. You're right. We can't bridle him. And look how skittish the poor thing is."

I try to go near the horse to pet him. I miss having a horse to take care of. But my mother tells me to stay away from him. "That horse has wild eyes. Someone has hurt him badly. You'd best keep away."

We take care of the horse anyway, naming him Fox, the color of his fur. Gradually, he seems to get used to us, although his nostrils still flare and he whinnies nervously whenever we come close to him.

We plant one crop that spring: potatoes. We borrow horses from the Oleniczaks and the Hädes—both of whom have also had their best horses drafted—to pull the machine that digs holes in the ground. Then one rainy, chilly March day, we spend hours walking behind it, carrying separated potato sprouts in our aprons, dropping them in the holes and stomping down the dirt with our boots. By the end of the day, we are muddy and shivering. My back and legs ache. But at least we will have a crop of potatoes this fall. We can't plant grain, though; the ground will have to be left fallow. "Maybe that will be good for the soil," says my mother.

"But what will we feed the animals?" asks Heinz.

"We'll have to see about that later," says my mother. "There's only so much we can do. One day at a time; that's the only way we can live. One day at a time."

It's rye harvest time in 1934 and I'm an infant in Mami's arms. She is in a black dress and white headscarf. My father is seated on the far right. To the left, on the horse, is my godfather Wilhelm. In front of the horse, from the left, are a girl Hugo knew, my sister Paula, Hugo, and Helmut. My godmother's family is also in the picture.

Hugo holds Bello, then a puppy. Paula holds me, while Helmut stands beside us.

I'm about three here, holding flowers beside my home in Doelitz. The war hasn't yet started. I'm wearing a hand-me-down dress sent by Aunt Bertha in America.

My brother Helmut, with his bicycle outside our home in Doelitz in about 1938.

Heinz (left), Helmut (right), and I with our grandmother in about 1938.

Mami (right) is working in the fields with neighbor women
and my godfather, Wilhelm (center).

Sometime during my first year of school in Doelitz in
1940, my rucksack on my back. I wore the same dress to
school every day until I outgrew it; then Mami would make
me a new one. I wore my hair in braids until I was 14 and
confirmed.

Here I am at home with Helmut (left) and
Heinz (right).

I am visiting my brother Hugo in Ludwigslust, where he attended school for the deaf. It is about 1940.

Mami and me, in front of our neighbor's house, in about 1940 or 1941.

Helmut (left) with Heinz, wearing their work shoes. They most likely have just finished mucking out the bull barn, one of their daily chores.

Mami is in the fields with my father (in the foreground) and Jan.
This picture was taken when my father was home on leave from the war.

Helmut is beside Bello, who is hooked to a wagon. I'm in the wagon with my cousin Rolf. Mami stands just behind the wagon; next to her is Rolf's mother. We are outside the train station in Doelitz.

My favorite horses Max (left) and Moritz, with Heinz riding him. Moritz was drafted by the Nazis.

My Confirmation Day at age 14 was a big occasion. Left to right, top: Wolfgang holding Brig-itte (daughter of Marie Oleniczak); a family friend; Hugo; Heinz; Helmut. Bottom row: Willi (missing an arm due to a war injury); Ruth; Paula; me; Klara; a distant relative; Henni; and another distant relative.

Another Confirmation Day picture. I'm on the top row, on the left.
Next to me is Klara. In the front row are Ruth (left)
and Henni (right). Fanni also snuck in the picture (lower right).

Henni and me on our bikes in 1949.

Here I am as the Doelitz "harvest queen" in 1950,
shortly before I escaped.

Mami outside our house, with her little dog, Fanni, and another dog, Purzel, in 1951.
This picture was taken after I had left home.

It's early summer, 1952, and I'm working as a
waitress at Schimcke's restaurant in Kassel.

From left: Aunt Bertha, her friend, Ingrid, Aunt Liesel, Dora, Uncle Paul. This was taken in about 1948, when Aunt Bertha visited her relatives in Kassel. They are sitting in front of an old bunker used during the war.

I'm getting ready to board ship in Hamburg and am just about frozen with fear! From left: Ingrid, me, Aunt Liesel.

Another nervous-faced picture, taken just before leaving Germany on Sept. 12, 1952.

The ship Italia, just before setting sail. I'm in the crowd on deck,
waving good-bye. Herbert is behind me.

Herbert and I on board the Italia, having drinks with other passengers. Herbert has a lump in
his cheek from an olive he is holding there—the first olive he ever tasted in his life (along with
his first-ever martini). He later spat the olive into the ocean. When this picture was taken, I had
no idea we would ever see each other again after the voyage was over, much less be married
for 50 years and counting!

19

Many people say that the Russians soon will be taking over our part of Germany. Unless the Americans get here first, that is. Some people say the Russians are monsters who will burn Doelitz to the ground, steal everything we have, murder us in our beds if we're lucky, and, if we're not, they will kidnap us and take us to Russia to be their slaves. Even Maria says that much of the Russian Army is made up of drunken, ruthless gangs.

I have a hard time truly believing these stories, which seem so exaggerated, so unreal. It's hard to imagine that men exist who would do those things, especially to children; men who would so easily burn and steal and kill and rape.

I learned about rape last week. My mother took me aside after supper. She led me to a bench in the flower garden and took my hand in hers and her hand was so cold and her face so serious.

"Tilli, I told you before about relations between men and women," she began. "Now there's something else I need to tell you about."

She sighed and then I learned about a different kind of sex, one I hadn't heard about before. When a man forces a woman to be with him, it is called rape, and it is one of the most terrible crimes in the world.

"I wish I didn't have to tell you about it. I wish it didn't exist," my mother said. "But I have to warn you. People are going to be talking about this. You're going to hear this word, because sometimes soldiers rape women when they take over their towns."

I felt numb. My mother drew me close. "But please don't worry, Tilli. I will protect you. I will always keep you safe."

Afterward, I tried not to think about what she had said. But just as she had predicted the word kept coming up whenever people told their terrible stories about Russian atrocities. Even Maria is saying it, that the dreaded Mongols love to rape girls. Young girls, girls like me.

After I am done hand-washing the socks and underwear, I walk slowly through the barnyard, trying to clear my mind of the ugly images Maria's words have put there. I try to focus on happier things, on my studies at school, on the English I'm learning.

But tonight, as I try to fall asleep, pictures fill my mind: pigs coupling in the barn, the bull going after one of the cows. Then I see tall faceless men chasing my friends, chasing me, and I can't escape them no matter how fast I run.

And then, as I am tossing and turning, my mother's breath steady beside me, I hear the siren. My mother stirs, reaches to me, grabs my arm, and squeezes reassuringly.

The planes come, flying overhead so close that I can hear the rattling whir of their propellers. I try to count them, but it is impossible, like trying to isolate each bee from a swarm.

Thunder. Bombs, so loud, so close. The windowpanes rattle; the floor is shaking beneath us. It is deafening. Never has it been this loud before.

My mother sits up straight in bed. "Dear God," she says. "Please God, protect us."

I jump out from under my covers and run to the window. Are they bombing the neighbors? How close are they? I have to know.

"Tilli!" yells my mother as I pull back the thick black shades. But all is darkness. I can't see anything; I can only hear the thunder, the terrible thunder.

My mother grabs me away from the window. "Don't ever do that again!" she screams, pulling me back to the bed and squeezing me against her and I grab her too and shut my eyes and try to shut my ears.

The thudding continues, over and over, closer, closer. I hear myself moan. My teeth are chattering and I can't stop them I can't stop anything I can't control anything Oh God. Oh God. Help me, God.

My mother envelopes me with her arms as if to surround me with a wall that can't be penetrated. Thudding, crashing, then footsteps running downstairs, shouts from the living room, the Pommerenke boys are screaming and crying. Heinz flings open my mother's bedroom door, gasping for breath. "It's Gnoien!" he shouts. "Gnoien's on fire!"

We run upstairs. The planes sound like they are going away. We pull back the corners of the window shade in my old bedroom window and take turns looking at what appears to be a brilliant red and yellow sunrise to the east, just visible through the trees. Only it is in the middle of the night and what we are seeing cannot possibly be the sun.

The next morning, when the sky lightens, we can see clouds of thick black smoke rising from Gnoien and the air is strong with the smell of burning wood and metal. I don't go to school. Soon we get the word from neighbors who went to fight the fires: some homes and businesses were damaged, but the biggest casualty—what appears to have been the chief target—was the field hospital, my old grade school that had been housing wounded soldiers. Despite the big red cross painted on the roof, the bombers hit it anyway, and now dozens of people are dead. Patients who couldn't leave their beds, and the doctors and nurses who wouldn't abandon them, who refused to leave when the warning sirens went off.

Ilse, Eva, Inge, all my friends, my teachers. My God. Are they dead or alive?

I will have to wait to find out, because school has been canceled, suspended indefinitely due to the escalation of the war. Gnoien—the little town they said no one would care to bomb—is no longer safe.

◆   ◆   ◆

Over the next few weeks, as the warm breath of April caresses us, as the crocuses and tulips open in vivid bloom, the war crumbles to its conclusion.

In the middle of it all, I turn eleven. There are no more birthday parties for me, although my mother somehow remembers to make me a cake.

Three days after my birthday is Hitler's birthday, but this year, for the first time since the war began, no one pays any attention to it. We don't put out our flag or listen to long speeches on the radio or hold ceremonies of any sort.

I worry at first that somebody from the State will punish us, but nobody cares. That's what my mother says. Some Party officials are already running away, fleeing Germany altogether. Some are even killing themselves.

The Party is pretty much dead, I suppose, which means—in a way—that we are free now, finally free from Hitler. But if we are free, it is at a horrible price, and it doesn't bring any relief from our daily terror. I don't feel free at all.

Injured people fleeing Gnoien and Rostock and other cities crowd the roads, walking, limping, stumbling; the lucky ones have horses and wagons. They drive by steely-faced, ignoring the pleas of those on foot, the requests for rides that would swamp them if they started giving in. I don't know where all these people are going. I don't know if they know. Some of them just give up and are later found dead, lying beside the road, usually missing their shoes and sometimes their clothes, which others passing by have stripped from them.

Soldiers, too, are appearing in ever-greater numbers: more wagonloads of injured, bloody men, looking for doctors and hospitals, plus now the deserters, men who have decided on their own that this foolish, horrible war is over and that they are going home, the State, the Party, Hitler be damned.

One afternoon, I hear Jan say to Mami, as they pull weeds in the vegetable garden: "I think it's time. You can't put this off any longer."

I am working in another part of the garden, kneeling a few rows behind them. My ears perk up at Jan's words. Something in his voice scares me.

"You can't just sit here and wait for them to get you," Jan continues. "Who will protect you? You've got to be ready. You've got to start packing."

"Now?"

"That way you can be ready to leave, if the news is bad."

My mother sets down her garden spade. She folds her hands together, her head bent, and prays. Then she stands up. "You're right, Jan." She turns and calls out: "Tilli! Heinz!"

My brother walks over from the horse barn. Jan and my mother then lead us into the bull barn. Jan stands in front of a wall of hay bales as tall as his head and starts removing the bales, one by one, until I can see that something is behind the wall. It is a wagon. But not an ordinary hay wagon. The wheels have been changed—instead of wood, they look like they have rubber on them, like a truck. And the sides of the wagon aren't open wooden planks any more. They have been covered with a braided, grassy material, and there is a canvas roof over the wagon bed.

My mother turns to us. "You know the war is almost over. The Americans are close. But so are the Russians."

"Are we going to leave?" asks Heinz. "In that? Now?"

My mother nods. "You know Jan has been fixing up that wagon for us. I think now is the time to start packing it. The Americans are in Schwerin. That's not too far away. I'd rather take my chances with Americans in charge than wait to see if the Russians come here."

"But how can we go anywhere? Fox can't pull that wagon. The heifers can't, either. We've tried that."

"We're going to try again. And if the heifers won't pull it, we'll just have to take turns pulling it ourselves and walking beside it."

"But what about Helmut?" Heinz says, frowning.

"What do you mean, Heinz?" asks my mother.

"He is coming home, you know. If the war's almost over, that means he'll be back soon. What if we're not here? What if we're wandering around the countryside in a wagon? Then what will he do? And Paula, too? What if she doesn't stay with the count, what if she tries to come home?"

"Oh, Heinz," says my mother. She tries to give him a hug, but he shakes her away and glares at Jan.

"Jan and I have decided that we need to start packing today," she says. "You two need to go inside and get your things. Bring everything here to the barn. We're going to have to pack food and blankets, but not too much or it won't all fit."

"But Mami," I say. "Heinz is right. What about Helmut and Paula?"

"We will have to rely on Helmut and Paula being able to take care of themselves for a little while, Tilli," says my mother wearily. "And on God watching out for them."

Heinz and I file into the house, not speaking. I take my spare dress out of the cupboard, plus my sweater, my extra apron, underwear and socks. I don't know if I should bring any of my books. I probably won't be able to read in the wagon.

Doris.

I remember her suddenly, guiltily. As I've grown older, I've paid little attention to my doll. She still sits in the corner of my mother's bedroom, facing the bed, almost hidden by a chair.

I take her out of her stroller and hold her in my lap on the bed and think about Wilhelm, who gave her to me, so long ago. It is hard to picture his face. When he was drafted, I was only five. That seems a lifetime ago. I was a small child when the war began. It has been going on almost since I can remember.

And now it is about to end.

What else is about to end? My home as I know it? My friends?

My life?

I leave the stroller in the corner, grab my stack of clothes and Doris and, my arms full, slip outside to the bull barn.

"So many things, too much, this will never work," Jan is growling, his scowl, as always, firmly in place as he bends inside the wagon, trying to arrange the things that my mother and Heinz have already brought to him.

Jan looks up at me. "What's that?" He grabs Doris from my arms, holding her in his hairy, dirty hands. "A doll? You think you can bring a doll? Are you crazy? We have to pack only important things!" Jan is yelling now, waving Doris in the air.

"Don't hurt her!" I cry. I drop my clothes on the muddy ground and reach for Doris. "No! Give her back!"

Jan shoves Doris at me. "Get rid of this thing. Hurry up about it. We've got lots of work to do."

My chin is wobbling. My eyes burn. I clutch Doris to my chest. Suddenly she is the most important thing in the world to me. I can't imagine leaving her here, innocent, abandoned. I kiss her cool porcelain cheeks and rub my face against her silken hair.

My mother greets me at the kitchen door. "What's the matter?"

"Jan," I choke out. "He says I can't take Doris."

My mother smiles and wipes my face. I feel like such a baby. But I can't help it.

"Don't worry, Tillilein," my mother says gently. "Don't worry. Why, how could we leave Doris? She's part of our family."

We finish packing the wagon that night. Jan doesn't know it, but my mother wrapped Doris in a blanket and set her right on top of a stack of other blankets, right where I can reach her if I need to.

By the time we go to bed that night, we're ready to leave.

The next morning, though, my mother says the time is not right. Rumors have been flying all over town with different stories about what the Americans and Russians are doing, and my mother doesn't want to lead us into a trap.

We wait like this for a few more days. And then the rumors, spread by refugees to the townspeople, solidify into truth: the Americans have decided to withdraw across the Elbe River. There is no way we can get that far in our wagon. Unless the Americans change their minds, our plan to leave is dead.

My mother keeps the wagon packed and checks it every day, lightening the load when she can and making sure that our provisions are fresh, just in case.

◆   ◆   ◆

At the end of April, a dirty and exhausted Paula appears at the door. "Mami," she says in a low voice, almost a whisper. She looks ready to collapse.

"Paula!" My mother runs to her. "Thank God you made it home. I've been so worried about you!"

"It was getting so bad there," Paula says. "They were going to come after the count. He's on the run. He had to leave everything. At least his wife and daughter were sent away months ago, to safety. I can't believe what I saw on the road. So many sad, lost people. And dangerous people, too."

"At least you are safe with us," says my mother.

She tells Paula about the wagon and our plans to leave. "I'm glad you got here," my mother says. "I hated the thought of leaving without you."

"You can't think of leaving this house now," says Paula. "You don't realize what the road is like. What the country is like. We wouldn't have a chance. We'd starve or be attacked or who knows what?"

"Is it really that bad?" my mother asks.

Paula glances quickly at me. "I'll tell you all about it, Mami. Later."

The next day we unpack the wagon. We are not leaving, no matter what happens with the Russians.

Besides, there's a new problem: a group of people in Gnoien—mainly old men and some women—are trying to organize a fighting force to defend the town against the Russians. Anybody who is able to wield a shovel or a stick or a rock is supposed to join in planning a line of defense.

My mother thinks this is crazy. "They can't be serious," she says to Herr Pech, who has come to discuss what we should do. "Somebody had better talk some sense into those fools. Otherwise, we will all die."

Herr Pech nods. "We don't have a chance against the Russians," he says gloomily, running his hands through his shock of wild white hair. Ever since his son went back to the war, Herr Pech has lost his fire. He isn't animated any longer, like he used to be when he and my father would scream about Hitler's latest foolishnesses. Now he is just tired.

"I tried to tell them," he continues. "The Russians have guns. We have nothing. We can't win with sticks and stones. We'll just make it worse for ourselves. But they don't want to listen. They just want to fight back."

After Herr Pech leaves, my mother goes to Gnoien, to see for herself what is going on. I hate to see her step outside the house. What if the Russians come while she is gone?

I try to picture my friends from Gnoien and their brothers and mothers and grandparents, all lined up in a chain around the outskirts of town, holding brooms and shovels. Or maybe the plan is to hide out behind buildings and launch surprise raids? And will I be expected to help out, too? Will I have to fight the Russians?

When she gets back, though, my mother tells us that she doesn't think the group of hotheads leading the movement in Gnoien will prevail after all. A lot of people are so angry about the bombing of the field hospital that they want to take some sort of action, to exact revenge of some sort, even if it ultimately fails. But others, like my mother, appear to be convincing them that this is foolishness.

For the next few days, the talk of defending Gnoien continues, and my mother keeps going to meetings. I find myself wishing we had taken off in the wagon. I think I would rather be on the move than just sitting still, waiting for soldiers who might or might not come. Or, worse, having to man some kind of doomed fighting line, trying to beat off an army with broomsticks.

Finally the group that wanted to defend Gnoien is defeated and the resistance movement is over.

"It was close, but we out-voted them," says my mother. "Thank God we won."

She smiles bitterly.

"Now we can surrender in peace."

20

I am in the kitchen drying the dinner dishes. The Pommerenkes moved to the villa yesterday, so we have our living room back. Maybe I can sneak off to read in my favorite chair for a while. Or sleep. I am so very tired. Mami looks ready to take a nap, too; she's sitting at the table with her head drooping. She sometimes does this after dinner, resting for fifteen minutes or so before going back to work.

Paula takes the plates from me and stacks them in the cupboard. Now and then she catches spots that I didn't dry so well. She rubs them with the corner of her apron, but she doesn't yell at me about it, like she used to. She has been so quiet since she came back home. She is always frowning and hardly an hour goes by that she doesn't mention Erich's name. Erich is still missing in the war; no one has seen or heard from him in months.

"You'd think May would bring better weather than this," says Frau Hoppe, drinking down the last of her barley coffee and handing Maria her cup to wash. "Here it is, the first of the month, and it's so cold. Makes my bones hurt. Sometimes I can barely walk. My knees get so puffy—"

Frau Hoppe drones on. I tune her out, tune the damp dishes out. I am walking in a sunny field filled with violets. Max and Moritz are there. I am braiding Max's mane.

"Run! Hide!"

My dream shatters. Voices are screaming, yelling, words I can't make out, voices in the distance, terrified voices.

"What's happening?" says my mother, jumping up.

Jan and Heinz burst into the room. "The Russians are here!" Heinz screams. "They just went through Teterow, taking everything, even the cattle! They will be here any minute!"

"Dear God," says my mother.

"The Russians are really here?" says Paula, cradling a plate against her chest.

"Girls, get ready," says my mother. "You're going to have to hide."

"Hide where?" I ask.

"The bull barn, in the hay. Where the wagon is hidden."

"Now?" I ask. "We have to hide now?"

My mother stands at the window, peering out. A boy is running past, shouting: "Russians! Hide! Russians! Hide!"

I go to the window, too. So do Paula and Maria and Ruth. From the kitchen, we can see where the highway from Teterow ends and our road begins.

"What?" says Frau Hoppe. "What do you see? Are they coming yet? Jesus, help us. What will we do? What will they do? Can you see anything yet?"

"Look," says Paula, pointing.

A herd of animals: pigs, bulls, and horses, plodding down the road. A man in a yellow uniform is hitting them with a stick, yelling. Behind the animals are wagons. A row of wagons filled with men, all in yellow.

My mother swings into action. "Heinz, go tell Frau Oleniczak. Get the girls here!" she shouts. Heinz runs out the door. Then my mother starts throwing food together, grabbing the bread left over from dinner and wrapping it, along with some sausages and apples, in a towel.

Paula and Maria and Ruth and I stand, frozen, at the window. As the wagons grow closer, I can more clearly see the men in yellow. Some are driving the wagons. Others are crowded in the back. They are whooping and yelling and holding long rifles. Some are waving glass bottles in the air and tilting their heads back and drinking.

The wagons stop at the Brewers' house, which is the first on our road. Some of the men jump off the front wagon and go to the door, their guns out. They shout something I can't understand, go inside, then come out, dragging Frau Brewer, who is screaming.

"Now!" yells my mother. "Go! Quickly!" She shoves the towel filled with food at Paula. Paula is paralyzed. I can't move, either. "Come on!" My mother pushes us away from the window.

Klara, Trudy, Wanda, and Marie Oleniczak come running in, led by Heinz. Klara comes over to me. "Tilli, I'm so scared," she says, her voice breaking.

"Me, too."

We rush outside to the bull barn, the farthest barn from the house. Jan meets us there. He pushes us behind the bales and boxes, into the corner where the wagon had been hiding. It is no longer there; I don't know where it is.

"Cover yourselves with hay," he orders. "Be quiet. No noise at all."

Jan drags bales of hay in front of us, stacking them into a wall. Heinz helps, his breath harsh and fast.

Paula and Ruth and the Oleniczak girls and I pull bunches of hay onto our legs, then try to cover each other as best we can. Pieces of hay scratch my neck and tickle my cheeks. I can see golden light above me, through the bits of straw on top of my head.

"They're going to run us through with their swords," Trudy says, her voice strangely calm, almost matter-of-fact. "They take their long swords and go sticking through the straw trying to find bodies."

"Quiet!" Jan yells, his voice faraway and muffled. "Stay quiet!"

Ruth sniffles. Paula moans. I bite my lips together so no sound comes out. I hadn't heard this story before, about the swords. I imagine the men in yellow slashing away at the bales of straw until they catch skin and flesh and blood.

The barn door creaks shut and the golden light goes away and it is dark. I strain my ears but can't hear anything except our ragged breathing.

"How long do we have to be here?" I whisper.

"Shhh," hisses Marie.

There is nothing to do but close my eyes and wish I were somewhere else. I can't worry about what might be happening outside, to Heinz, to Maria. To my mother.

Hours pass. Occasional loud sounds, yells and shrieks, erupt like bombs in the silence, before falling away into an uneasy quiet, until the next explosion.

"What's happening?" I whisper.

Paula starts to cry. "Trudy's right. It's true about the swords. This is the first place they'll look for us."

"Would you please be quiet?" says Marie.

We burrow deeper into the straw. I try to sleep. But sleep is impossible. Wild images whirl in my mind and I jump at every strange sound. There is too much to be afraid of.

There is a sudden, loud bang, nearby. A crash. Voices, deep voices, very close, and feet, stomping in the dirt.

I try not to breathe. Male voices yell, words I don't understand. The barn door flings open so hard it crashes against the far wall.

I try to sink further under the hay, without moving. I will myself invisible.

The men's feet make crunching noises as they walk through the barn. I hear things being pulled off shelves. The walls sound like they are being kicked. More of those gruff voices and clinking sounds, like glass cracking, and crunching boots and a laugh, two laughs, how could they be laughing? and the creak of the barn door as it shuts.

And then there is blessed silence.

◆   ◆   ◆

The next morning, my mother comes in, swiftly pulling back the bales of hay guarding our corner. "Mami!" Paula and I cry out.

My mother's face is black, as if she has smeared dirt on it, and her mouth is set in a grim line. She wraps us in a quick hug, not saying anything.

"Frau Horn, is everything all right?" says Wanda.

My mother pushes Paula and I back. "We've got to move you," she says briskly. "Come on. Everyone get up. You can't stay here."

"Where are we going?" I ask.

"The secret attic, where we've been hiding the surplus food. They didn't find it last night."

"They were in our house?" Paula says.

"They came in and took things," my mother says slowly. "They took the radio and all the bikes. They took my watch. They had armloads of watches."

"Did they hurt you?" Paula asks.

"No. We're all right. But they were looking for Hitler things, to see if we were Nazis, and I forgot to take down the Hitler picture. I threw it in the woodstove right away, and they didn't do anything to me. They seemed to be in a hurry. They went through the barns real fast but I wouldn't be surprised if they come back tonight, for a better search. After it gets dark, I'm going to move you into the attic."

"We have to wait here all day?" I ask. I don't know how I can stand another day in here.

"I'm afraid so," says my mother.

"Is there room in that attic for all of us?" Paula asks. "It's just a crawlspace."

"I think you'll fit. I'm putting bags of straw up there for beds. And I'll have food for you. But you'll have to be very quiet."

"For how long?" I ask. "How long is this going to go on?"

"Tilli, don't whine!" my mother snaps. Then she reaches for me. "I'm sorry. I know you're scared. I just don't know how long this will keep up, or what to expect."

She gives me a hug and some of the black on her face rubs off onto mine. She wipes my cheek and smiles.

"What is that stuff?" I ask.

"Ashes," she says. "We're all doing it, all of the women. We rub ashes on our faces so the Russians will think we're old, too old for them. Then maybe they will leave us alone."

My mother leaves. We spend the rest of the day trying not to move and speaking only occasionally, in whispers. Heinz brings in more food and tells us he hasn't seen any Russians all day but he's heard that they've taken over the villa and kicked out the refugees that were there, except for the ones—the women—that they wanted to keep.

Finally it is dark. My mother comes in and we stand up, stiff and sore, then hurry with her across the barnyard to the house. As I rush through our house to the stairs, I see the gray, empty spot on the living room wall where the Hitler picture had been. Now there is nothing left on that wall but a shadow.

We run up the stairs, passing Heinz and Helmut's bedroom. Where is Helmut sleeping tonight? Is he alive? We hurry past sacks of rye and wheat, past my old bedroom, to a ladder propped against the wall. It leads up to a dark opening cut into the wooden ceiling: the door to the secret attic, raised like a hidden altar over the rest of the house.

We scurry up the ladder, squeezing ourselves into the dim, dusty space. As she had promised, my mother has put burlap sacks filled with straw on top of the wooden planks, so we have something to sit on. A plate with sandwiches is in the middle of the space, a water pitcher beside it. In a corner is a chamberpot, a black bucket that we all must share.

Sitting on my knees in the straw, the roof scrapes the top of my head. From ceiling to floor there is about a four-foot space, except for the point where the roof peaks, where I can almost stand up. There is no light, no window. The air is stuffy and thick. I am in a coffin. Panic surges through me.

"When I need you, I'll bang with this broomstick," my mother calls from below. She points to an old broom, resting in the corner next to the ladder. "If I bang twice, that means be quiet. They said we can't lock our doors any more. The Russians can come in any time they want. There won't be any knocking on the front door to let you know they're here. You will have to always listen for their footsteps and their voices because I don't know if I will always be able to warn you."

Paula and Ruth lift the ladder into the secret attic, laying it on its side near the opening. We call good-bye to my mother, then Paula slides a square piece of wood with rope handles across the opening. It slips down neatly into the hole, sealing it tightly, casting us into darkness.

We go back to our silent waiting, huddling together. I find myself wondering what it was like when the soldiers, the Russian soldiers, came through our house last night. Did they open our cupboards? Did they touch our china? My books? Doris? Did they touch Doris?

Can they really just walk into my house whenever they feel like it?

I picture my mother tossing the Hitler picture into the fire, Hitler's stern face licked by flames, eaten away into nothingness, and that makes me happy. I feel sorry for the pretty girl in the painting. I wonder who she was and what she is doing now.

I want to talk to Klara, but I'm afraid even to whisper. I hug my knees tightly to my chest. We are all breathing so loudly. My ears fill with our sounds; how can the Russians not hear us? And what about the lines in the upstairs ceiling, where Jan cut out the secret door? What if the Russians notice those lines?

What about Maria? Maria isn't hiding with us. She said the Russians were her people and wouldn't hurt her and since she spoke their language, she could maybe help protect us. But what if they hurt her anyway?

Mami isn't hiding, either. Is she really safe? What if they hurt her, too? Why do the Russians hate us so much?

As I strain my ears, trying to hear if they are any closer to our house, my fears circle my head like vultures, swooping around, around, over, lower, perching on my shoulder, whispering in my ear. Finally I am so exhausted that I fall asleep, lying down on my burlap sack between Klara and Paula, all of us curled together like sausages in a row.

Suddenly I jolt awake, my heart racing. It must be a cloudy night, because there is no moonlight or starlight coming through the cracks in the roof above me. For a moment, I can't think where I am, why I am so uncomfortable. Why I can't stand up.

Then I hear voices beneath me. They're back. Glass crashing. Shouting. Fanni barking, then squealing in pain. Laughing, harsh laughter. Where are Mami and Maria and Frau Hoppe? I don't hear them, only the men.

The other girls sit up, too. Ruth starts to cry again. Wanda puts her hand lightly over her mouth, a cautioning look on her face. Ruth nods silently: she will be quiet. Klara squeezes my hand.

I hear Maria's voice, from somewhere below us. She is yelling something. More thuds, as if people are falling down. Chairs scraping on wood, doors slamming. Why can't I hear my mother? It is only men's voices, yelling, hooting, laughing.

On and on, for hours, the voices rise and fall. What do they want? Why are they staying so long?

Then, suddenly, it is silent again.

Even though they must be gone, we don't talk to each other or move. We are like statues, kneeling statues, frozen in our fear. Klara's fist is in her mouth. Her cheeks look wet and she is blinking furiously. I wish there were something I could do or say to help her. But there is nothing.

We sit like this for seconds, minutes, hours. Paula silently passes the sandwiches and water. I drink some of the water, but have no appetite for food.

Trudy crawls over to the chamberpot. I try not to look or hear. The rest of us use the pot, taking turns. It is awkward and messy and smelly and so embarrassing, but we have no choice.

The darkness begins to lighten. Pinpricks of rosy dawn find their way through the holes in the roof-tiles. I hear the rooster crowing, Fox neighing, Bello barking. The light turns golden bright. It must be sunny outside. I wonder when I will see the sun again.

Somehow I sleep. Dreamless, deep sleep. When I open my eyes it is warm and stuffy and feels like afternoon.

Everyone else is awake. Klara and Trudy are holding hands; Ruth is stroking Paula's hair; Marie's fingers run across the top of her rosary beads, making the slightest of clicking sounds.

Thump, thump. "It's me!" my mother calls softly, tapping on our floor with the broom she left propped against the wall downstairs.

Paula, who is closest to the opening, pulls on the handles and lifts the piece of wood from the opening. Then she and Marie pass down the ladder. My mother climbs up, carrying a bundle of food.

Her face is still dark with ashes. I crawl to her and wrap myself in her arms. She kisses the top of my head and for a moment nobody says anything.

"How are you all doing?" my mother asks, turning to look at each of us as best as she can in the shadows.

"Fine," I lie, echoing the others.

"I wish I had more food for you," my mother says. "If I can get back up here tonight, I'll bring more. Or Heinz will. But this may have to last you until tomorrow."

There's an edge to my mother's voice.

"What is it?" Paula asks. "What's wrong?"

"Jan left today. The Russians said he had to go with them. He is free now."

I don't know whether to be happy or sad about this—I never really liked Jan, but I don't like the idea of no man around the farm during the day to help my mother. To protect her.

"And that's not all," says my mother. She pauses, her face grim.

"Mami, what? What is it?" asks Paula.

"The burgermeister came by this morning. There's going to be a dance at the villa tonight for the Russians. Our new friends, he called them. Can you believe that? Friends! We're supposed to be welcoming them to Doelitz. All the women in Doelitz are invited."

"What?" says Paula. "You're not going, are you?"

"If we don't go, the Russians—our new friends—say they will burn Doelitz to the ground."

"Oh my God," says Wanda.

My mother laughs bitterly. I have never heard her laugh like this before. "Who could refuse such a polite invitation from such charming gentlemen?"

"Can't you stay here?" says Paula. "Can't you hide with us? Don't go!"

"I'll be all right," my mother says. She waves at her face. "We're all going like this, with as much ashes and dirt on us as we can, and we're wearing our oldest and smelliest clothes. They won't want us."

"Is my mother going, too?" asks Trudy, her voice small.

"Yes, dear. We all have to go. We can't risk not showing up. I did want to warn you, though, that I won't be here tonight. In case anything happens."

After Mami leaves, it is a long time before I can slow my thoughts, my endless circling vulture thoughts. I fall asleep, but my sleep is broken with nightmares, filled with sirens and unseen men chasing me and flames on all sides.

"Shhh," Wanda says, shaking my arm. "Shhh."

I shake the dreams from my mind and listen and then I hear them, soft foot-steps, the floor creaking below us.

There's a tap on the door to our secret space and I let out my breath: it's the sound of the broomstick; it must be my mother. Paula slides open the door and lets down the ladder. Instead of my mother, another girl climbs up. It's Dor-othea, Lori Pech's young aunt, covered in a black shawl and scarf. Her face, like my mother's, is smudged black.

My mother stands below, on the first few rungs of the ladder, calling up to us in a low voice. "Dorothea has come to stay with you. I'll see you in the morning. Be careful!"

We help Dorothea find a spot in our cramped space. She blinks, trying to adjust to the darkness, and holds her arms tightly around herself.

"What's happening out there?" whispers Paula. "Have they had the dance yet?"

"It's starting now," Dorothea whispers back. "Everyone is on their way to the villa. The Russians are all there. I took my chance to run. I've been hiding in our root cellar but that isn't safe, so your mother said I could come up here with you."

Dorothea slumps against the wall, looking exhausted.

Paula offers her half a sandwich. She waves it away. "I haven't slept since they came," Dorothea whispers. "I'm afraid to close my eyes. I'm afraid of what I'll see."

Dorothea starts to cry. Paula puts her arms around her and they sit together silently.

We resume our vigil, waiting, listening. I don't hear anything for hours. No soldiers yelling. No screams. Once I hear a soft thud below, but quickly realize that it is only a cat, pouncing on a mouse.

Finally we hear the front door open and footsteps walking slowly through the house. I smile. It's my mother; I recognize her sounds, so unlike the men, who burst in, the door slamming, their voices thick and loud. Her footsteps, soft and steady, continue to her bedroom, and then there is silence.

I drift to sleep, relieved. Maybe the dance helped, somehow, and the Russians are at peace and will leave us alone and I can go back home again.

◆   ◆   ◆

I am by myself in the park, next to my dreaming rock, gathering wildflowers. The sun is strong and hot overhead and I am going to take a nap on my rock and then I'm going to bring these flowers to my mother and life is so sweet and I am so happy.

The sun splinters and crashes out of the sky and now I am awake and it is dark, not sunny, and the crashing is real, glass is smashing, and there are voices, men's voices. They're back and they're yelling. They sound so angry, running through the house, flinging open doors, breaking glass, shouting and laughing.

Ruth starts to cry, her shoulders shaking. Dorothea puts her hand over Ruth's mouth to silence her sobs.

"No!" Maria shouts from somewhere below us, her voice rising high and sharp above the voices, the angry, laughing voices.

I freeze, my breath in my throat.

Another crash. Glass again? China? I can't tell. A man yells harshly and something heavy bangs, thuds, against the floor, so hard the wood floor quivers beneath me.

Maria is yelling in that other language now, the men's language. The men's voices are high with fury, yelling back. More thuds and thumps, the sounds of struggling.

And then Maria's voice, her scream, carrying over all the other sounds, soaring right up to us and landing helpless in our laps. I press my hands into my ears as hard as I can, but still I can hear her, still I can feel her pain and terror.

"Oh no," Paula whispers, her eyes wide, horrified.

"Those bastards," says Dorothea.

"Shhh," says Wanda. "Shhh!"

I lie back down on my bed of straw. I am so useless. All we can do is nothing. That is our only function. To say nothing, to be completely still; if possible, not to be at all. At least for a while. We have to be lifeless, we have to be wraiths, spirits in hiding, if we are to have any hope of saving ourselves.

21

My mother is wearier and sadder than ever. It is the morning after the dance and she is here, bringing us our breakfast and news of the night before.

"I'm all right, I'm all right," she says, as soon as she sees us.

"What about Maria?" Paula asks.

My mother shakes her head. Her eyes are full of such agony that I can't stand to look. I put my hands over my face.

"I couldn't help," my mother says. "I couldn't do anything to stop them."

"What happened?" Dorothea asks.

"They were angry, because of the dance. A Russian commandant saved us. He's in charge of the men here. He speaks German and seemed from a better class, seemed nice, actually. Maybe that was a lie. I don't know. But he kept his men from getting us. That's why they came back later."

My mother pauses again.

"What happened?" Dorothea repeats.

"They are keeping their horses right there with them, inside the villa. Inside the ballroom, all those horses on that beautiful parquet floor. Can you imagine that? Horses in the ballroom."

My mother looks like she might start to laugh and I wonder what's wrong with her.

"We got there looking as bad as we could. I even put ashes on my teeth. Everybody looked as bad as me, or worse.

"They had music playing on the radio. And they had a table full of bottles of vodka. No food, just vodka. The commandant welcomed us and offered us something to drink. But we told him no, German women don't drink. The other men seemed angry at this. I think they wanted to get us drunk. But the commandant said, 'As you wish.' He was very polite.

"Then I had to dance with a couple of young soldiers. 'Where's all the young ones?' one of them asked me. 'Where are your girls?' I told him everybody was there, that there were no others, but I could tell he didn't believe me.

141

"We danced outside, under the linden trees, just like a spring festival dance. It only lasted a couple of hours. I think when they saw we wouldn't drink anything, they wanted to call it off.

"The commandant thanked us for coming. We gathered near the door and it looked like the men were going to crowd after us, maybe get us when we were outside, when we weren't in a group any more. But the commandant ordered the men to line up at attention, so they had to watch while we all hurried out. I ran home. I think if the commandant had not made them stand like that, they would have come after us."

My mother sighs. "And then you heard what happened. They came back later, drunker than ever and frustrated and mad. So even though Maria is one of their own, this time they..." She can't finish.

"How is she?" I ask.

My mother looks at me with dead eyes. "I don't know. She won't talk to me."

I feel sick. The dark ceiling not three feet from my nose is sinking in on me, the gray stone walls are closing in and, as I look through the hole that my mother entered, as I spot the rooms below, including my old bedroom that I miss so terribly, it is all I can do not to dive through that opening into free space once more.

◆   ◆   ◆

That night, just after the sky grows dark, my mother brings two more girls: Eva and Claudia, friends of Paula's, also wearing dark clothes. Over the next two days, always in the late afternoons or early evenings, when the Russians are less likely to be roaming around, she brings more girls, until there are thirteen of us, crammed shoulder to shoulder in this tiny space. I am the youngest. Dorothea, at twenty-five, is the oldest. I don't know Paula's friends very well. Many have been away working for the past few years.

Each of the new girls brings news. Most of the houses in town have been stripped of everything from sheets to kettles. The Russians have grabbed whatever they can carry away. Our house, by comparison, has been left practically untouched; other than our radio, bicycles, and watches, nothing valuable has been taken.

"I wonder why they left so many of our things?" Paula asks.

"It's because of the Oleniczaks," Dorothea says.

"What do you mean?" asks Marie.

"Because you're Polish. They aren't hurting anybody who is Polish." The Oleniczak house is connected to ours, so the Russians must think we are Polish, too, which is why we haven't been robbed as thoroughly. That hadn't stopped them from hurting Maria, though, and from coming into our house almost every night to drink and eat sauerkraut and other food stored in our root cellar.

We learn from the new girls that the Russians made the shopkeepers in Gnoien take everything in their stores and put it onto the street. Then they went through it, picking and choosing bolts of cloth, tools, and food. What they didn't want, they burned. "The businesspeople are all ruined," whispers Claudia.

The Russians hunted down the Nazi Party officials and prominent Party members. Two officials, including Corporal Ring, hung themselves before the Russians could get to them. The other officials who were captured were either shot or are being kept prisoner and probably will be sent to Russian concentration camps.

I don't know what to think about the Nazis being punished. I hate the Nazis. I hated Corporal Ring. But I hate the Russians, too.

The Russians have raped many women in Doelitz. One of them is Gretel Theis, Anna Theis's sixteen-year-old daughter, who used to come to our house at Christmastime and help bake cookies. The soldiers found her hiding in her root cellar. They dragged her out and threw her on the ground and beat her and took turns with her and beat her some more.

Another horrible thing happened to Herr Schlorff, my old schoolteacher, the gentle man the boys called Herr Wartski. Herr Schlorff was home when the Russians came through. They wanted his gold wedding band, but his knuckles had swollen with age, and it was stuck. The Russians didn't give up: the soldiers took Herr Schlorff's finger and ripped it off his body. Then, ignoring his screams, they laughed and went out the door, waving their bloodstained trophy.

◆   ◆   ◆

After about a week in our secret space, my mother lets us out for some exercise. I am so eager for release that I nearly scream with joy. We climb down the ladder, one by one, our legs wobbling. It is a sunny spring day and even though the shades are drawn, the light that passes through is almost blinding. We step through the upstairs rooms blinking and waving our arms and stretching. I go to my old bedroom window and pull aside the curtain, just to see the sky again, but my mother quickly stops me from peering out, warning that someone could easily see me if I did this and had I lost my mind?

After our exercise break, everyone else goes back up to the secret attic, but my mother lets me come downstairs to get more food. It feels so strange to be in my house again. I can see where the walls have been gouged. The floor in the dining room is scratched and the wallpaper is torn. What have the Russians done to make these marks?

In the kitchen, Maria is frying potatoes. "Hello," I say. Maria says hello without turning to look at me. "How are you?" I ask.

Maria turns to face me. There is a red welt on her cheekbone and her right eye is swollen shut. She meets my gaze with her left eye, her expression stony.

"Oh, Maria." I don't know what to say. I give her a hug. She is stiff in my arms.

"You'd better go back upstairs," she says. "You don't want them to find you. They are bad, bad men."

"I just want to sit here a minute." I curl up in my old spot on the bench, thinking about the person who used to sit here—the young girl who loved to sneak books at the table—and about the family that used to exist.

"I'm going outside for a minute," Maria says. "You'll be getting back upstairs, right?"

I nod. She leaves. A few minutes later, Mami comes in. "Tilli, why aren't you upstairs?"

"I just wanted to be here for a minute, that's all. I miss it. I miss our family."

My mother sighs, frowning. "So do I. But you've got to go back."

The door opens. I look up, expecting Maria. Instead, in walks a tall, blond man, wearing a mustard-yellow uniform.

A Russian soldier.

I shrink into my seat. My mother puts her hand to her throat, then smiles directly at the man, trying to hold his gaze. He hasn't seen me yet. Maybe he won't.

"Hello!" she says cheerily.

"Hello. You have eggs today?"

"Yes, yes I do."

My mother has told me about this Russian, whom she has nicknamed the Egg Man. Besides the commandant, he is the only nice one she has met. He has come a few times to get eggs and each time, instead of just taking them, he has given her sugar in exchange. He also speaks German and treats her respectfully.

"Come with me and you can pick out your own eggs, fresh from the hen," my mother says, trying to lead him outside.

The Egg Man starts to follow her, then turns to glance around the room. That's when he sees me.

"Well, hello there," he says, smiling, his eyes pale gray and unreadable.

I nod at him, still too frightened to speak.

"Are you coming?" says my mother, a worried look on her face.

"Yes, yes," the Egg Man says, his eyes still locked on mine. "Good-bye, quiet one."

As soon as they are out the door, I run upstairs and close myself back into the safety of our hideout.

That night, we hear the usual crashing and hollering from the various Russians coming into our house. But the next morning, when my mother brings us our food, she says we had a new visitor, one who hadn't come before.

It was the Egg Man.

"He came by himself. He was drunk, too, but he was still polite. 'Where is that girl who was here today?' he asked me."

"Oh, no!" I say.

"I told him that no girl lived here. But he either didn't understand me or didn't believe me. 'I want that girl, that quiet girl who was here,' he said. Maria talked to him in Russian. He kept shaking his head. He walked through the house, looking, but even after he didn't find you, he wouldn't leave. He sat down and said he was going to wait for the girl to come back. He was here for hours before he finally left.

"Tilli, you can't be downstairs like that again. What if he comes back looking for you again?"

◆　　　◆　　　◆

One morning a few weeks after the Russians came and our lives in hiding began, my mother brings sad news. "Maria is gone."

"What!" Paula and I gasp.

"They came to get her—three Russian soldiers," says my mother. "They made me take them to her. She was peeling potatoes in the barn. She had a bucketful of scraps and a pile yet to peel. She wouldn't look at them, or me. She just kept peeling while they stood there.

"'Now,' one of them said. He was getting mad.

"'I have to finish,' she told them. Then she said something in Russian and he said something in Russian. Then he yelled 'Now!' again.

"They made her stand up and walk away. Just like that. She left with them. She was crying and crying and so was I."

"Oh, Mami," I say.

"I couldn't think of anything to say to her. Maybe I should have written down our address, so she can write us someday. She was so scared. Who knows what is happening in her country right now. If she even makes it home. It's a long ways away, a tough trip to make, especially when you're pregnant."

"What? Maria's pregnant?"

"After the soldiers were here that night, she should have had her period, but she didn't. She thinks she's pregnant."

Jan had left the day after the Russians arrived. That didn't bother me at all. But Maria was my friend. I would have liked to say good-bye to her.

I find myself thinking a lot about Maria, about her courage and her strength. She could have hidden with us, but instead she helped protect us. She worked hard for us. If there is any justice in the world, she will make it home to her family.

Two days later, my mother has more upsetting news. This time, it's about Bello. "I wish I didn't have to tell you this. But the Russians killed Bello today."

"How?" says Paula. "Why? Did he bite them?"

My mother shakes her head. "No, he didn't do anything. He was in the yard, just being alive. And a group of them walked by, waving their bottles and guns around, and one of them just decided to shoot him. Heinz saw the whole thing. They all cheered when he went down. 'Nazi dog!' one of them yelled and then they all laughed. They kept walking down the road. When they were out of sight, Heinz ran out to help Bello, but it was too late."

As the endless hours pass, Paula begins talking about Erich more and more, until he is all she speaks about. Every day, she smiles and says that Erich will be here before sundown to rescue us.

"I can't wait to hold him," she says, a strange light in her eyes. "It's the hardest thing, not being able to hold the one you love. I just wish I looked better."

Paula rubs at her hair, as if that would do any good. None of us have had a bath or even a good washing with a rag since the Russians came. We are dirty and smelly, our hair rumpled, our clothes wrinkled.

"He'll take us all with him. Mami, too," Paula says. "We will all be free. We can go live on his farm. He's such a good farmer."

Oh, Paula, I want to say to her. Pull yourself together. We need you.

"My brother will be back soon, too," says Dorothea one day. Her brother, Frederich, is Lori's father, who has been missing in action since shortly after returning to the war following his injury. Lori used to be so certain he would be coming home on the train, even though everybody else thought he was dead. She had been right. Maybe Dorothea also has the power to predict the future? Or maybe Paula's ramblings have us all wishing for what we cannot have.

I wonder if madness is contagious. I hope I don't catch it. Although maybe I would be happier lost in a joyful delusion like Paula is than trapped in this dark prison.

One morning, just as the blood-red rays of dawn are shooting into the attic, the Russians burst in the front door, yelling drunkenly and giggling.

My mother and Heinz are in the meadow, milking the cows, which they do every day before dawn. I don't hear a sound from Frau Hoppe. She is alone to defend our house. I hope they don't hurt her.

"Erich," Paula calls, sitting up abruptly and smiling. "He's here!" She starts to stand, bumping her head on the ceiling.

Trudy and Wanda and I lunge at Paula, trying to push her down. Dorothea puts her hand over Paula's mouth. "Quiet, Paula," she whispers fiercely. "It's Russians, not Erich."

But Paula is beyond hearing. She struggles against us. I am too weak to hold her down. Marie and Claudia take over. We are all awake now.

"No, no, Erich," moans Paula, every time she pulls one of the girls' hands free from her mouth.

I hear thumping and creaking close by, near the stairs leading to the attic. The Russians are shouting things I can't understand. At least they are making noise of their own. If they were silent, they would be able to hear Paula. We hiss again at her to be quiet, but she is somewhere far away, unreachable.

Paula lunges suddenly at the rope handles on the trapdoor, nearly reaching them. "Erich!" she calls.

Wanda picks up a burlap sack and holds it over Paula's face, pushing her down. Dorothea and Ruth grab her legs, which are twitching. Her arms spin wildly and I can hear her deep moans, even with the sack on her face.

I notice all of a sudden that there is no sound from below. Have the Russians left?

Then I hear their voices, no longer yelling and giggling, but low and serious. I hear footsteps close to the stairwell.

Have they heard us?

More silence below. What are they waiting for? Are they listening for us?

I hold my breath. We are all as quiet as we can be, except for Paula, who keeps thrashing around. Marie helps Dorothea and Ruth hold Paula's legs still. Claudia and Trudy grab her arms.

A footstep, then two, creaks on the staircase.

Please God, please God.

The moment is frozen; I am frozen. The Russians beneath us, listening. The thirteen of us, trying not to be heard, except for Paula, who is lost to madness.

And then the soldiers leave. Just like that. The footsteps go back down the stairs. The front door slams. They are gone.

Wanda pulls the sack off Paula's face. "Are you okay?" she whispers. "Paula, I'm sorry, I'm sorry."

Paula is finally motionless, except for the heaving of her chest as she sobs, sounds from the deepest part of her, sounds of a pain, an agony, that are unbearable to hear. I cover my head with my arms and try not to cry.

"Why didn't you let Erich in?" Paula finally says, when she can speak again. "Erich was here for me and you didn't let him in. This was my last chance."

"Paula, that's not true," I say. I look in her glazed, tear-swollen eyes, trying to find my sister. "Paula, listen to me. Erich is not here. There were Russians here, only Russians. Erich is not here."

"I will never see him again," whispers Paula, her voice flat and dead. "And it's your fault."

She closes her eyes. She doesn't say anything more. She falls asleep and doesn't wake up until that night.

"I have such a headache," Paula moans. "Is it safe to talk? Are the Russians here?"

Paula is back. She never mentions Erich again.

22

Minutes, seconds, days, hours, months, week, spring, summer, what's the difference? It's July already. We have been in the attic since May. Except for our brief exercise breaks, we have been confined for almost three months.

The nighttime visits by the Russians are becoming fewer and farther between and less violent when they do occur. Many of the soldiers have moved on; some of them have been relocated to Gnoien. My mother is beginning to relax a little. She no longer wears ashes on her face and sometimes when she brings us our food, she is humming again.

"Mami, can't we please go downstairs?" I ask one day. If only I could see the sky again, the yard, flowers. Our kitchen.

"Remember the Egg Man, Tilli," she says. "It's still dangerous."

"But what if you or Heinz watch the road? We'll be careful. I promise. Please!" The other girls echo me.

"Frau Horn, I have to get out of here!" bursts Elfriede, who usually is so quiet. "I am going insane!"

"Well—" My mother hesitates. "Things are a lot better—"

We wheedle and beg until finally my mother relents. I get to be first. I am only allowed to be downstairs for thirty minutes. Heinz will be posted outside the house, near the back, while my mother will be just outside the door, pretending to weed the flower garden but really keeping an eye on the road and listening for my brother's warning cries.

I creep downstairs, looking forward, backward, all around. I am so weak. My dress hangs on me. It seems somehow to have gotten larger. I see my legs moving on the stairs and marvel at how bony and white they look. They don't look like my legs at all; they look like Frau Hoppe's knitting needles.

Just getting downstairs to the kitchen tires me out. I curl up on the bench, in my favorite spot, to rest and look around. I marvel at the little things: the songs of the birds, the fresh new smell of the air, so sharp and clean, compared with the dusty dankness of our hiding place. Hot, wet dirt. Flowers. Manure. It is heaven.

149

After that, we begin taking turns coming down. My mother lets two girls at a time, then three. The Oleniczaks go in pairs: Klara and Trudy, Wanda and Marie. Their parents come over here to visit them so that they won't have to go outside.

Edytha's mother also comes to visit her daughter. Frau Weyer has shiny dark hair just like Edytha's. They could be sisters, except that Frau Weyer's face is fallen and shadowed with worry.

All of us are happy to taste freedom again, but it makes it that much harder to shut ourselves back in the attic. I am greedy. I want to run and jump and scream scream scream. I don't ever want to be quiet and still and *not-there* again in my life.

At last it is my turn to go downstairs again. I wander through the house, from room to room. Frau Hoppe greets me, spinning away at the wheel, chattering as always, but I don't mind listening to her as I roam.

"They say it might be safe to travel to Berlin once summer's over," she says. "I can't wait to see my Elsie. I've got to find her. I'm sure she's all right. My Elsie is a survivor, like me. She's young and strong, too. She doesn't have my sciatica, which has been—"

I go to my mother's bedroom, which I shared with her so long ago. It looks the same: the faded brown comforter, the flowered chamberpot, the picture of dying Jesus on the wall beside the bed.

Suddenly, Heinz and my mother burst in the kitchen door, yelling. "Tilli, hide! Someone's coming!"

A Russian. A Russian who has come too quickly for them to warn me.

There is no way to get back upstairs. I am right beside my mother's window. The first place the Russians would look is under the bed. There is nowhere else to hide in her bedroom. I am trapped.

Unless I leave the house. Why not? I climb out the window, drop to the ground, then crouch and run alongside the bushes to the Oleniczak's gate. I lift the latch, run to the house and climb in an open bedroom window.

Frau Oleniczak stands there, a broom in her hand, staring at me. "Tilli? Is that you? What's wrong? What are you doing here?"

My mother screams. A giant scream, then another.

Oh my God. The Russians have her, they're hurting her.

Frau Oleniczak and I stare at each other in horror. There is pounding on the Oleniczak's door. "Hide. Hide!" hisses Frau Oleniczak. She points to a closet door. I start towards it when the person pounding on the front door begins shouting.

It's Heinz. "Tilli!" he is calling. "Tilli! It's okay, it's okay!"

Frau Oleniczak opens the door. Heinz is grinning from ear to ear. "Tilli, Helmut's home."

We run back to our house. My mother and Paula are in the kitchen, holding each other. No, I realize, there is someone between them: Helmut. My mother is sobbing and smiling and saying, "Thank God, thank God," over and over again.

I join the embrace. When it is over and we step back, I get my first good look at Helmut. I am stunned at the change in him. He has a beard, long hair, deep circles in his sunburned face, and he is bone-thin and barefoot and shirtless, wearing only a pair of torn, filthy pants held up by a rope.

But those eyes are his. Those lively, sparkling eyes.

"Hello, little sister," he says, winking at me. "I made it."

It is wonderful having Helmut back. When he has time away from his chores, he climbs into the secret attic and tells us jokes, trying to cheer us up. He also tells us how he made his way home.

Soon after being drafted, Helmut and a group of other boy-soldiers were captured by Americans. "I think they felt sorry for us, when they weren't laughing at us," says Helmut. "They weren't bad to us. At least we got to eat."

After a week in American hands, Helmut escaped, but was captured not long afterward by Russians, who treated him more severely. He escaped again, this time finding refuge with an elderly German farm couple who had lost two sons to the war. He stayed with them for a while, helping with their farm and trying to figure out how to make it home. At last he left, but once back on the road, he was captured a third time, by another band of Russian soldiers, even more cruel than the first. These soldiers took his clothes and starved him and the other prisoners, until Helmut escaped yet again. After that, it took a week of walking through the country, surviving on grass and dandelions and stream water, and hiding whenever he saw troops, before he finally made it home.

Shortly after Helmut's return, the Russians begin posting notes on buildings and trees. Official orders, printed in ungrammatical, misspelled German, saying that the Russian soldiers no longer will be harming German girls. German girls are now safe, say the official papers.

"Well? Do we believe them?" says my mother, scratching her head. She and Helmut sit with us in the attic, trying to decide what to do.

"I wouldn't trust a damn thing they say," says Helmut.

"I haven't seen that many Russians on the road lately," says my mother. "They haven't been by at all in the past two weeks."

"That may be true," says Helmut slowly. "But once is all it takes. The officers are in Gnoien. They don't keep track of what their men are doing here."

"You're right," my mother says, turning to us. "They aren't as crazy as before, but some are still around, looking for women. It's still not safe for you to leave here."

We all groan.

"Frau Horn, what about those of us who live close by?" asks Edytha. "Can't you see if our mothers would let us go home? We could stay inside."

"All right. I'll check with them to see what they want me to do."

My mother puts the ladder down and gets ready to climb out, back to the real world.

That's when I start to cry. I don't mean to. But I think if I don't taste fresh air again soon, if I can't feel the sun on me, the wind in my hair, I am going to die. I feel like a turtle, living inside my shell, which protects me, but which is growing so hard and thick that soon I don't think I will be able to break out of it.

By early August, I barely notice the passing of the days. My eyes feel clouded, my mind fogged. I lie on the straw and don't talk when the other girls whisper to me. I don't have an appetite. I stare at the roof tiles and count the holes where the light comes through. There are nineteen of them. Nineteen holes for light in the entire roof. Imagine that.

My mother is alarmed.

"Maybe Tilli should come down now," she says to Paula. Her voice sounds far-off. I stop paying attention to her words. I only notice the rolling lilt of the voices around me, as if I were underwater, catching only vibrations of sound. I wonder if this is how things are for Hugo, if this is what he hears. It's really rather pleasant.

"Tilli!" My mother is shaking me. Her voice is loud and sharp. Shouldn't she be whispering? "Get up! You're going downstairs."

I nod weakly. Then my mother's strong arms are under me. She and Heinz are lifting me, carrying me down the ladder.

The sun is so bright, so hot. I blink and shiver at the same time. My house looks so strange, so foreign. It's hard to believe that I once lived here.

Gradually, I become adjusted. The fuzzy feeling fades, my eyes focus again. I sit in the kitchen and watch my mother make supper. I am too tired to move, but I enjoy just being there, smelling the potatoes frying.

Heinz and Helmut joke with me at dinner, trying to get me to smile. They are looking at me with such worried expressions. Don't they know that I'm fine now?

That night, I sleep again in my mother's bedroom. It is wonderful being so close to her again and being able to stretch my arms and legs without disturbing people on all sides of me. I can have privacy when I use the chamberpot. Though I can't go outside yet, air comes in through the open window, sweet air on my cheeks.

Above me in bed it seems like miles to the ceiling. Moonlight splashes through the window, across my comforter. Delicious moonlight. And stars too; I can see out the window to the heavens. I am no longer underground. That's what it felt like, being in that attic for all those weeks. Even though we were in the highest part of the house, it felt like being buried alive in never-ending darkness.

Now I am free. I am out of my shell; I am alive once again.

Soon after I come down, Edytha and the Oleniczaks and Dorothea, who all live close by, go home. They slip across the yard in the dusk, wearing dark clothes and shawls over their heads.

The only girls still upstairs are Paula, who comes down every day to fetch food and water, and her friends who live further away from us, and Ruth. My mother says she hopes within a few weeks to be able to let them down, too. She just doesn't trust the Russians yet.

Meanwhile, Helmut's return has given new hope to our neighbors that their missing sons might be on their way back, too. Herr Pech comes over sometimes to chat. He talks more and more about Frederich, whom he is sure will be back with the other returning soldiers before you know it.

Often, I see German soldiers walking past our house. I watch them from the window, making sure to keep my face hidden. Many of the soldiers are wounded. Some of them stay for a few days with Frau Häde, who is hoping to see her missing son, Heinrich, any day now.

"Those soldiers stay at poor Frau Häde's house for a few days, eat her food, fill her with stories about where they saw Heinrich last," my mother says angrily. "But it's all lies! They don't even know who Heinrich is. They just want food and shelter—they're just preying on her. I hope Frau Häde isn't giving them anything else, anything valuable, but I wouldn't be surprised if she were. She thinks if she does these good things, God will reward her and send Heinrich home. But she's never going to see Heinrich again. He's almost certainly dead."

Paula, who is downstairs getting fresh water, puts her hand to her mouth. I can see the old faraway look coming on, like a veil closing over her face.

"Paula," says my mother, taking her by the shoulders. "Paula, I'm sorry, but Erich's gone. You have to accept this."

Paula shakes her head and runs out of the kitchen. I hear her feet pounding up the stairs, back to the secret attic.

"Mami, how do you know Erich is dead?" I ask.

"There are so few survivors, so very few. I don't want Paula to waste away in some deluded fantasy, like Frau Häde or Herr Pech. She's got to accept it."

I can't say I blame Paula, though. If I were Paula, I wouldn't want to bury my hope so easily, either.

It is a strange August, with no crops to tend, except for the potatoes, which won't be ready to unearth for another month or so. Our days do not have the normal rhythms of late summer; the needs of our rye and our oats and our wheat and our soybeans and our sugar beets, once so all-consuming, are no longer there.

My brothers spend their days taking care of the vegetable garden and the animals, always scanning the horizon for soldiers. I stay inside almost all the time, doing chores like washing the floors or shelling peas. Gradually, Paula and Ruth and the other girls starts spending more time downstairs, too, even going outside to help in the garden now and then. But every night, they go back to the attic.

My mother begins churning butter so that all the extra milk we have won't go to waste. The milk can't be sold, but we are allowed to trade butter. It fetches a few things, but not much, because nobody has anything to trade in return. Everybody in Gnoien, whether they were rich before the war or poor, is now in the same circumstance: barely able to find enough food to eat each day, some living in broken-down buildings ruined by the bombs. Most of the nice houses are occupied by Russian officers, who threw the owners out, leaving them to wander like refugees, begging for any shelter they can find.

When my brothers tell me this, I wonder what my wealthier classmates, like Eleanor and Margaret Timm, are doing now that their good fortune has left them. It must be hard on them; I imagine it is more painful to have once had something and lost it than never to have had anything at all.

"I wonder how Victoria is doing," I say to Paula.

"Yes, I wonder how she is, and the count, too," says Paula, staring pointedly at my mother, her eyebrows arched. "Well, Mami?"

"What?" my mother asks innocently.

"Come on, I know the count was planning to come here," says Paula. "Did he? Did he make it okay?"

That's when I find out that while my mother was hiding us upstairs, she also was hiding the count in the barn. His family wasn't with him, though. He had sent them away before the war ended.

"He stayed with us for a couple of weeks, but then he took off again, and I have no idea what's become of him," says my mother.

My mother also tells us that after the Russians came, Henni and her sister dug a hole for themselves in their meadow and spent much of the first two months of the Russian occupation in the dirt. The Oleniczaks hid their son, Karl, who had deserted the Army, in another underground shelter in their yard, first from the Nazis, then from the Russians.

We have all been hiding. The whole village, cowering in dirt and darkness and fear.

After supper one evening, little Walter Weyer, who is about eight years old, comes to our door. "Frau Horn, can you come to our house?" he asks, breathless from running. "Edytha is sick. My mother says she needs your help."

"Of course," says my mother, drying her hands on her apron. "What's wrong with her?"

"I don't know," says Walter, shifting from foot to foot. "She's real sick. Can you hurry?"

"I'll be right back, Tilli," my mother calls, hurrying out the door.

But she is gone for hours. She returns just before supper, which Paula has started. She sinks down in a chair, looking tired.

"How's Edytha?" I ask.

"It's a bad fever. I put cold cloths on her, all over her. She's gotten so thin. Being in that attic can't have helped. Poor thing."

"Is she going to be all right?"

"I don't know. Right now, she's delirious."

"What does that mean?" I ask.

"It means she's seeing things that aren't there. It means her fever is very high."

Helmut and Heinz come in. "Who has a fever?" asks Helmut.

"Edytha Weyer is sick."

"She isn't the only one," says Helmut.

"What do you mean?" asks Mami.

"In Gnoien today, I heard about a few cases of people with high fevers. The doctors have been very busy. They have all these wounded people, soldiers and people still recovering from the bombings, and now there's some sickness going around."

"I wonder if there's a connection," says my mother.

That night, Walter Weyer comes again, pounding on the door around midnight. At first, I think it is the Russians, come back to haunt us, and leap out of bed in terror. Then we hear Walter calling us.

"Please come, Frau Horn, it's even worse!" he cries.

Mami leaves. In the morning, she is still gone.

"We did the milking without her," Heinz says worriedly. "I wonder what is going on over there."

"Why don't I go find out?" says Helmut, starting to get up.

Just then, my mother pushes open the kitchen door and walks in, her eyes wide in her pale face.

"Edytha is very bad," she says. "She is in a coma."

"A coma?" I ask.

"It's like you're almost dead," says Heinz.

"Can't you do anything for her?"

"I don't know what else to do," says Mami, frowning at her hands. "I'm afraid that Edytha has typhoid fever. She's in God's hands now."

The typhoid epidemic sweeps through town with vicious speed. My mother spends much of each day traveling to her friends' houses, helping with their stricken children. Hertha Hunsinger, the seventeen-year-old daughter of my god-mother, Tilla Hunsinger, is so sick she is hallucinating. Dorothea also falls ill.

My mother goes to all their homes, helping as best she can, giving the sick homemade wine mixed with raw eggs, wiping down feverish bodies with wet towels, cleaning everything with disinfectant. She comes home each night exhausted.

Hertha dies one day. I have never known anybody close to my age who died. Hertha and I sometimes played, when her mother came over to visit my mother. I liked Hertha. It's shocking to think of her now as a spirit in heaven, with an empty body, soon to be buried.

The night before the funeral, my mother goes to Frau Hunsinger's house and dresses Hertha. Frau Hunsinger begged my mother to do this for her; she couldn't bear to do it herself. So my mother put Hertha in her Sunday dress and stockings and combed her hair, tying it with a white ribbon, in a way that she hoped Hertha would have done herself.

The next morning, we all walk to the Hunsinger home on the other side of the park. It is the first time since the war ended that I have been outside. No Russian soldiers are in sight. I hope they won't bother a funeral procession.

Inside the house, Frau Hunsinger is dressed in a black shawl, her wide pink face splotched with red, her eyes swollen. She offers me a piece of cake. I don't eat it.

We hear slow, steady thuds as Heinz and Helmut help Herr Hunsinger carry a freshly made wooden box down the stairs. *Hertha is in that box.* I feel numb, removed somehow, far away behind my eyes. I watch my brothers and Hertha's father carry her coffin through the kitchen and outside to the wagon, which is covered with flowers. Even the horses are wearing wreaths of pink and orange and white blossoms.

My mother leaves Frau Hunsinger's side for a moment and makes her way to me. "Are you all right?"

I nod.

"It will be over soon."

The wagon starts to roll. We walk behind it, a crowd of about thirty people, down the road to the cemetery. Frau and Herr Hunsinger drive the wagon; Frau Hunsinger clutches her mouth and tries not to sob.

My legs tremble as I walk. *Hertha will never walk on this road again.*

A hole with a pile of black dirt beside it—a wound in the ground—is waiting for us at the cemetery. Herr Pastor Scharnweber is standing beside the hole, holding a Bible and a basket of flowers.

We watch as the men lower the wooden box into the hole. Then the pastor hands each of us a flower. I receive a brilliant orange tiger lily. When it's my turn, I toss my lily on top of the coffin, on top of all the other flowers, and I try not to picture Hertha lying inside.

Herr Pastor Scharnweber gives a sermon. I don't listen. I gaze around me, at the deep blue sky and the dark green grass and the orange and yellow and white and purple and blood-red flowers, brilliant colors, so vivid, that Hertha will never see again.

Frau Hunsinger doubles over as Herr Pastor Scharnweber gives his final blessing. "Ashes to ashes, dust to dust," we echo. "Amen. Amen."

The Hunsinger family picks up shovels. Frau and Herr Hunsinger, bent with mourning, and Hertha's sister, Emmi, who is thirteen, pale and shaking. They take turns scooping dirt from the mound and tossing it on the coffin below. The dirt is soft and doesn't make much noise when it hits the coffin. Pretty soon, there is no sound at all.

I wonder what it is like in heaven. I hope Hertha is not alone, that someone is holding her, comforting her. Maybe she is happy. But I wonder how she could be happy if she weren't with her mother. I can't imagine being happy if I were somewhere alone, without Mami.

My mother holds my hand on the walk home. "Thank God, we've come through this war all right," she says. "When you think about it, we're all here, in one piece. Except for Hugo. And your father, of course."

We haven't heard from either of them. Hugo's town was in American hands for a while. We are hoping the family he was staying with has taken care of him. Somehow I don't worry about my father; I don't even think about him.

That night, my mother is awakened once again. I don't know why people always seem to get sickest in the middle of the night. This time it is Lori Pech at our door, come to see if my mother can help Dorothea. Strong Dorothea, who helped us get through our time in the attic, is slipping farther and farther away.

The next morning, I wake up with a headache. I don't often get headaches. It is a dull throbbing behind my eyes. My throat hurts, too, like someone scratched it with a potato peeler while I slept.

My mother comes in during breakfast, once again having been up most of the night.

"Dorothea is dead," she says flatly. A picture flashes in my mind of Dorothea in the attic with us, telling stories, smiling. But I don't feel anything to think of her being gone. I feel incredibly numb, as if I'm nothing but a shell, skin over cotton, empty and floating.

My mother sits down, folds her hands in her lap, and closes her eyes. Her lips move in prayer for Dorothea.

"Is there anything I can do to help?" I ask, when she is finished.

My mother comes over to me. She leans against me, her cheek cool against mine.

She jumps back, puts her hand on my forehead. "Oh my God," she whispers.

"What?" I ask, frightened by the look in her eyes.

"Tilli, you have a fever."

23

August—October 1945

The bears are after me again. I don't know why they want me. But here they are. Their breath is hot, so very hot, hot all over me, their tongues on me, too. Hot and wet and I can't get away.

I scream but no sound comes out. I try to run but I can't move.

One of the bears whines. It changes: it is no longer a twisted, growling beast. Now I see that it is Bello. Bello back from the dead. The other bears change to dogs, too. And then they jump on Bello, their teeth flashing. "Bello!" I cry.

But he is gone. And all is black night.

Nighttime and again I am in the attic. The ceiling is pressing down on me, close to my chest. I am trapped. Somebody is tugging at me.

The Russians, come to get me.

I know that I have to fight. "Tilli, Tilli," they call. How can they know my name? They are pushing on my head, on my body. Lifting me, moving me. I know that I have to struggle, to fight them.

Only I don't have the strength. I can't move.

Once again, the darkness claims me.

◆　　　◆　　　◆

"Mami, what's happening?" I croak, my throat so very sore.

I am upstairs again. I can smell grain and the tang of ham and sausage from the old smokehouse. What am I doing here?

I try to rise up, but fall back onto the pillow.

"Tilli, you're sick, but you're going to be all right," says my mother. She has a cold, wet rag that she brushes against my forehead. So cold.

I shiver violently, my feet knocking against the wall. I hold myself tightly, trying to stop the shivering, and the next thing I know, it is darkness again. Max and Moritz are there. Dorothea is riding Max. I am jealous. I want to ride him, too.

We are beside the pond in the park. The horses are hot and sweaty. It is summer. I love to ride them into the water to cool them off.

Dorothea, high atop Max, thunders past. I try to run after her. She shakes her finger at me as she rides.

"This is my job now," she says. "Go home. Go home."

Paula is here. She is yelling at me. Why does she always yell at me?

"Have some of this. Drink it, drink it. That's good," she's saying. She's pouring something sour and awful between my lips, holding my mouth open with one hand.

I spit and shake my head. Paula sighs. She isn't even angry.

Then all of a sudden it is night again. My mother's face appears overhead. She looks very white, like a ghost, or maybe a star. Very white and far-off. I have to strain to hear her, to make her vibrations into words that I can understand.

"I think Tilli is going to die," she says.

How can that be? How silly. I'm only eleven.

Then I allow myself to float away. I know I shouldn't, but I can't help it. I want to touch those stars over my mother's shoulder. They are glimmering, glistening, so beautiful, like jewels.

I grab one, snatch it out of the blackness. I look down at it. It is a Russian soldier's face, laughing and leering, a man with shiny sharp teeth and wicked eyes, who suddenly changes into a ferocious dragon with hot fire shooting out of its mouth.

I scream and again I am gone and everything is dark once more.

Months go by, or maybe just minutes.

Slowly I return to consciousness, to myself. I have a sensation of landing back in my body, a thudding feeling, a coolness all over me. I try to sit up, but I feel dizzy. I rest and try again. Still dizzy. So I just rest.

Outside, I can hear my brothers talking. They must be outside the door, waiting to see me. I look around. I am in the old smokehouse room upstairs. How odd. I wonder why I am here. And why don't I smell meat? My nose is filled instead with the bitter scent of disinfectant.

"You know the potatoes can't wait any longer," Helmut is saying.

"But Mami has to take care of Tilli," Heinz says. "Tilli is getting better, I know it. We can harvest next week."

Potato harvest already? How long have I been sick?

I must have typhoid fever, I realize. But I don't feel so bad, not any more. Just tired and weak.

My mother walks in, talking over her shoulder to my brothers. "We can do the harvest next week, Helmut. A week won't matter."

She is carrying a glass of something reddish-orange. She sits beside me, still looking back at my brothers. She must be used to me not responding.

"Can I help with the harvest?" I ask.

My mother stares at me. My brothers rush into the room and stare, too.

"Can I help?" I ask again, my voice barely a croak.

"Tilli, you're back!" my mother cries. She feels my forehead, my cheeks. "Your fever has broken. You're going to be all right. Thank God!"

I hear my brothers cheering. I smile.

Then my mother frowns. "But wait. You said you wanted to help with the potato harvest? In that case, you must still be sick. My Tilli wouldn't want to work in the potato fields for anything." My mother winks at me, then laughs so deeply tears come to her eyes.

It takes a few weeks before I am strong enough to walk around. I guess that's normal after typhoid fever.

So many people have been ill, but for some reason, most of those who have been sickest are young women. Several have died. Others are like me, weak and struggling to recover.

Edytha came out of her coma and is fine—except that she lost all her dark hair. It fell out in clumps on her pillow, until she was bald. Strangely, her hair is coming in blond and curly. Nobody can explain it.

One good thing about having typhoid is that the Russians have left us alone ever since my mother first wiped the front door with disinfectant. That's what everybody has been doing when somebody in the house comes down with the typhoid. Even people who don't have somebody sick in their house have been wiping disinfectant on their doors. The strong smell keeps the Russians away. I wish we had thought of doing this earlier.

Maybe it's because of the typhoid, or maybe it would have happened anyway, but the Russians seem to have lost interest in terrorizing us. They have been busy putting up red flags around town, at the villa and in the park. The flags show a hammer and a sickle, the symbols of Russia. The Russians also have been hanging pictures of their leader, Stalin, who has fierce eyes and bushy eyebrows that remind me of Jan.

I get better and soon am able to help with chores. My life starts slipping back into a normal routine, like it was before the war ended, only without the fear of bombs and planes. The only thing missing is school. It's the middle of September and I'm tired of reading the same books over and over again. I miss my teachers and my friends.

"When can I go back?" I ask my mother. "I need to get back to school."

"It's still too dangerous for you to go to Gnoien," she says. "But I've been thinking that maybe you could go back to your old school here in Doelitz."

"With Herr Schlorff?"

"That's right. How would you feel about that?"

"I don't know. I guess it would be okay. Are you sure I can't go to Gnoien?"

"I'm sure."

The next week, I return to the one-room schoolhouse that I left after first grade. Herr Schlorff greets me at the doorway with a warm handshake. Immediately my eyes go to his other hand, his ring hand. Was the horrible story I heard after the Russians came really true?

It was. Herr Schlorff keeps his hand at his side, curled a little, but I can tell that it is disfigured. Only a stump remains on his ring finger, a pinkish-red stub where a finger had once been.

Herr Schlorff ignores my staring, which I know is rude, but which I can't help. He shows me to a seat in the back of the room, where the sixth grade sits.

As I take my place at a scarred wooden desk, beaten and battered by so many students over the years, I can't believe that I used to be a student here. The room is so much smaller than I had remembered, and more crowded, full of bored boys and girls who don't pay the least bit of attention to the mild-voiced teacher.

Herr Schlorff tries to give me work to do, but everything he proposes I have already mastered. The eighth-graders here are working on math and reading lessons that I learned in fourth grade in Gnoien.

I go to school for two weeks. Finally, I can't take it any more. Even though it is nice to see Klara and Henni and talk with them at recess, the rest of the school-day is just too interminable to sit through. My skin crawls with boredom and annoyance and frustration.

"Mami, it's a big waste of time," I complain. "I would learn more sitting in the park watching the trees grow. Are you sure I can't go to Gnoien?"

My mother talks to Herr Schlorff. When she gets back, she is frowning. "He says there's nothing he can do for you here. He says you are too advanced."

"See? Please, can't I go back to my own school?"

"But you have no bicycle, remember? The Russians took it."

"I don't care. I'll walk."

"I don't know. I just don't know." My mother ponders the problem for a few days before deciding to let me go to Gnoien again.

At last, I think happily. I will be back with my friends. Now everything truly will be back to normal again, only even better, because finally the war is over and even though the Russians are here, there are no more bombs, no more threats, nothing really to fear.

◆   ◆   ◆

There is a fine mist in the air, just a tickle in my face, as I set off on the road home from school. It's been a good day. I got a one on my English test, and Fraulein Meyer doesn't give out ones very easily.

It has been wonderful being in Gnoien again and seeing all my old friends. Ilse is like a different person, so light and happy, because her father returned safely from the war and her family is together again.

Nobody has talked very much about what it was like when the Russians came. I think no one wants to relive those memories. We all have had terrible experiences and now we all just want to forget and get on with our lives.

I have been back in Gnoien for a week. My teachers have been quite kind and understanding, allowing me extra time to get caught up with the rest of my class.

It's funny, though, what has changed and what hasn't. We used to start the day with Heil Hitlers and hearing some message or other from the Party about how great Hitler was or how well the war was going or how lucky we were to be part of such a great land and how we needed to do our duty as good Germans. Now the teachers say the complete opposite.

"We have to respect our Russian friends because they have given us Communism," said Fraulein Meyer the other day.

I couldn't believe she said this with a straight face, after telling us all those years during the war that Nazism was the perfect system.

"Our Russian friends have given us freedom from the Nazis," Fraulein Meyer continued. "The Nazis put people in concentration camps and were very cruel to them. The Russians have freed them and they have freed us. Now we have to go their way in Communism."

I stared at her in amazement as titters of laughter broke out around the classroom. Fraulein Meyer ignored us, staring straight ahead as if somebody from the Communist Party were watching her. She is performing, I realized suddenly. She is the perfect puppet teacher: wind her up and she says what they want her to say.

"Joseph Stalin is a great, great man and we are lucky he has befriended our country," she said.

The next day was the same, in her class and in others, as our teachers gave us the new Party line. One even led us in a song:

Do you still have a Hitler picture?
Do you still have a Hitler picture?
No, no, we already have one.
We have one of Stalin.

I told my mother about the shift in what the teachers were telling us. "Have they really changed their minds so suddenly?" I asked. "They used to seem so positive that Hitler was good and the Nazis were good. Now they are saying just the opposite."

"Don't pay attention to them," she said. "They are just doing what they have been ordered to do."

"What do you mean? Why can't they say what they really believe?"

"If they don't say what the Russians tell them to say, they could certainly lose their jobs, and probably worse."

"Worse?"

"The Russians have their own camps, you know, just like the Nazis did."

I ponder this as I walk home from Gnoien, kicking at the clumps of dried brown leaves that have collected at the side of the road. I wonder how it must feel for Fraulein Meyer, who has always seemed like such a tough, capable person, to have to spout this nonsense that the Russians give her to say. I know she has no choice, but still it's disappointing to see her act this way.

I turn a corner in the gently curving road, my eyes on the dying leaves, red and brown and pale yellow, dried and curled toward the sun.

That's why I don't notice them right away.

Until it's too late.

Three Russian soldiers, pushing bicycles. One of the bikes is wobbling, its tire flat.

They are singing and laughing and I see that one of them has the bottle, the ever-present bottle of vodka that they all drink.

I asked my mother once why the soldiers drank so much. She made a face. "Stalin gives it to them. Bottles and bottles of vodka. He knows if they are drunk enough, they'll do anything he tells them to."

When I see the soldiers, I feel my heart stop. The air seems to freeze around my face, to catch in my throat.

They haven't seen me yet. There are no other people on the road. Usually, there is somebody else around. But I am alone, with no one to help me, no house to run to. I look for somewhere to hide. Maybe if I lie down on the ground, flatten myself, they won't see me.

I run to the ditch at the side of the road. There are scraggly bushes all along it, some still with a few stubborn leaves that refuse to let go. I lie down, trying to slide under the half-dead bushes, pressing my rucksack against my chest. I look up at the sky and pray as I have never prayed before. Dear Jesus, sweet Jesus, God help me, oh please please please.

The sky is gray and heavy with clouds. The mist continues, a fine rain, like spray. I close my eyes and feel its coolness. *I am sweet and pure and my heart belongs to Jesus alone. Dear Jesus please help me.*

But it doesn't help. None of it helps. The prayers, the hiding. Nothing works.

They see me. They shout. They laugh and come closer. I hear them. I don't open my eyes. I try to will them away.

And then they are on me.

They rip my clothes off me. My dress, torn right down the middle, their hands scratching me, their rough hairy hands. Their smells, sour and dank, worse than any overflowing chamberpot.

I can't breathe. I separate from myself. I try to float in those clouds, to find the meadow, the happy meadow, Victoria's castle, her playroom with the leather walls and the fireplace, so safe, so warm.

The pain brings me back, a horrible pain, splitting me, ripping me apart. Again again again again. Oh God.

Somehow in the pain and terror, I pass out. I enter the blackness, the deep darkness of my fever days, only this time the vicious animals chasing me are real. This time, they have caught me.

PART III

24

I used to think that those months spent in the secret attic were the worst time of my life. But after what happened in the road that day in October, I realized how wrong I had been.

That day, that day that changed my life forever, I somehow managed to stumble home to my mother, clutching the ripped pieces of my dress around me, blood dripping down my legs.

When she saw me, my mother screamed. She grabbed me and held me and started sobbing. "I'm sorry, I'm sorry," she gasped. I was sobbing, too. I hadn't thought after all we'd been through that I had tears left. But there they were.

Then my mother rubbed her eyes dry and took me into the washkitchen and gently oh so gently cleaned me.

Not that I ever really got clean, though. I am still not clean.

She dressed me in my only other dress, my Sunday dress, and threw the pieces of the one the Russians had ripped into the stove to burn. Then she walked me to Gnoien, muttering to herself. "Father, help us. Father, help us."

I didn't want to go. It hurt to walk, hurt terribly. Even worse was passing the spot where it happened. My heart raced and I thought I was going to get sick when I saw that ditch, those helpless dead leaves.

But my mother said we had to see the doctor right away. So we went to Doctor Schumacher's office near my school.

Doctor Schumacher was the mother of Karla Schumacher, a girl in my class. She was about my mother's age, with long, slender fingers, cool to the touch, and a slow, methodical way about her. She did not seem shocked at what had happened to me; she just asked me in her steady voice to please lie down on her examining table. Then she touched me in that private, pain-filled place, and I thought that I might die. I wished that I could die.

Afterwards she told me that I was lucky I was a tall girl, so big for my age. "There does not appear to be any damage," she said, wiping her hands on a towel.

"However, there may be problems later. Unfortunately, the Russians often carry venereal diseases. Do you know what these are?"

I nodded. I had heard that Gretel Theis, who became pregnant after her rape, also came down with syphilis, which leaves red sores on your body and which can eventually kill you. "I know a little," I said softly.

"Good," Doctor Schumacher said, then told me what I needed to know. Once again I thought I would be sick.

"I'm afraid we don't have any good medicine for this," she said. "I can give you suppositories. And you must be sure to keep that area very, very clean."

I didn't know how this would be possible. It felt to me like it would be dirty forever.

On the way home, my mother, who had been quiet, started to talk. "We'll get through this, Tilli. I am so, so sorry that I let you go to school. Helmut was right. We can't trust the Russians. They said they wouldn't do this any more, but they lied and I shouldn't ever have believed them. This is all my fault."

"No it's not. It's my fault. I wanted to go to school."

"It's not your fault! Don't ever say that or think that!"

We were quiet for a few minutes. Then my mother said, "I don't want you to go to school in Gnoien again. At least not for a long time."

"Good. I don't want to go to school. I don't want to go anywhere but home."

So I went home, where I stayed for the next two months. I never told Paula or my brothers what happened, but I think they probably guessed. At every loud sound, I jumped, worse than ever before, even after the air-raid drills and the bombings. Every stranger passing by made me want to run back to the secret attic again, where I could hide. No man could come near me; I couldn't stand anybody touching me, anybody except for my mother.

My father returned to our family at the end of October. He simply walked in the house one day, with no warning. He had been in Norway and had never been involved in any fighting, but had been required to spend the last few months in a discharge camp, waiting to be released.

"I had a necklace for you," he told me, hugging me tightly and kissing my cheek, as if he loved me. He didn't notice how quickly I pulled away from his rough, hot touch. "It was a very pretty necklace. I was going to bring it to you, but they took it away from me at the camp."

I didn't know whether to believe him. My heart was closed to him, after everything he had done to my mother.

I didn't tell my father what had happened to me. The only ones who knew were my mother and Doctor Schumacher. But just because nobody knew didn't mean it hadn't happened, that it went away. It replayed itself over and over in my memories, my thoughts, my nightmares.

For months after the attack, I had a discharge, dark and foul smelling. No matter how much I cleaned myself, it wouldn't go away. I was sure I had syphilis, just like Gretel. The soldiers had invaded my body and left a vile, vicious germ, infecting me from the inside out.

I hated the Russians. I never knew I could feel such a deep, passionate loathing for anybody. But inside me there boiled a sea of hot anger.

How could they have done this to me, a child? How could any creatures on this earth be so evil? They didn't deserve to live. If I were a man, if I had a weapon, a gun or a sword, I would go after them. I would kill them. I would watch them bleed and beg for mercy. And I would enjoy it.

On New Year's Eve, the night before 1945 became 1946, I stayed up with my family. They were drinking dandelion wine, laughing, playing cards. I sat quietly, empty as always, watching them.

"10, 9, 8, 7, 6—" They counted back, using a watch that Helmut had found on the ground one day. It was a perfectly good watch; nothing had been wrong with it except that it needed to be wound, something the Russians who stole it apparently didn't know how to do. So they tossed it aside; they had plenty of others that they had stolen to take its place.

They used it, then they tossed it aside. Just as they had used me and then thrown me away.

The gold secondhand clicked stiffly, pulling time along behind it. I wished I could turn time back. If only I had not been on that road that day. If only I had been there a few minutes earlier or a few minutes later. If only.

My father was smiling, my brothers were smiling, Paula was smiling. My mother looked worriedly at me.

"Happy New Year!" they shouted, holding up their wine glasses. I didn't join in their cheers. I couldn't imagine ever being happy again.

I returned to school in Gnoien in mid-January, three months after the attack, rejoining my class after Christmas break. I hadn't wanted to ever go back to Gnoien, but I knew I had to get on with my life. I couldn't stay hiding in my house forever.

As much as possible, I avoided walking by myself to Gnoien. Whenever I could, I rode the milk wagon on its morning run. To do so meant getting up before 5 a.m. Otherwise, I wouldn't have time to get dressed, eat breakfast and peel potatoes before the wagon stopped at our house to pick up the milk my mother had collected. On days that I missed the milk wagon, I would trot along its route until I caught up with it.

But even on the wagon, even sitting safely beside the driver, whenever we passed Russian soldiers I was filled with terror. I tried not to look at their faces. I didn't want to recognize any of them.

I could only ride the milk wagon in the mornings. In the afternoons, I had no choice but to walk home by myself. Most days, there was someone else on the road. I tried to stay as close to them as possible.

Sometimes, though, I found myself alone on the road. Alone as I walked past that ditch, as I relived that day. And there was nothing I could do to change any of it.

Gretel Theis's baby was born dead. I don't know if she loved it or not, since its father was one of the Russians who had raped her. Its body was covered with red blisters and boils.

At school, I kept having to hear my teachers, one after the other, tell us how wonderful the Russians were and how evil the Nazis had been. I believed them about the Nazis, but I would never find the Russians wonderful.

According to the newspapers and my teachers, the Russians found horrible atrocities when they liberated the Nazi concentration camps. The newspapers printed pictures of starving, bone-thin, naked people who had been kept in the camps—mostly Jewish and Polish people, even children. My mother and her friends were horrified to think of the suffering the Nazis caused, how families had been torn apart, how so many innocent people had been tortured and murdered.

It made me feel sick, too. "Couldn't somebody have done something to stop it?" I asked Mami. She reminded me that anybody standing up to the Nazis would probably have been taken away and most likely killed. I thought of what had happened to my father and to Frau Zell's husband, the minister who refused to honor Hitler and had been sent to a concentration camp, never to return, and I knew my mother was right. Maybe everybody in Germany who hated Hitler had been as afraid as we were and had decided they had no chance against the Nazis. Maybe if we had all joined together it would have made a difference, but how could that have been accomplished?

It was the same thing with the Russians now ruling us. They were in so many ways just like the Nazis. Before we feared Hitler and the SS—the secret police. Now we were terrified of Stalin and what his soldiers would do to us if they found us disobeying any of their edicts.

In the early spring, the Russians announced that everybody in Doelitz was to report to the villa to be photographed. We took turns standing in front of a wall while an unsmiling Russian with a big camera shot our pictures. Then we were issued identification cards, our official papers that marked us as subjects of Russian rule. We were ordered to carry these identification cards with us always. A Russian soldier could stop anybody at any time and ask to see his or her card. Failure to produce the card could result in imprisonment, or worse.

I kept my card in my rucksack. I barely looked at it when I got it. I didn't want to see myself this way, as a pale face in a box, as a Russian possession.

In school we were required to learn two foreign languages. Our teachers, under orders from the Russians, urged us to learn Russian so that we could communicate more clearly with our "friends."

I refused to learn Russian. I thought it was the ugliest language in the world and the idea of Russian words in my mouth, in my mind, made me ill. So, one day I waited after school for Fraulein Meyer and asked her what I should do.

Fraulein Meyer looked around to make sure no one was listening. Just like under the Nazis, we had to watch what we said around other people. Already there were spies among us. It was rumored that some of our neighbors—although I couldn't imagine who would do this—were taking money and getting special favors from the Russians for informing, for telling who was loyal and who was not.

"Instead of taking Russian, I don't see anything wrong with you taking extra English lessons," said Fraulein Meyer. "You can take English twice a day and get really good at it."

"That would be great," I said. "Because I am going to America some day."

"You are?"

"I am going to live there. I know it."

My dream of moving to America had become more than an entertaining fantasy. It had formed into a hardened, definite goal. I thought about it every day. I wanted to live in a free land, with no soldiers attacking innocent children, with no more terror and worrying about what I thought or said or did. This was my future. It had to happen. It just had to.

"How would you like to come to my house after school and get even better at English?" Fraulein Meyer asked. "I am tutoring promising students. And you are one of my most promising."

"I am? Really?"

"There's a fee. I'm sure we can work it out. Some food—potatoes, perhaps? Or butter?"

"I'll ask my mother."

To my relief, my mother said yes, and I started spending two afternoons a week at Fraulein Meyer's cozy apartment, both learning English and—more importantly to me—finding out everything I could about America. Fraulein Meyer loved to talk about America, about her time there, and she told her stories over and over again.

"Do you know what Americans do when they get holes in their stockings?" she said, leaning toward me in her flowered pink armchair, grinning. "They throw them away!"

I shook my head in amazement at the carefree prosperity in America.

"And do you know what they do when the sole of a shoe comes off? They don't repair it. Oh no. They throw the whole pair of shoes away!" Together we laughed at such heedless wealth.

Fraulein Meyer didn't like everything she encountered during her stay in America. For one thing, the children that she cared for were different from German children. "They were nice, but spoiled," she said, her lips pressed together disapprovingly. "They didn't have any work to do and they had so many things—clothes, toys and more toys. Anything they wanted, they had."

American food was not as good as German food, Fraulein Meyer claimed. She missed spicy ham and sourdough bread and German potatoes. On the other hand, they had great desserts in America; they ate dessert after every meal. American ice cream was truly wonderful. "We don't have anything like it here," she said, grinning at the memory. "Ahh. They had chocolate ice cream. Was it ever great."

At home, Fraulein Meyer was different than at school. She was relaxed and funny. She also seemed to really believe in me, that I was smart and that I would indeed get to America some day. During those too-short times in her apartment, I was almost happy. My heart was not as sore, as heavy, as it was the rest of the day. As we practiced our English verb conjugations, as I memorized simple phrases—*I am going to the store; I have gone to the library*—I pretended that I was already there, a free person living a free life, reborn fresh and new and pure in America.

"When I get to America," I told Fraulein Meyer one afternoon, "I am going to put Doelitz and Gnoien and the war and the Russians so far behind me. I am never going to speak German again. I'm going to forget all I ever knew and speak only English."

Fraulein Meyer frowned. "Oh no, Tilli, no. You don't want to do that. A wise person never forgets their mother tongue. It will still be useful to you. You'll see. And besides, you don't want to forget Germany. Never forget Germany."

As the months passed, I found myself settling into a routine—chores, school, chores, sleep—that was almost peaceful, except for the quiet menace of Russian soldiers watching us, and the fear that unseen spies were listening to our thoughts.

My mother bought a new horse, trading for it with butter and honey since we had no money. The horse's name was Astra and she was beautiful, with a sleek chestnut-brown coat. She looked like a riding horse, not a workhorse, and she was little more than a colt, fresh and high-spirited.

"What's the good of getting a horse like that?" my father complained.

"I like her lines," said my mother. "Besides, there aren't very many horses around any more. The Russians took all the good ones, the ones that weren't drafted."

"But that horse won't be able to do any work for three years, at least."

"Can you do better? Go ahead. Try to find a mature workhorse. At least with this one, we will have a good horse in a few years."

Because Astra was so young, her duties were to graze in the meadow and nap. I didn't mind this in the least. It gave me time to pet her and braid her mane. Although I knew I shouldn't let myself, after losing Max and Moritz, I was already in love with Astra.

We also got a new dog, to replace Bello. His name was Purzell. I didn't like this dog at all—there was something rough and selfish about him and he never wagged his tail or acted friendly. He also wasn't smart like Bello and couldn't pull the milk cart like Bello had. Even so, said my mother, he served his chief purpose: to act as a good watchdog.

Only a few Russian soldiers were in Gnoien by then, with none in Doelitz any longer. They had left the villa to the refugees—after first placing a large red star in the ground, made from rocks painted red, surrounded with red and white stones and flowers. It reminded me of the bulls-eye in the middle of a target. The soldiers didn't come around at night any more and I hadn't heard any reports of them attacking anybody in a long time. I didn't know if the wild ones had left or for some reason had temporarily calmed down and could yet erupt in violence again.

I was still having nightmares every few nights. I wondered if they would ever leave me. I still was jumpy, too. At least the awful discharge had stopped and I no longer feared that I had syphilis. One day I even started my period. I was walking home from school, felt sick, went to the bathroom in a ditch at the side of the road, and discovered blood. I was scared at first but my mother told me I was fine, that now I would have to deal with pain and white linen squares every month, but that it was normal and good and not to worry.

At school, we didn't have enough books and paper and pencils for regular lessons, so we spent many of our days in the woods looking for herbs—chamomile and lindenberry blossoms—to take back to school, where they were dried in the attic and used for medicines or tea. Sometimes we gathered bucheggern nuts, which were pressed into oil. I liked walking in the woods, though I was terrible at spotting plants. I tended to get wrapped up in the beauty of a particular tree branch or pattern of light through the leaves. Or else I liked just being still and listening to the sounds of the woods, to the animals and birds and the breath of the wind through the forest.

Jan wrote to us once. The letter was written entirely in French and I had to have one of the teachers at school translate it for me. It didn't say anything surprising: Jan had made it home safely, everybody in his family was doing well, and he sent us his best wishes. It was good to hear that Jan was all right, but what I wished was that we could receive some news about Maria, although we never did.

Frau Hoppe left in early March of 1946. Paula took her to Berlin on the train. They stayed with the Bergs, whom my mother had befriended when they came to Doelitz during the war looking for food. Besides getting Frau Hoppe settled, Paula had another mission in Berlin: she brought jars of our butter and honey with her, then traded them for kerosene and cloth, thread and pencils and other things we needed.

"Butter is like gold in my hands," Paula said when she came back. "The people there are so hungry. They are trading everything they own. At least Frau Hoppe found her daughter. She's living in the basement of a wrecked building. I guess that's where Frau Hoppe will live now."

Paula's successful trip to Berlin seemed to energize her. She was almost fully herself again: capable and strong, not the destroyed Paula of the attic. She never mentioned Erich again, not once.

Soon after her trip to Berlin, Paula brought home a new boyfriend, Willi, who was staying with his aunt while recovering from his war injuries. Willi had lost an arm in the war and his leg also had been badly injured, leaving him with a permanent limp.

After he and Paula started seeing each other, Willi began working with my brothers in the fields, doing all his work with his remaining arm, which rippled with muscles. Willi fit right in with Heinz and Helmut, he joked as much as they did, and it seemed from the start as if he were a member of our family—which he became when he and Paula were married in mid-June of 1946.

Their wedding was the first big social event in the village in years. Everybody talked about it for weeks before and after it happened; it seemed that their marriage was a sign of hope that life could go on, that everything could be normal once again.

Paula and Willi actually had two weddings: a legal, official ceremony at the burgermeister's office in Gnoien, held on a Friday afternoon with my parents and Willi's parents as the only witnesses, and a church ceremony the next day in Boddin, attended by at least half of Doelitz.

While Paula and Willi were in Gnoien for their first wedding, all the neighbors came to our house for one of my favorite wedding rituals. Everybody brought bags of old dishes and glasses and clay pots, which they emptied onto the ground in front of our house in a giant pile. I added a cracked preserve jar.

"Ready?" shouted Trudy.

"Ready!" we answered.

Then we each picked up our dishes and, one at a time, took turns heaving them at our front door, where they crashed and clattered and cracked apart. If something didn't break, we picked it up and threw it again.

It was terrific fun, more fun than I had had in years. I felt exhilarated and alive. We were laughing, shrieking, whooping. We didn't have to stay silent any longer. We didn't have to hide or watch what we were doing or saying. Just throw, smash, throw, loud smash after glorious smash.

When we were done, glass and pottery shards covered a wide swath of yard in front of the door, ending in a huge glittering mound, right at the doorway.

Paula and Willi came walking up the road from Gnoien, holding hands, and grinning. Willi's parents and my parents, who were wearing their best clothes, walked behind them. They burst out laughing when they saw the mess we had made.

"You know you can't go to the church and get married until you clean this up," teased Elfriede, handing Paula and Willi two brooms and a dustpan.

Then everybody except Paula and Willi climbed over the messy doorway into our house for the reception. My mother served glasses of a sugar-beet and raspberry alcohol she had made, plus plates of cakes and cookies. I wasn't allowed to have any alcohol, but I stuffed myself on sweets.

When the party broke up a little after midnight, there were still glimmers of glass and shards of pottery lying around. The next morning, Paula and Willi, with my mother helping, spent another hour on their hands and knees, picking through the dirt until, at last, the yard was clean and they were free to go to church and be married in the eyes of God.

The Russians decided we should no longer farm wheat and barley. Instead, they forced everyone in Doelitz to plant poppies, hemp and tobacco, crops that we knew nothing about.

At first, I liked the poppy crop, mainly because the red flowers were so beautiful, much prettier than plain yellow-brown stalks of grain. But when it came time to harvest the poppy seeds, I changed my mind. Poppy seeds were grown for their oil, which could only be collected by pressing them. My mother set up a big wooden press in the kitchen. I would sit in front of it for hours, trying with all my might to turn the stiff handle so that the golden oil would come dripping out; my shoulders and my back and my wrists would ache, and I would fume at the Russians who were forcing us to grow such a troublesome crop.

My mother, on the other hand, was happy with the poppy seeds, because we were able to harvest much more than the 100 pounds the Russians ordered us to turn in. We had so many seeds left over that we could make dozens and dozens of bottles of oil, which was as valuable as honey or butter, and could be traded for all sorts of things that we needed.

Paula wanted to use the poppy-seed oil to hire a plastic surgeon she had met in Berlin. She was determined to finally do something about the scar on her face, the old purply-pink line that ran down one side of her cheek and neck, left over from the tuberculosis operation she'd had when she was two. I thought she was crazy and so did Willi and my mother. Paula always wore her hair over her scar and nobody ever noticed it. But for some reason it was bothering Paula terribly, and she stubbornly insisted on having the operation. Finally Willi agreed, more to stop the fighting than because he had changed his opinion. Our evenings grew quiet and peaceful again, as Paula saved our oil for her surgery.

The hemp and tobacco crops didn't present nearly as much difficulty as the poppies. The dried hemp stalks we simply collected and turned in to a processing factory, which made them into rope or string. The tobacco leaves we hung to dry all over the farm, so that it looked like we'd been invaded by brown bats, asleep upside down on our clotheslines and our fenceposts. We had plenty of tobacco left over after turning in our quota to the Russians and my brothers soon took up smoking, as did many other people in the village. Most people had never tasted tobacco before and they liked it. Helmut would just about smack his lips as he crumbled the green leaves into a piece of newspaper, then rolled it into a bulky wad, set it on fire and inhaled the thick smoke.

One afternoon when Henni's family was gone, she came over and dared me to come smoke a cigar with her. I followed her up the street to her house, my heart pounding. My mother, I knew, would definitely not approve of this. We went into Henni's dark basement. Henni had already rolled us two fat cigars, the tobacco blackish-green in the newspaper wrapping. She handed me mine.

"Ready?" she said, her eyes gleaming like a wild cat's.

"I guess," I murmured.

Henni stuck her cigar in her mouth. I did the same. She lit a match, touched her cigar, then mine. I took a breath. Sour hot smoke filled my mouth, stung my lungs. I started coughing and couldn't stop.

Henni arched her eyebrows, leaned back against the basement wall, and continued calmly smoking. "You'll be all right," she said. "You just have to get used to it."

Thud! Thud! The pounding on the door upstairs was firm and heavy. It reminded me of soldiers, of Russians crashing down doors in the night.

Henni's eyes opened wide. "Who's that?" I choked out, between coughs.

"I don't know," said Henni, looking worried. "We're not expecting anybody."

We put the cigars out in a pail and ran upstairs. Slowly Henni opened the door. There on the front step stood Herr Lang, one of her father's friends.

"Is your father home?" he asked.

"No," Henni said.

Herr Lang frowned, looking suspiciously at us. "Are you sure?" He sniffed the air. "I smell his cigars."

"Oh, he was here, but he just left," said Henni. "You just missed him."

Herr Lang went away. Henni closed the door and then she and I started laughing, so hard that we collapsed on her kitchen floor, tears running down our cheeks. Even though my stomach was upset and my throat hurt from the tobacco, it felt so good to laugh again.

The winter of 1946 was one of the harshest, coldest, snowiest winters we'd ever had. Everyone said so. The snow kept falling, the temperature dropping. We had very little kerosene, only a small basket of smelly brown coal, and only the wood we could find outside to keep our stoves going, our house warm. We also were running out of hay and grain for the animals.

Still, we were much better off than the homeless people trying to survive in the big cities with no shelter, no fuel, and no food. Relief workers came almost every day, looking for old clothes and food and things that could be burned for heat. My mother donated what she could, which wasn't much.

My father complained that we would all have been better prepared for this difficult winter if we hadn't been required to grow the Russian crops.

"Poppies, for God's sakes," he snorted. "These damn Russians have people with no farming experience trying to tell us what to grow."

"Maybe it was a test," Helmut said. "To see if they can make us obey."

"I wouldn't doubt it. Have you heard what they did to Joseph Schott?"

Joseph Schott was a farmer who lived near Gnoien with his wife and five young children.

"No, what happened?" Helmut asked.

"He disappeared one night, a couple months ago," said my father. "The Russians took him in for questioning. He hasn't come back and they won't tell his family anything."

"Why did they take him?"

"He refused to change his crops. He complained to too many people. He wasn't loyal enough for them."

My father stood up and got his coat. "You know who took him away? Officer Schmidt. Remember? Officer Schmidt, who used to be a Nazi." My father wrapped his scarf around his neck, laughing bitterly. "They sent him to a camp for awhile, to clean out his brain. Now he's back, working for them. From Nazi rat to Communist rat."

My father opened the door, letting in a blast of screaming wind and thin white pellets of icy snow. He left without saying where he was going.

"I hadn't heard about Herr Schott," said Helmut. "But I have heard stories in Gnoien about other people disappearing."

"Where are they disappearing to?" I asked.

"The same as before," said Helmut, his voice low and angry. "It's all the same as before. To the camps. Or to their graves."

Paula left for Berlin in early January, during a break in the heavy snows that were regularly pummeling us. She took the train by herself, carting a suitcase filled with jars of poppyseed oil. Two weeks later, she was back, holding her head stiffly. Her jaw was swollen and purplish green. To me, she looked worse than before. Paula was happy, though. She said the surgery had gone well: when the swelling was gone, we would all see a big difference.

The snow and ice picked up again the day after she got back, so much snow that school was canceled. A cold wind whipped across the fields and smacked our house, whistling through chinks in the walls and windows, and even extra bricks in my bed couldn't keep me warm. Everyone in the village was burning their brown coal, so that in the mornings a mud-colored haze rested along the treetops. The snow looked gray-brown and dirty, even as it fell.

By the end of January, Paula's face did look much better. The swelling and bruises had faded and the scar was fainter, though I could still make it out if I was looking for it. Paula began carrying herself differently, with pride and confidence, and she seemed happier, and that was all that mattered. As far as I was concerned, the operation had been a success.

One afternoon in early spring, my teachers marched us to the movie theater in downtown Gnoien, where I got to see my first film.

When it began, I was in awe. I couldn't believe how big the black-and-white people were on the screen in front of me, how fascinating it was to eavesdrop on their lives. Then I began paying attention to the storyline. The movie was about a fifteen-year-old girl who fell in love with an older boy and contracted venereal disease and died. This was the reason our teachers had taken us out of school to see this movie—to warn us about venereal disease.

The movie relieved me in one way: From its description, I was sure I hadn't had venereal disease.

In another way, though, the movie tore me apart. The actors were only images on a wall, but they were somehow as real as my classmates. I had tears in my eyes, sitting in the dark, as the heroine of the movie lay on her deathbed.

And then suddenly the tears were for something—someone—else. Suddenly a different movie was playing in my mind, a movie that never stopped playing in the private theater of my deepest memories. Even though I had in many ways recovered from that day in October 1945, that movie was still playing. If I stopped what I was doing or thinking at any given moment, I could tune it in. Sometimes it came on when I wasn't expecting it, playing flashes, sounds, horrors in my mind's eye, until I forced another thought to take the stage, to keep the memories behind the curtain, as far away as possible.

25

"When you're confirmed."

I had heard those words from my mother for so many years. When I wanted to cut my hair instead of wearing it in schoolgirl braids, she said it: "When you're confirmed." When I wanted to dance in public, at the harvest festival or at weddings: "When you're confirmed."

And now, finally, my confirmation day had arrived. The day when, in my mother's eyes at least, I was almost a woman.

Aunt Bertha sent me material from America to make two new dresses for my special day, one black and one blue, as was the custom. Thank God for Aunt Bertha. We'd started receiving her boxes again after the war ended. If she hadn't sent the material, I don't know what we would have done.

Confirmation required two dresses because there were two events—the confirmation test on the Sunday before the ceremony was scheduled, and then the ceremony itself. We were all supposed to wear blue for the test; we stood in front of the entire congregation and answered questions from Herr Pastor Scharnweber about what we had learned. I answered the questions correctly, thank God. I had been so nervous I wasn't sure I could speak, but everything went smoothly.

The next week, on confirmation Sunday, I wore the new black dress my mother had made from Aunt Bertha's material and the silver cross necklace my mother had given me the night before. We rode to church in our wagon, which was decorated with flowers and ribbons. Even my father went to church, one of the few times he had set foot in the Lutheran church in Boddin.

After the service, we rode back home and set out cake for our neighbors and friends. Tilla Hunsinger gave me a heart-shaped silver jewelry box. Other people gave me cards or flowers.

Then my father presented me with a large hydrangea plant, one huge white blossom already open, as big as a face and ten times bigger than the daisies and roses and other flowers I had received. There was a strange look on his face when he handed it to me—a look of satisfaction, of triumph. He didn't even really look at me, just turned and stared at my mother, at the neighbors. My mother's face grew red. We all knew that there was only one place nearby that sold such expensive and exotic plants: the nursery run by Lotti Kreitz's father.

Right after my father came back from the war, he stayed away from the Adventist church, and from Lotti. He and my mother didn't get along very well, but he had at least seemed to be trying to be a family man. Then, one morning, Lotti came to our door, looking for him. My mother was out milking. Paula opened the door, saw Lotti, then got my father. He and Lotti went off together.

Paula still hadn't forgiven herself for doing that. "Why didn't I just send her away? It was so early and I wasn't thinking clearly or I would have told that woman what I thought of her."

"It wouldn't have mattered," Heinz said. "She would just have come back another time. If he didn't want to see her, he didn't have to. He didn't have to leave with her."

I had never heard my mother talk to my father about Lotti. But the awkward distance between my parents had become a tension-filled battle zone, where I didn't dare walk for fear of intercepting a shot filled with bitterness and contempt. Mostly it was my father doing the firing, but sometimes my mother unloaded her own weapons, too. When they hurt each other like this, I would leave the room, the house, wherever they were, and try to put as much distance between us as I could.

I hated my father more for his confirmation present than if he had given me nothing.

The day after confirmation, I went to Gnoien's only beauty shop and had my braids clipped off and my hair styled to just below my chin. After it was cut, I felt bold and free. I decided to go all the way and have a permanent wave. The beautician rolled my hair and poured sour-smelling, burning liquid on it and lowered a heavy, hot, cone-shaped machine on my head. Three painful hours later, I was a new person, an almost-grown woman, with short, modern, sophisticated curls. I felt like my feet were curled, too, with the extra swing in my step as I pranced back to Doelitz, the newfound sensation of air at the back of my neck tickling me so much that I almost burst out laughing.

"Tilli? Is that you?" said Lori Pech, walking with her grandfather. "You look so different! I can't believe it's you."

Herr Pech stared at me suspiciously, as if he thought that I might indeed be an imposter.

I passed more neighbors as I walked home. "Tilli Horn, what in the world has happened to you?" shrieked Frau Häde, her mouth dropping open.

My mother just looked at me, her face expressionless.

"Well? What do you think?" I asked impatiently.

"You know what I think. I think your hair was perfectly lovely the way it was before."

But I didn't let her bother me. I was feeling too wonderful, too grown-up. After all, I had the hair to prove it.

Besides being the age of confirmation, fourteen was an important age as far as the Russians were concerned. They demanded that every child of fourteen or above join the Communist version of the Hitler Youth Party—called the Free German Youth, or FDJ. I kept getting notices at school and messages sent to our house reminding me that it was time for me to join the FDJ. The Russians said that anybody who wanted to continue their education would have to prove their loyalty by joining.

I kept hoping that something would happen, that there would be a change in policy, or that maybe I would slip through some loophole, because, as much as I wanted to go on in school—to the school in Teterow that came after high school, then perhaps even on to a university to school—I would not join the FDJ. I simply refused to do this.

Alone in Fraulein Meyer's apartment, I asked if she thought I was doing the right thing.

"I shouldn't be saying this," she said, sighing. "I should tell you to go along, to join the FDJ and be safe. But you need to know that if you join the FDJ, you can forget about going to America. Americans won't let Communists into their country. And I know how much you want to go to America."

That sealed it for me. There was no way I was going to give up my plans to move to America. There was no way I would give in to the Russians. They had forced me once; they weren't going to force me again.

A month after my fourteenth birthday, my father left my mother, for good.

What really hurt was that he took Astra with him.

I had just come home from Gnoien, from my English lesson with Hannah Meyer. Before I even got to our house, I heard yelling, my mother and father yelling, their voices carrying their hurt and rage beyond our yard, beyond our street, out into the village. I hurried to see what the trouble was.

"You don't need me!" my father was shouting, standing in the yard, his feet crushing a few of my mother's lilies, which had strayed from the borders of the flower garden. He was holding his suitcase, the one he took with him when he went off to fight in the war. "You and your farm! Always this farm! Never anything for me!"

"I hate you! You're nothing but a lazy, selfish pig!" My mother's face was so twisted I hardly recognized her. I had never heard her use words like this before.

My father's face was red, his eyes lit with rage. He looked like our bull before he charges. He started to move toward Mami, his hands in fists. I caught my breath, wondering if I should jump in front of him to protect her. My mother didn't look frightened, though, just furious. She stood firm, her arms folded over her chest. She glared at him and he stopped a few feet from her.

"Go to your woman, then," she said. "Go on. Go! And don't ever come back!"

"First I'm taking my horse," said my father, heading off to the barn.

"Oh, no, you're not!" my mother shouted, rushing after him.

I didn't follow them. I just stood there, woodenly, as my father came back from the horse barn, leading Astra by the reins. She followed slowly, her heels dragging, her eyes twitching in panic. Helmut and Heinz walked behind her, my mother between them.

"That's my horse! My horse! You can't have her!" she screamed.

"Just watch me," my father said, smiling.

"Mami, let me at him," Helmut said. "I'll get Astra back."

"No, no," said my mother, resting her hand on his chest. "No, it's not worth it. He's not worth it. Don't fight your father."

My father marched through the gate, down the road, without a backward glance. Astra plodded along beside him, her tail twitching nervously.

Mami rubbed at her face. "Let's get cleaned up for supper," she said, her words as soft as sighs.

26

Although I felt a bond with Aunt Bertha from all her letters and presents over the years, I had never met her, and only knew what she looked like from old, grainy photographs my mother kept in a black leather album.

Now, though, she was coming to Germany, and we were going to see her.

When my mother told us that Aunt Bertha was coming for a visit, I assumed she would be staying at our house, and I asked my mother which room she would sleep in. My mother shook her head and said it wasn't that simple. The Russians would not allow anybody to go in or out of the parts of Germany that they controlled, which included Doelitz. We were prisoners, after all, and Aunt Bertha couldn't enter our prison.

"Then how can we see her?" I asked.

"Because she's an American citizen now, Aunt Bertha can go to any place in Germany that America controls," Mami explained. "She's going to Berlin, to the western zone. We're going to see her there."

Paula and my mother then began telling me all about Berlin, which was a very complicated place. It was completely surrounded by Russian-controlled areas, like an island in the middle of the Red Sea. However, only part of Berlin itself was Russian-controlled—the eastern half. The rest of Berlin was shared by the Americans and their allies.

As Russian prisoners, we were only supposed to go into the Russian zone, just as Aunt Bertha was expected to remain in the American zone.

"Then how are we going to see her?" I was thoroughly confused.

Paula said that people in Berlin crossed between the zones frequently, even though they weren't supposed to. The city was such a chaotic place that the soldiers couldn't keep order. They stomped around with their machine guns looking fierce, but in reality, they couldn't very well stop and search millions of people for their identification papers.

My mother had decided that the risk of our getting caught was very small and she wanted to see Aunt Bertha very badly. So, the morning after spring break began at school, my brothers—including Hugo, who had made his way home earlier that year—and Paula and my mother and I got on the train, heading for Berlin. Willi stayed behind to run the farm.

The train was crowded as always and we had to stand, holding metal poles and swaying as the cars rattled over the tracks. It was hard, especially since we were carrying so much food: bags of potatoes and apples, bread, hams, sausages. My mother explained that we needed to bring food because of the current Russian siege of Berlin. The Russians no longer wanted to share Berlin with the Americans and were blockading the roads all around Berlin, trying to keep food and other supplies from reaching the city, in hopes of starving its residents into turning the entire city over to Russian control. We were bringing food for the Bergs, with whom we would be staying, as well as ourselves.

We rode most of the way to Berlin in silence, the train jutting and swaying. I was alternately excited and frightened. I'd never been farther from home than Victoria's estate and I didn't know what to expect. I watched the countryside pass, field after field, mixed with wilder, untended patches of woods and scrub grass. Next came villages and small towns, where the train stopped to let people on and off. The crowding never eased. My legs and back ached from standing in one spot for so long.

After several hours, I found myself dozing off, sleeping as I stood, hypnotized by the scenery rushing past and the motion of the train and the music of the wheels on the track.

"There it is," Paula said suddenly, pointing out the window to a brownish-gray haze. I jumped awake and started looking more closely around me. We were not in the country now. Instead, we were passing rows of gray houses mixed with gray factories, silver-brown smoke curling from their chimneys.

"That's Berlin." Paula pointed to a faint row of tall buildings at the edge of the sky. The train snaked its way closer. The air was thick with coal fumes; I started coughing. Around us were more trains, all feeding into the city, streams into a river.

And then we were in the middle of Berlin. On all sides, everywhere I looked, were buildings so tall that, from the window of the train, I couldn't see their tops. The fronts were all that remained of many of the buildings. The bombs that hit Berlin during the war had torn off the sides and backs of the buildings, exposing remnants of offices and apartments, places where people had once lived and worked. I didn't see a single building that had escaped damage. Some had only one wall standing, while others had been leveled into patches of charred, blackened ground. Next to many of these patches stood neat piles of bricks, like senti-nels guarding the ruins.

"What are those piles for?" Helmut asked Paula.

"The rubble women put them there," she said, as the train clicked and clacked its way through the smoky haze.

"What are rubble women?"

"Almost every woman still alive in Berlin after the war ended became a rubble woman. Right after the war, there were almost no men in the city—they were either dead or being kept prisoner. The women had to clear the streets of the rub-ble left from the ruined buildings. Many women spent all day cleaning mortar off bricks and stacking them up so they can be used again someday. So the city can be put back together."

The whistle sounded and the train jolted, then stopped.

"This is it," Paula said. "Come on. Let's go."

We followed her out the door onto the station platform, which was marked "Russian Sector," then stepped off into chaos.

Cars. There were cars! And trucks. Honking, honking. Soldiers marching, guns at their sides, suspicion in their eyes. People, so many people, huddled, wan-dering. No sunlight, no grass, no trees, where was the sky?

I found it hard to breathe, to think. My heart lurched and tripped over itself. I felt dizzy.

"Come on, come on," Paula said, walking quickly. "This way." She didn't look around, didn't seem bothered by the noise and confusion and ruined build-ings and gray thick air. I guessed she had seen it so many times on her earlier trips that it no longer struck her. My mother, brothers, and I, though, found it diffi-cult not to just stop and stare.

As we walked, I kept noticing all the Russian sentries. Even though Paula kept assuring us that everything would be all right, I couldn't stop worrying about them. I fingered my identification card in my pocket as we followed Paula down street after street. In the Russian Sector, this card would help me—but what if they found me with it in the American Zone?

We passed long lines of people standing, waiting, people with dead looks on their pale faces. Paula said they were most likely waiting for bread or coal. They might have to wait all day long and still, even though they had ration tickets, they might not get any food. Supplies were just too low. I clutched the bag of potatoes and bread that I was carrying, feeling guilty.

After awhile, we reached a tram stop and stepped onto a crowded elevated train car, which rattled past more crumbling buildings, then passed a sign: American Zone. The train stopped and we got off. I didn't see any soldiers. Nobody stopped us or asked to see our papers. We were there illegally; we could be arrested. But nobody cared.

We walked for another fifteen minutes, then reached the apartment where Aunt Bertha was supposed to be waiting for us. She was staying with old friends of hers, the Schencks. Their building was one of those with only the front wall still standing. I was amazed to think that anyone could live in such a place, but Paula said they were there, so we weaved through the piles of rocks and rubbish, climbed a stairway open to the sky, walked down a hallway to a door. Paula knocked. After a moment, a woman—Frau Schenck—opened it and led us into a dark, dank basement room.

Because of the darkness, at first I didn't see the short woman with Frau Schenck. Then, before I knew it, I was being hugged and squeezed by someone who felt just like my mother.

"Tilli! I'd know you anywhere," said the woman, who was my mother's height, with a round, smiling face, curly brown hair and glasses. "I'm your Aunt Bertha."

For the next three days, we spent as much time as we could with Aunt Bertha. We slept in another broken-down building with my mother's friends, the Bergs, but each morning we met Aunt Bertha at the Schencks' apartment. My mother and Aunt Bertha talked for hours, catching up on their lives, as we walked along the destroyed streets of Berlin. Amid the devastation, we managed to find a few nice spots, some parks and flowered areas where life was not entirely blackness and ruin. Some of the shopping areas, too, had been partially rebuilt. Aunt Bertha took us to a shoe store and bought us all new, crepe-soled shoes.

"Thank-you, Aunt Bertha," I said, then blurted impulsively, as I hugged her: "I wish I could go back to America with you!"

"Tilli!" said my mother.

"Do you really want to come to America?" Aunt Bertha asked, looking at me closely.

"I've wanted to for so long, especially since the war began," I told her, speaking in English.

Aunt Bertha looked surprised. "You speak English very well," she answered, also in English.

"I've been taking extra English lessons in school. I want to go to America so badly!"

"Tilli, talk in German so we can understand you," my mother said impatiently.

"Why do you want to come to America?" Aunt Bertha asked, switching to German.

"Because," I began. My mother and Paula and my brothers were staring at me. It was so hard to put my strong feelings into mere words. "Because I want to be free," I said slowly. "I want something better. I don't want any more war. I don't like being afraid all the time. And I hate the Russians. I hate them!"

"Regina?" Aunt Bertha murmured to my mother, her eyebrows raised in a question.

"If this is what she wants to do, I think she should do it," my mother said. "She deserves a better life."

"Then maybe I can help," Aunt Bertha said. "Tilli, if you can get out of Germany, I will pay for you to come to America. I will sponsor you."

I started to leap with joy, but the worried look on Aunt Bertha's face stopped me.

"I don't want to give you false hope, Tilli," she said. "The hard part is going to be getting out of here. The Russians have you pretty well surrounded here in Berlin. I'd take you with me now if I could, but you can't fly out of here without the right papers. I don't know if there's any way to get papers, whether you can buy them or what. Your best bet might be to get to western Germany somehow, then apply for permission to legally emigrate."

"Maybe Herr Berg can help," Paula said. "Maybe he can find a way for Tilli to get papers."

"That's a thought," said my mother. "He has a lot of connections. We'll work on it and let you know."

That night, we said good-bye to Aunt Bertha.

"I'm so glad I got to meet you," I told her.

"I hope to see you soon in America," she said. "You'll make it. I know you will."

My mother and Herr Berg stayed up that night for hours, talking. I curled up on a blanket on the floor. I heard my name being mentioned, but couldn't make out what they were saying.

The next morning, we rode the train back to Doelitz. This time it was easier. We didn't have the heavy bundles of food to carry. Plus my mind was filled with new, exciting dreams to occupy the tedious hours. Dreams of America.

Before Berlin, Aunt Bertha had been a face in a photograph, a signature on a card. Now I knew she was real, she loved me and she was going to help me get out of this country that I hated.

Two months later, during my summer break from school, I left my family and took the train to Berlin. Herr Berg had agreed to try to get me the papers I needed to fly out of Berlin, fly over the Russian ring encircling the city, fly to the west, where I would stay with my Aunt Liesel in Kassel until Aunt Bertha could arrange my passage to America.

Although I was glad to be leaving Russian rule, it almost killed me to say good-bye to my family. Especially my mother. I watched her out the train window, her face drawn, her eyes squinting as the train pulled me away from her. She looked so small, so faraway. Already, I missed her so. But I couldn't think about that.

Because the Russian siege of Berlin was still going on, I brought as much food as I could to Berlin, to give to the Bergs. It didn't last us long, though. Soon I was trying to survive on the same diet the Berliners had been forced to live on for months: dried potatoes, powdered milk, stale bread—all of which had been air-lifted into Berlin by the Americans, who were trying to save the city's two million inhabitants from starvation.

The second day I was in Berlin, Herr Berg took me to Templehof Airport to see the American planes in action. We joined a crowd gathered on the low hills encircling the airfield, loud with the droning whine of airplane engines. I craned my head back and in flew a fat-bellied white plane with an American star and red and white stripes painted on its side. It swooped onto the runway, gliding to a stop. American soldiers dressed in green jumped out and began unloading box after box, a mountain of brown and white boxes, as the crowd on the hills cheered.

Less than five minutes later, another plane shot in, pulling up parallel to the first. More soldiers jumped out, more boxes of food, more cheers.

A few minutes later, another plane arrived. And another. Every five to ten minutes, a new plane landed, another one left. There was a steady stream, arriving, dropping food, flying off into the gray sky.

"Without the Americans, we would all die," said Herr Berg.

"That's right," a man standing beside us said. "First they destroyed us. Now they are keeping us alive."

"They did what they had to do to win the war," said Herr Berg. "They stopped Hitler, they saved us from him. I don't blame them for that. They don't need to be doing this now, bringing us food like this. This is what I admire them for."

As we rode the tram back to Herr Berg's apartment, I thought about what he had said, and decided that I was even more determined, if that were possible, to live in America, a land that would reach out to save the lives of millions of people in the city of its enemies an ocean away.

After a month of trying, of pulling every string he could, Herr Berg finally gave up. He couldn't find any way to get me West German papers. Without them, leaving for America from Berlin was impossible.

I was still a prisoner.

"I'm sorry, Tilli," said Herr Berg, and I knew that he meant it.

Two days later, my mother sent me a telegram. Since my plan to escape had failed, it was time for me to come home and help out on the farm. We had threshing to do, after all, and every hand was needed.

I felt like crumpling her telegram in my hand. I wished it had never arrived. For one thing, even with the lack of food and all the despair permeating Berlin, I had been enjoying the adventure of living away from home, more or less on my own, with no tedious farm chores to do. For another, I hated threshing: sitting for hours on top of a beast-like, roaring threshing machine, shoving in prickly stalks of grain, being careful not to get my hands chewed off.

More than that, though, going home now meant I truly had lost my chance to be free. Maybe I would never get another one. I might never again get as close to America as I was right then, living in the American Zone in western Berlin.

"I guess you'll be leaving us, then," said Herr Berg. "Tomorrow?"

I nodded glumly.

"I'm sorry again that we couldn't make this work," said Herr Berg. "I sure envy you, though. Getting to go back to the farm, to your nice little village, instead of having to stay here in all this mess, with no food to speak of. I think you're really quite a lucky girl."

I nodded again, although I didn't feel lucky in the least.

The next day, I watched the shattered hulk of Berlin recede from the window of the train. For once, I had secured a seat. I didn't have to stand for the trip, but could lean back and close my eyes and dream of what might have been.

27

More than anything, I loved to dance. I practiced the steps—waltzes, fox trots, cha chas—for hours with my brothers in the barn. I loved losing myself in music, losing my body as I became one with sound, my movements taking control of my mind, erasing my thoughts and my worries, dulling my pain, leaving only pure sweet rhythm.

My mother had never let me dance in public before, but now that I was confirmed and the harvest dance was upon us, she had no choice but to give me permission. I couldn't wait. I was ready to be happy.

My brothers, Paula, Willi, my mother, and I rode the wagon to the villa, bringing cake and homemade ale to share. I could hear the music even before we went in the door. The sounds wafted out, calling me. I jumped·out of the wagon and rushed to the door. "Tilli, slow down," complained my mother. "Help me carry this."

I got the cake and set it on a long table covered with food that was set up just inside the villa's main ballroom, the wood-floored room where the Russians had once parked their horses, which was now filled with couples spinning to a band playing folk songs. Mami stopped to talk to Tilla Hunsinger. At first I waited by her side, but then I couldn't stand still any longer. I shot Heinz a pleading look. He laughed and took my hand.

"Shall we?" he said, grinning, and then there I was, one of the adults, a woman now, my skirt lifting around me as Heinz swung me and twirled me, just as we had practiced so many times in the barn, when only the cows and sheep were there to see us.

Soon, other boys were dancing with me. I lost track of how many, and whom, and what music we were moving to. I couldn't get enough. People went on and off the dance floor to get something to eat or drink, but I didn't stop. I couldn't stop. I was hot and thirsty, but I didn't care. My body had never felt so good, so right. I was no longer betrayed by my tallness, my too-big feet. Instead, I felt fluid, graceful, the music pounding in time to my heartbeat, in rhythm with my soul. I was a set of chords, a song swirling on a parquet floor. I'm free, I thought wildly. *I'm free.*

Hours later, the dancing stopped. It was time to name the Harvest Queen. A group of adults huddled together. Then, Herr Burger, Henni's father, made the announcement: "The Doelitz Harvest Queen of 1948 is—Tilli Horn."

Everybody clapped and smiled at me. At me! Heinz squeezed me tight.

"Come here, Tilli," Herr Burger called. "Christian, Paul, come here."

Christian and Paul—two boys from the village who were my age—raised the crown over my head: a three-foot woven arch, made out of barley and oats and straw and rye, interwoven with blue bachelor's buttons and red and white poppy blossoms and other flowers I couldn't stop to identify, yellow and orange and lavender. We marched outside, everybody following behind, then went down one street and up another, singing and shouting in joy.

I kept the crown. After a few days, the flowers withered and died. But at least I had my memories of one of the happiest days of my life.

Soon after the festival, Hugo left. He had been repairing shoes in Gnoien and he liked his job, but he couldn't stand living in the east, under the thumb of the Russians. He planned to cross the border in Bavaria, where the mountains met Germany, and settle somewhere in the west. I wanted him to take me with him, but he said it was too dangerous.

My mother was tense for weeks after Hugo left, until at last we got a letter from him, saying that he had arrived safely and had never once encountered a Russian soldier. "Thank you, God," whispered my mother, handing the letter to me.

I wondered sometimes how my mother could stand it, all these leave-takings, never knowing whether her children would be back, or whether she would ever see them again, or whether they would die before they reached their destinations.

Not long after we heard the good news about Hugo, I saw Astra, for the first time since my father took her from us.

I was on my way to Ingeborg's house with several jars of honey, which were my mother's payment to Ingeborg's mother for some sewing she had done for us. I walked slowly through Gnoien's downtown, keeping my eye out for any of my friends who might also be running after-school errands. I didn't feel like hurrying home to my chores just yet.

As I passed through the town square into the area where farmers parked their horses and wagons, I saw Astra, tied to a hitching post, saddled and bridled, alone.

The last time I had seen Astra, she'd had only a rope tied around her neck. She had never been used for work; she had only been cared for and loved, especially by me.

I have always thought that horses have the most human spirit of any animal, except maybe dogs. It's something about their eyes, the way they look at you. At least that's the way I felt about Max and Moritz, and the way I had allowed myself to feel about Astra. I hadn't opened up my heart since, not to Thunder, our new horse, or to Fox. I didn't want to be hurt again.

"Astra, how are you girl? Astra, it's me."

Astra turned her head to face me. She nickered, pulling her lips up to show her teeth, and I could almost believe it to be a smile. She shook her brown mane and stamped her front legs.

I stroked her shoulders. Her fur was not nearly as soft now. And she didn't feel as well-muscled, either. Instead, she seemed thin and almost bedraggled.

Her eyes were the same, though: black and liquid-soft, seeing me, seeing my heart.

"Oh Astra," I said, resting my cheek against her nose. I wished I had some oats to give her. I closed my eyes, feeling the rumble of her breath.

When I opened them again, my father was walking towards me, an almost frightened look on his face, smiling awkwardly, guiltily.

I stood away from Astra. "Good-bye, girl," I whispered.

Then I turned and walked quickly through the square, heading for the road home.

"Tilli, wait!" my father called. "Tilli, please."

I walked more quickly. I didn't look back.

◆   ◆   ◆

It was September 1949, six months until graduation from high school, and Fraulein Meyer was scared.

"They're getting worse," she said quietly. "So much worse."

We were in her living room, getting ready to begin my English lesson. She had seemed so pensive, so lost in thought, that I had asked her what was wrong.

"Who is getting worse?"

"The Soviets. They're coming out with more rules every day. Rules to drive you mad, things we can and cannot say, songs I'm not supposed to play. I don't know if I will even be allowed to keep teaching English. They are ordering everybody to learn Russian. We have to report things to them, things about our students."

"What things?"

"They want to know about the students who won't join the FDJ, why they won't join, everything about them."

Fraulein Meyer's eyes were deep with warning. She took my hand. "I didn't tell them about you, Tilli. But I know they're going to keep asking."

Ilse and all my classmates had already joined the FDJ, officially becoming young Communists, even though none of them believed in the Party doctrines in the least.

"Tilli, you need to join, too," Ilse said firmly. "Otherwise you can't go on in school. You're so smart. You can do so much. Don't let them stop you. Just join—it doesn't mean you believe in it. It just means you know how to play the game."

"Ilse, I can't," I said. "I just can't."

There was so much Ilse didn't know about me and couldn't understand. She didn't know about the rape and how I felt about giving in to the Russians and why I hated them so much and how I planned to go to America, which would never admit a Communist.

I hadn't told Henni these things, either. Henni had also joined the FDJ and had gone to her first meeting a few weeks earlier. "They aren't so bad, Tilli," she said. "It's just like the Hitler Youth, only more like parties, with cookies to eat."

We were riding bikes through the park. My brothers had found a broken-down bike abandoned by the Russians and fixed it up enough for my mother to use; I had borrowed it and Henni and I were taking our usual Sunday excursion. We stopped to admire the violets and marigolds, which still held their blooms, nestled amid the rocks along the path.

I tried to ignore the hammer-and-sickle rock sculpture that the Russians had left.

"What will you do if you can't go on in school, if you can't go to Teterow?" Henni asked.

"I don't know," I said.

We got off our bikes and sat in the grass. Little children ran past us, so carefree and happy. I closed my eyes and felt the breeze touching me, lifting my hair. What would I do? Whatever would I do?

We got up and rode on, into the woods, past my dreaming rock. It was cool and dark there. The ground was a mass of moss and vines and wild blossoms. All around us, birds were calling to each other, singing their private music. Everything was so intensely beautiful. I felt a sharp pang of sadness, a yearning so deep I would have cried if I had been alone. But I wasn't and the moment passed and then I was home again, going about my daily life.

The next few months flew by. Before I knew it, I was taking my final exams. The results came back the following week: I passed, as I'd known I would.

I went to see Herr Principal Gross, hoping for a miracle. "I can go to Teterow now, can't I?"

Principal Gross frowned. "Tilli, if I were making the decisions, of course you would go," he said softly, almost whispering. Then he stood up, speaking loudly, as if I were a stranger. "I am sorry, fraulein, but you must be a member of the FDJ to advance in school. Please see a Party official immediately."

There didn't seem to be anything more I could say or do.

"It's so unfair," I told my mother. "Nobody I know who has joined the FDJ believes in it. It's just a joke to them. How can I be hurting the Communists if I get a better education? It doesn't make any sense."

"I know, I know," my mother said. "Please try not to worry. We'll figure something out. I'm not going to let you waste yourself on the farm."

My mother alone understood me. Even though she had chosen the farm life for herself and loved it without reservation, even though she would undoubtedly prefer for me to stay with her for as long as I lived, she knew what I needed, which was to leave her and go somewhere where I could be free.

For the rest of the summer, she wrote letters to friends around Germany, trying to come up with a plan for me. I went to the department store in Gnoien, the bakery, the hardware store, hoping someone would take me on as an apprentice. But all the businesses had been taken over by the Communists, who had put managers in charge that supported the Party and did whatever they were told to do. As soon as they would find out that I was not a member of the FDJ, I would be turned away.

"I'm sorry," I would hear, over and over. "I'm sorry, but my hands are tied. Even Herr Frieburg, my mother's good friend who ran the farm bureau and sold most of our grain, shook his head gently.

"I'm sorry," he said. "There's nothing we can do."

After school was finished, I spent the next nine months in Rostock, the harbor town about thirty miles away, learning to be a secretary. My mother had found the school, one of the few in existence, it seemed, that would accept students who had not joined the FDJ.

But when I came home, once again I was met with closed doors. Even with my secretarial certificate, I was not employable.

Just after sunset on a drizzly, damp early September evening in 1950, I was curled on the kitchen bench with an old romance novel, only half paying attention to the story. My thoughts were elsewhere; my mind was running like a trapped mouse, circling endlessly. *What will I do? What will I do?* I was dizzy with it, with my unsolvable problem. *What will I do?* The words echoed in time with the raindrops beating against the windows.

And then, without warning, a loud pounding on the kitchen door.

Mami and I jumped. Fanni, who had been sleeping in the corner, leapt up and started barking. We were not expecting visitors. Sudden knocks in the night were rarely a good thing.

I put my book down and opened the door.

Standing before me, holding her jacket over her head to keep back the rain, was Henni. Her eyes, usually so merry, were filled with fear.

I flinched: at the sudden rush of cold, wet air; at the certainty that something was terribly wrong.

"Henni! What—"

"I have to talk to you," said Henni, stepping quickly into the kitchen.

Mami, her hands wrapped in dish towels, smiled and said a polite hello; her eyes, though, betrayed her alarm. Henni grabbed my arm. We sat down together on the bench.

"What is it?" I said. "What?"

Henni stared at me. Water trickled like tears from her tousled hair onto her cheeks and shoulders. "I've just come from the FDJ meeting," she said, twisting to look over her shoulder, as if she feared somebody had followed her into our kitchen, or was listening at the window.

"Tilli, they talked about you."

Henni paused. For a long, frozen second we were still. I knew what she was about to say. A sudden picture flashed before me: the self-important Party officials, sitting in straight rows in the old, ruined villa house, passing their judgments, feeling the thrilling force of their petty power. They were no different from all the smug, smirking Nazi officers who told us what to do during the Hitler years.

Henni looked down at the puddle forming at her feet, at the water spreading across the wooden planks of the kitchen floor.

Then she said it, all in a rush. "They said if you don't join now, they are going to send you away. To the island. To Usedom."

I had, of course, heard of Usedom: the Isle of Usedom, located in the Baltic Sea; a place where the Communists had built a concentration camp for people who didn't go along—for people like me. Communists took people to this concentration camp to give them the opportunity to "concentrate" on becoming Party members.

"Tilli, if you don't do something, they're going to come and take you away," Henni said. "Oh, can't you just come to the meetings anyway? You can pretend you agree. What difference will it make?"

"No!" I opened my mouth to try to explain, to tell Henni how I hated the Russians, how I was sick of not being able to say what I believed, how I no longer could abide States and Parties governing my thoughts. But Henni interrupted me. "I know, I know," she said, sighing. "I know this is something you just can't do."

We sat beside each other in resigned silence. "Well, I'd better go," Henni said. "I'm not supposed to be here. No one knows. If they knew I was here—" She stood, blinking quickly.

I gave her a hug. "Thank you for warning me," I whispered. "Good-bye."

Henni opened the door and slipped away, into the wet night. I watched from the window as she hurried down the road toward her house, her head swiveling back and forth. I didn't see anybody behind her, anybody following her, but our road was lined with big trees and bushes—plenty of places for a spy to hide.

"That was very brave of Henni," my mother said.

"What will I do?" I asked. I felt on the verge of panic, my breath coming quickly, my heart racing, a cold feeling settling in my stomach.

"Don't worry. I won't let them take you away."

But that's what you said about the Russians before they came here—that you would protect me, that you wouldn't let anything happen to me, and look what happened.

I didn't say this to my mother, I hated myself for thinking it, but I couldn't help it. I knew now how much hope there was in the things adults told children, and how little truth.

Mami moved back to the table and began wiping up the stray bread crumbs, her arms moving with strong, angry strokes over the dark, scratched wood.

"But what can we do?"

"Let me figure this out," she said. "You'd better stay inside for the next few days. Don't talk to anyone. Just stay out of sight. And if anyone comes while I'm not around—anybody official—you need to be ready to go back upstairs again."

Upstairs. To the secret attic, that elevated coffin space that I swore I would never go near again.

28

I seem to be spending my entire life in hiding. Trapped, always trapped.

I am in my bedroom now, my bedroom upstairs. I measure it with my steps. Ten steps forward, ten steps around, back and forth and back again I go, pacing, pacing. I can't lift the curtain; I can't look out the window. They might see me. I can't go outside. I'm not even supposed to go downstairs, in case somebody comes to the door unexpectedly. In case they come for me and I must hide.

I don't think I could live if I had to go back to that attic.

"My thoughts are free, who can guess them—" I try humming my mother's song to myself, to calm myself as it seems to calm her. *"They fly by like nightly shadows—"*

The song doesn't work for me. My thoughts might be free, but I'm not.

I'm trapped, trapped, trapped.

I lie down on my bed, close my eyes and try to escape to the land of my dreams, to my future, to my wonderful grand existence in America, where I will be free and happy and safe, living in a sparkling house with new clothes and crystal vases full of roses and candy whenever I want it and I can run outside shouting my thoughts to the stars and no one will care.

My impossible future. I have to laugh at myself. My future is as far away and fanciful as the castles of sand I built when I was a little girl and still believed in the rescue of princesses.

I get up and peek out behind the curtains to see the world outside my window. The rain is continuing, off and on. It's the annual autumn rainy season, I know, but somehow it seems more somber, more mournful and chilly than I can ever remember it being.

Yesterday I caught a glimpse of Henni, walking along the road with Trudy. We exchanged looks and I saw a question in her eyes, as if she were trying to ask me what I was going to do, but I let the curtain drop. When I looked again, she was gone.

I don't sleep very well. Memories swirl across the horizon of my mind: the harvest dance, my new confirmation dresses, my father's hydrangeas, losing Astra, air-raid sirens, bombs crashing, Russian boots thudding on our stairs, Maria's screams, the soldiers on the road that cold October day.

I try to put it all out of my mind, to shut everything back in its box. It's over, it's all over and done with, time to move on. But my mind won't obey. My future is too uncertain. When I do manage snatches of sleep, I have nightmares and wake paralyzed with fear. I would rather not sleep at all than endure nightmares like these.

My mother is keeping very busy and, when she is with us, acts quite distant and preoccupied. One day she leaves the house and doesn't come back until suppertime, not telling us where she had been. A few times, in the midst of her bustling, I suddenly find her paused, just standing and staring at me, as if drinking me in, as if engraving the memory of me in her mind. I know then that she has found a way for me to leave. I am not sure where I will go, exactly, but I know that very soon I will be leaving this town and probably not coming back. I wish I could talk to Henni and Klara and my other friends. But it isn't safe: for them, or for me. I can't expect them to carry my secrets. Even if it means I won't be able to say good-bye.

Thursday afternoon, my mother beckons me to her bedroom, away from the kitchen and the window and the door, away from the others' eyes. We sit on the bed in the shadows and she takes my hand in hers. Her hands are so rough and lined with calluses, toughened by years of hard work. It makes me sad to look at her hands and think of the life she has had. She deserves so much better.

"It's settled," she says. She has her matter-of-fact face on. Brusque, no-nonsense. It's the face she uses when she doesn't want her heart to show. "I know someone who can take you across the border. You're going to leave Doelitz. You're finally going to get what you wanted."

She pauses. Her eyes are dark and unreadable. "But it is not going to be easy."

I nod, as if I know what she means. In reality I have no idea what to expect. But I want to appear brave, ready to meet whatever challenges she has set for me.

"Here's what you will do. Tomorrow morning, Willi will take you on the train to Wernigerode. From there, you and Willi will go west through the woods to a farm. You need to give the farmer—his name is Richard Burger—some money."

From her pocket she pulls several silver coins—western currency. How in the world has she found western money? What has she sold or done to get it? I want to ask but she is still talking.

"I will hide the money for you so they don't find it. They will probably search you on the train. But you should be okay. After you get to Herr Burger's farm, he will help you go over the border. He has fields, potato fields, in the west. He can cross and he can hide you. Willi can't come with you across. After you are on the other side, you will go to Kassel on the train. Liesel says you can stay with her until Bertha can get you to America."

I don't know what to say. I am reeling.

My mother gives me the directions to Herr Burger's farm and to Aunt Liesel's apartment and she tells me what to pack and how to act and what to look out for. She says she can't write any of the directions down; it would be too dangerous for me and for Herr Burger if the Russians were to find them. I will have all night to go over these things, to commit them to memory.

I try to concentrate on what she is saying. But I am so shocked my mind freezes, my attention wanders.

Jesus is watching me from His perch on the cross. Even in the dim light, I can make out His brown eyes, so wise and yet so puzzled, so pained, and I can see the blood trickling from the holes in His bent and broken wrists. I have looked at this painting so many times in my life and still it disturbs me.

My eyes drift from Jesus to the rest of the bedroom, making their practiced arch from corner to corner, from the wardrobe where my mother keeps her clothes to the nightstand to the flowered curtains covering the small window.

"Tilli?" Mami is saying, frowning.

"I'm sorry," I whisper.

Mami sighs. "I'm sorry, too. I'm sorry it has to be this way."

Then she hugs me, tight and hard, and I never want to let her go.

◆   ◆   ◆

I can't fall asleep. Rain continues to pound the roof; wind slaps against the windows and howls through the nearby trees. But the storm is not the reason I am still awake.

Under the bed is my little cardboard suitcase. I packed three pairs of socks and underwear, plus the silver jewelry box my godmother gave me for confirmation. Inside it is the necklace my mother gave me. That's all I can think to bring. I wanted to bring my new winter coat, the one my mother made me last year, but she said I couldn't. It's too bulky and might attract suspicion, so I am leaving it for Paula.

It really doesn't matter, though, what I take with me. The possessions that I value the most—my family, my friends, our animals, the woods and ponds and fields and flowers—none of these can fit in a suitcase.

I remember when we were going to flee Doelitz in the wagon and Jan didn't want me to bring Doris. I thought then that I couldn't live without Doris. It makes me laugh, now, to think how important a doll was to me. I don't even know where Doris is any more. I've lost her, along with the girl who loved her, the child who is no more.

Tears burn my eyes and I bite my fist to keep from gasping. Then I hear my mother's footsteps on the stairs. My door creaks open and in the near-darkness she comes over to me. I close my eyes, ashamed suddenly of my tears, and pretend to be asleep, trying to make my breathing slow and steady. My mother stands for a long time, then walks back to the doorway.

"Goodnight, Tilli," she whispers. "I love you."

I don't answer. I am too afraid of my emotions.

My mother slowly goes back down the stairs. And then, somehow, with the rain cascading against the windows and the wind beating against the walls, I fall asleep.

When I wake up, it's morning. Sunlight is bursting through the bedroom window. Last night's rain is but a misty memory. I open the window and take a deep breath, inhaling our farm: the rich wet ground, the musty smell rising from the fallen piles of leaves, the tang of the manure pile. The pigs are squealing about something, a sound like human babies screaming. Fanni is barking excitedly. I can hear the clatter of pots and pans in the kitchen and I can almost believe today is a day like any other. Everything seems perfectly normal.

Except that there, peeking out from the foot of my bed, is my suitcase. Today is anything but normal. Today I will not be washing dishes or peeling potatoes. There will be no more of that for me.

I dress quickly, putting on my faded, everyday dress and the white socks with yellow tassels that Paula knit for me from wool Maria spun. We have never heard from Maria. So many people have come through our lives and then disappeared.

Now I am about to disappear.

My hands tremble as I take my suitcase and go downstairs to the kitchen, where Paula is setting out plates. Willi sits at the table, sipping coffee. Waiting.

My mother has her back to me, her shoulders hunched over the stove. She is making soft-boiled eggs. She sees me and puts an egg on a plate, the yolk still runny and sunshine-yellow. "Here, you need to eat something substantial this morning," she says.

I sit at the table and pick at the egg and nibble some bread and take a few sips of boiled milk, which I can't stand, but Mami wants me to eat well and I should do this for her.

But I can't.

"I'm going to say good-bye to Heinz and Helmut," I choke out, then rush outside to the barnyard before I start to cry. My brothers are in the barn, cleaning out the horse stalls, carrying dirty straw with pitchforks, which they set down when they see me.

Heinz puts his arms around me and lays his head on my shoulder. Oh Heinz. How can I leave you? I bite my lips to keep from breaking down. Heinz pulls back, picks up his pitchfork, studies the hay. "Good-bye," he says, his voice low and husky. He goes outside.

Helmut is standing against a stack of fresh hay. "I'm leaving now," I blurt.

He comes to me and hugs me, saying nothing, the rough fabric of his shirt scratching my cheek. He smells of damp and grass and earth and horses and he is my brother and he almost was lost to us once and now I am leaving him.

A few stalks of hay hover briefly in the air above us, then float back down onto Helmut's head and shoulders, resting in his hair. He clears his throat, coughs, then turns away. When I leave the barn he is still standing there, staring into the corner.

Paula and Willi are waiting by the door as I walk back in. It's time.

"I put some sandwiches in your suitcase for you," my mother says. I nod. "Thank-you," I say stiffly.

We stare at each other. I don't know what to do, what words will fit this moment. Paula hugs Willi, then me. "Now you be careful," she says, her voice trembling.

My mother looks at me strangely, a remote, almost removed look in her eyes, mingled with a kind of desperation.

"I guess this is it," I say. I am surprised I can still speak.

Mami, my Mami, hugs me one last time. She is so warm, so soft, so strong. My fingers press her shoulders, feeling her bones through her thin, worn dress. She kisses my cheeks and then, as Helmut had done, abruptly turns away.

"That's it. Go then. Go."

Willi opens the door. I look back over the kitchen, the heart of what has been my home for sixteen years. Then I pick up my suitcase and walk out the door.

Willi and I pass silently through the iron gate, past my mother's flowers, their blossoms browned and drooping, heavy with water from the past few days' rain, living their last weeks of life before winter comes. The day continues to promise dry warmth, which is a good sign. I hope the weather in the mountains is the same. I don't feel like walking in the rain.

We pass Henni's house. I wonder how long it will be before she realizes I am gone, before the whole village knows.

"Looks like a nice day, eh?" Willi murmurs. I nod. I know he's trying to relax me, but all my thoughts are on this great and terrifying adventure. I feel so odd. I am almost sick with anxiety, yet at the same time, I can't wait for the train to get here. This is so different from my trip to Berlin. This is more risky, there are so many unknowns, so much danger. The Russians have hardened the borders. They are more fiercely determined than ever to keep us imprisoned.

The sun is breaking warm through the trees as we come upon the train station, the sunlight glinting off the metal roof of the building. We stand with a few other farmers, waiting. I am afraid they can see my thoughts, can somehow tell what I am trying to do, so I try to be impassive, to put on the stone face I have learned to wear over the past few years.

A whistle blast slices the silence. I jump. Willi touches my arm and gives me a reassuring smile. I'm so glad he's here with me.

"Ready?" he asks. "You're sure about this?"

I nod. This is it: no turning back. We shuffle up to the edge of the platform as the train rounds the bend and chugs to a stop.

Willi hands the attendant our fare. "Teterow," he tells him. We get two tickets and, to my surprise, are able to find seats. I sink down onto the wooden bench and slip my suitcase beneath me. We don't talk. I press my hands together, trying to stop them from shaking.

After a few stops, the train is full, with newcomers forced to stand. I know many of the passengers. They are farmers, shopkeepers, field hands, neighbors, and church mates. Yet even though we are together now in this small space, we remain silent. There is no chatter, no small talk, no friendliness. The war and all that has come in the past few years has bred aloofness and distrust into us. We are solitary travelers now, trained always to worry about who might betray us, even when we've done nothing wrong. We are all guilty, even though we are innocent.

I keep my face impassive, my eyes on the floor, the walls, the window.

The train thumps and sways. The wood is hard underneath me. Sometimes Willi has to catch me to keep me from sliding off the seat. I barely notice. I stare out the window, watching the countryside slipping past, taking me further and further away.

Gradually I become aware of something, a feeling at the back of my neck, a sense that someone is staring at me. I turn from the window and scan the train car. No one appears to be paying any attention to Willi or me.

Then I see him. Four rows back, staring fixedly at me: Juergen Bull. One of my old friends from school, whom I haven't seen in a year.

What is he doing here? What if he asks where I'm going?

Juergen smiles at me and looks as if he might get up. I almost smile back. I want to. But then I stop. Who knows what the Russians are capable of? What if they are looking for me already, come to take me to Usedom? What if Juergen is a Party member now? What if he gets off the train and sees a Party official and mentions that he saw me?

I know Juergen wouldn't knowingly turn me in. But I can't take that chance.

I look coldly and impassively at him, then turn back to the window. As I shift my gaze, I catch a shadow of hurt flashing over his face.

We continue our silent ride, the car hushed save for the creaking and rattling of the wood and metal on the rickety tracks. I no longer feel Juergen staring at me. The train stops at Teterow. We get off, wait a half-hour, then board another train to Wernigerode. I don't see Juergen again after that.

It seems like I have been on this train for a week. Each minute has lasted an hour, each hour a day. It is getting harder and harder to sit still. Willi, too, is shifting in his seat, clearing his throat, and sighing.

We are traveling through steep, wooded hills, lush with green-gold lindens and oaks just beginning to turn orange and tall, bluish-green pines. The air is chilly and damp, almost misty. Occasionally I catch glimpses of the ice-blue sky through the tops of the trees.

"We're in the mountains now," Willi says, as the train twists around yet another steep curve. "The Harz Mountains."

"Really? Then we're almost there," I say with surprise. I guess I had expected snow-capped mountain peaks like those in my storybooks, but all I see are tall, wooded hills.

We will be in Wernigerode any minute now, I realize with a burst of panic.

Suddenly the train screeches, bucks, then stops. Ahead, I can see a platform, but they are not opening the doors. No one is getting out.

We wait silently. Willi squeezes my hand.

The door to our car opens and in walks two Russian soldiers, dressed in full uniform, their guns drawn. They step slowly down the aisle, pausing to stare hard at each passenger. Willi and I are six rows back. The soldiers stop in front of an elderly man several rows ahead of us.

"Document!" one of the soldiers barks.

The man reaches in his pocket and hands over his identification papers. The soldiers motion to a package he is carrying. He hands it over. One of the soldiers tears it open, shaking out what is inside: a teddy bear with a pink ribbon around its neck. For a moment, I am afraid the Russians are going to rip it apart. They turn it over and over, examining it, their faces grim and hard. Then one of them drops it back in the old man's lap. They continue down the aisle, the heels of their boots loud against the floor.

"What are they looking for?" I whisper to Willi.

"Western things. Money. Anything suspicious."

Several more passengers are searched. "Document!" the soldiers shout, waving their rifles and motioning for their victims to empty their pockets.

I gaze out the window, trying to appear bored. The air has an unreal, grainy quality. The forest is so vivid, so green. Through the foliage I can make out what appear to be even higher hills—the free side of Germany. What if I never get there?

A soldier marches up to me, his eyes chips of stone, his face stiff. He motions with his gun to my suitcase, which is on the floor next to my feet. I bend to get it, my head swimming.

He knows. How can he know? Was there something in my face that gave me away?

I hand him my suitcase. He flips it open, pushing at my socks, his dark-gloved hands pawing my carefully folded underwear. I can't stand it. These men, touching me again. I want to scream.

He sees my sandwiches, wrapped in newspaper, the ones my mother made so long ago this morning. He unwraps them: black rye bread, heaped with sausage. He sniffs the sandwiches, then puts them back in the suitcase, which he returns to me, still open. He continues down the aisle, the leather in his boots crunching.

I feel a rush of hatred for him, for all the Russians, for what they have done to us, to me. My hatred is so intense I can taste it, bitter and sour in my mouth.

Then I smile.

Between the pieces of bread, tucked among the slabs of sausage, are my silver coins. My western money, without which I could not escape. The soldier missed it.

Finally the search is over. The soldiers leave. The train inches up to the platform. "Wernigerode! Last stop!" the conductor calls. We file off the train.

Another group of soldiers waits near the platform, their rifles hanging loose in their arms, examining us as we leave. I keep my eyes to the ground. Willi walks in front of me, his head up.

"Hey!" Willi cries, as a soldier shoves at him with the point of his rifle, pushing him out of line.

I freeze. The other passengers continue filing past me, past us, pretending not to see what is happening to Willi.

The soldier pushes Willi to the spot where the other Russians are standing. They begin yelling at him. He holds out his passport. They knock it to the ground.

Willi tries to talk to them, using the few words of Russian that he knows: Stop, No, Mistake. He gestures with his good arm, pointing at the train. The soldiers shove him and grab his arm and begin marching him off, away from the mountains, on the road to town.

Willi looks over at me, to where I am still standing, staring and sick. He forms a word silently with his mouth: "Go."

The soldiers don't notice. They don't see me. But they will soon, if I continue to stand there.

I have no choice. I turn away from Willi and begin walking towards the mountains.

29

I walk along the main road, searching for the path that my mother told me would run alongside the road at the edge of the forest. So far, I haven't seen it. My thoughts are spinning. What about Willi? Why did they take him? Will he be all right? Will they come after me?

What if the path isn't here? What will I do then?

Then I see it, a dirt trail leading into the woods. Beside it is a broken-down stone road, filled with holes and ruts, just as my mother had said there would be.

I glance back at the station. Workers are unloading boxes and other parcels from the train. A few soldiers are milling about. There is no sign of Willi.

"Please let this be the way," I whisper, then turn off the main road and start walking along the path into the forest, where it is cool and dark and feels safe, away from prying eyes. I collapse under an enormous pine tree. I need time to think.

What are they doing to Willi? Is there anything I can do to help him? Should I go back?

I don't know anybody in this area. I can't get back on the train; I don't have any money for a ticket. All I have is the forbidden western money.

I can't think of anything to do but continue with my plan. I feel terrible for Willi, I feel like I'm deserting him, letting him down somehow, but I know that I have to go on.

I begin making my way along the path, stepping over rocks and vines, up and down and around the hills, trying to make sure I stay due west. Luckily, the sun is shining and there is enough of a break in the dense foliage for me to glimpse it and gauge my direction.

And then I hear the sputtering of a motor, coming up rapidly behind me on the bumpy road that runs alongside the path. It is a fierce snarl amid the hushed stillness of the forest.

I turn to look. A smudge of mustard yellow; shiny black helmet; black boots. That's all I need to see.

A Russian soldier, riding a motorcycle, coming straight towards me.

Not again. Why me? Dear God, not again.

The path and the road are deserted. I have no one to turn to for help. There are plenty of bushes to hide under, though, and the forest is thick with trees. Should I run from the path to the trees? No. He is coming too quickly. He would see me and then he would be suspicious.

All I can do is walk straight ahead. Walk slowly, as if I belonged here, as if I am not terrified.

The motorcycle roars loud, louder, and then slowly the sound begins to fade. I look straight ahead, at the bushes and trees edging the sides of the path. In the corner of my vision is the road. The exhaust from the soldier's motorcycle is a gray plume as he passes by me, continues on, disappears.

He didn't see me. Or, if he did, he didn't care about me.

I sigh, feeling cold sweat trickling down my back. For the moment, at least, I am safe.

About mid-afternoon, I stop to eat, perching on a mossy rock as I unwrap my sandwiches. I pull apart the rye bread. My mother's coins glint at me, winking in secret triumph. I pick the coins out, wipe off the sausage grease, and put them in my pocket. With luck, I won't be running into any more Russian soldiers today.

After I finish eating, I pause for a moment on the rock, listening to the birds calling across the forest. The spot reminds me of home, of the forest at the edge of our fields, where we would hike, and where I would sometimes hear cuckoos cry. It reminds me, too, of my dreaming rock in the park in Doelitz, where I used to plan my wonderful life in America.

Now my dreams are taking their first baby steps toward reality. I try to take comfort in this thought as I begin once again making my way through the forest.

Already it is starting to get dark and cold. Shouldn't I be at Herr Burger's farm by now? Am I lost? What am I doing here, on this deserted road, so very, very alone? My feet, in their too-small shoes, feel blistered and sore; I begin to limp.

The path veers sharply to the right. And then, as I finish the turn, I see it: the clearing I have been looking for. I half-run, half-stumble into a field. A farm field. A few hundred yards away is a cottage, smoke curling from its chimney. Beside the cottage is a small gray barn. In the yard, two horses nibble grass. A man sits on the ground beside a wagon, doing something to a wheel.

It is dusk, almost dark. I walk up to the man, who is about fifty, with a broad red nose and puffy cheeks. I can't tell if he is friendly or not. What if he is the wrong man? What if he is someone who will turn me in?

"Herr Burger?" I whisper, my heart beating so fast it trips over itself.

The man looks at me suspiciously, not saying a word.

I hold out two of the coins my mother gave me. "Regina Horn sent me."

"Okay, yes," Herr Burger says. He points to the barn. "Over there."

I run into the small barn, which is filled with straw, and close the door behind me. There are no windows. I sit in the dark, shivering. None of this is real.

A few minutes later, Herr Burger comes in, carrying a loaf of bread and a jar of buttermilk. He sets them down in front of me.

"Thank-you," I say.

"No one knows you are here," he says. "Not even my wife. Stay quiet. We will leave at five tomorrow morning. You be ready."

He leaves the barn, shutting the door behind him.

After eating what I can, I lie down on a pile of straw, pulling pieces of it over me until I am covered, then close my eyes. Sleep, though, doesn't come. Thoughts and hopes and fears and memories chase each other in my mind. Sometimes I am so panic-stricken that I want to get up and run away, find my way through the woods again, beg for money for a train ticket, then go home to Mami, home where I belong.

At other moments, I am filled with elation. My dreams are coming true. I am going to my America, the land of picket-fenced houses and beautiful furniture and gleaming kitchens and chocolate ice cream after every meal; a place where there are no spies, no secret police, no such things as concentration camps, no soldiers invading the night. I will live there and make money and send clothes back to my family, like Aunt Bertha has done for so many years, and when I can I will send for them, all of them, and they will come to live with me and then everything will be perfect.

Over and over I replay my American dream in my mind, but still I can't sleep. The dream is just that. Just a dream, a pretty picture I have imagined, but not real at all.

What's real is this barn and this hay and my fear, more fear than I have ever felt before in my life.

I open my eyes to pale gray rays of light slipping through the cracks in the plank walls of the barn. It is dawn. Time to go.

I get up, try to brush some of the straw off my clothes and hair, grab hold of my suitcase and wait. A few minutes later, the barn door opens. "Ready?" says Herr Burger.

"Yes."

"Come here. Get in the wagon."

He tells me to lay on the bottom, which is covered with burlap potato sacks. "Use those sacks to cover yourself."

As Herr Burger hitches his horses to the wagon, I climb into the sacks, sliding my feet into one, my head into another. Then he throws more sacks on top of me. I hear him climb into the wagon seat and then the wagon starts to move, bouncing in and out of ruts in the dirt road. I can breathe fairly well, though I keep feeling like I have to sneeze, and I can even see a little bit, through the squares in the burlap, through the openings in the wagon's wood rail. I can see yellow-green fields passing by, clumps of trees, hills in the distance.

The steady squeak of the wagon suddenly stops.

I look to the side of the road. Yellow, mustard-yellow cloth. A gun, the end of a gun, waving.

And then the dreaded word: "Document!" The voice so harsh and cold. The voice of a Russian soldier.

Herr Burger hands papers to the soldier. I can't see his face, only the blur of his uniform. My heart is pounding so hard surely the soldier can hear it.

I am back in the attic again and the men are close by, so near to us that we can't breathe or they will hear us, find us. We have to shrink, become invisible. I did it before. I can do it again.

I flatten myself against the bottom of the musty, smelly wagon, trying to hold my breath, to quell the tickling in my nose.

"Where are you going?" the soldier asks Herr Burger.

"To my potato field," Herr Burger replies. "I'm going to get my potatoes."

Silence. I don't try looking out any more. I close my eyes and listen with every cell in my body, but I can't hear anything, *what is happening what does he want is he going to search the wagon now oh God please no.*

And then the wagon starts up again, slowly moving down the road. The soldier must have decided not to search the wagon. If he had lifted only a few of the sacks, he would have found me. But he didn't.

About fifteen minutes later, Herr Burger says loudly, without stopping the horses, "Roll off now, into this ditch."

I climb out of the burlap bags, grab my suitcase, then do it. I tumble out the back of the wagon and roll into the ditch. I stand to say good-bye and thank you to Herr Burger, but he is already past me. He never stops his slow, steady pace, never looks back, doesn't say a word to me, just keeps going, bumping and swaying down the dirt road before vanishing around a curve.

The road is empty. The land is the same on all sides: flat farm fields, hills in the distance, here and there clumps of apple trees alongside the road. A faint, early-morning mist drifts up from the dew-laden ground. The sun is beginning to break from behind heavy gray clouds.

Which way should I go? I can't tell what is east and what is west. Should I follow Herr Burger? But he was headed for his fields and I need to find a town, a train.

I climb out of the ditch and start running. It feels good to move again after holding myself so still and tight. I hope it doesn't start to rain. But rain is the least of my worries. What if I run in the wrong direction and wind up back across the border, in the land of the Russians?

Ahead of me is a sign announcing a nearby town. I don't recognize the name of the town; I hope it is in the west. I keep running. There is no one in sight, nothing but fields and trees and this crater-filled dirt road.

My side starts to hurt. I slow to a fast walk. After awhile, I come to a curve in the road, then another, and then I stop.

Standing stiffly in front of me in the middle of the road is a stern-looking man in a uniform, his arms crossed over his chest. His uniform is not yellow. It is an indistinct grayish color. He doesn't have a gun. But he looks angry.

I can't move. Am I about to be arrested? Is this how it is going to end?

And then the man smiles at me and the harshness melts off his face. "Don't worry," he says gently. "You ran in the right direction."

It takes a minute for his words to sink in. When I realize what he is saying, I want to cry, to laugh, to scream. I made it. *I'm free.* I stare at the man, fighting my emotions. He smiles patiently. I wonder how many times he has seen people like me.

"Where can I catch the next train?" I ask. He smiles again and gives me directions. "Good luck to you," he says.

I thank him and start walking. Some green apples lie on the ground beneath the trees lining the road. I pick two of them up and eat as I walk, the sour-sweet juice trickling down my chin.

I come to a small town and find the train station, which is bustling with chatting, busy people: families, children, old farmers, young girls. These people aren't afraid to talk to one another. They don't look over their shoulders, their faces stiff, their eyes shifting back and forth. These people smile and laugh; they are relaxed; they are free. *I'm free, too.*

I buy a ticket to Kassel with the last of my mother's western money and squeeze myself into the jammed car. It begins moving on the tracks. There are no soldiers in sight, no men with guns marching up and down the aisles checking our bags.

A few people glance curiously at me. I touch my hair and feel pieces of hay. I try to pull them out, to comb my hair with my fingers, but it is matted and snarled. I look down at my dress and see that it is dirty and wrinkled and covered with bits of straw and leaves. But I am too happy to feel embarrassed. I don't mind the stares. They are nothing compared to the fierce glares of Russian soldiers.

I will never have to see a Russian soldier again.

I am free.

PART IV

30

I wish I could say that once I made it across the border, all my troubles disappeared. But in some ways, they had just begun.

I was so happy as I walked along that road, eating those green apples, tasting the sweetness of freedom. Everything in my life had been building to that moment and that moment only: crossing into free land, leaving Soviet control behind me for good. I had focused so long on getting to that point that I hadn't thought much about what would happen next. In my dreams I had imagined escaping, then flipped forward to my shiny magazine-perfect fantasy life in America. I had never bothered daydreaming the in-between part. I had always figured that once I got to western Germany and Aunt Liesel's house, it would be a matter of a few weeks at most before I would be sailing off to America.

I was so very, very wrong.

But I didn't know that, then. All I could think about as I rode the train to Kassel was my freedom and how wonderful my life was going to be from then on. Even when the train pulled into Kassel and I saw how much damage was still left from the war, it didn't dampen my joy. Even the grayness of Kassel—everything hazy with smoke, filled with half-shattered buildings, brown weeds sprouting amid charred rubble—none of that infected me with its gloom. I didn't mind. I was free.

After the train dropped me off, I walked slowly through the deserted streets of the factory district, searching for Aunt Liesel's apartment building. A half-hour later, I found it. It was three stories, a medium-gray brick, and relatively undamaged, compared to many of the other buildings. Aunt Liesel had twice been bombed out of apartments, had lost all her belongings two times. This was her third apartment.

I climbed the stairs to the top floor and rang the doorbell. I heard it buzz, then nothing. No sound.

Was she gone? Was she on a trip? My mother probably hadn't been able to get word to her that I was coming. What if she had moved? I rang the doorbell again, then began knocking.

"Just a minute!" a woman called. I heard footsteps. Then the door opened and there she was: the same round face, same curly hair, though she was shorter and thinner than I remembered from her visit to Doelitz years before.

Aunt Liesel stared blankly at me for a moment. Then her eyes opened wide. "Tilli?" she gasped. "Tilli?"

"Hello, Aunt Liesel. I've escaped."

She grabbed me in her arms, shaking, crying. I began crying, too, letting go of the tears I had held in for so long, for too long.

"Look at you!" she exclaimed. "How on earth did you get here? Come in, come in."

Aunt Liesel led me into her apartment, then pulled me down next to her on a faded sofa, held my hands and stared at me. "Are you ever dirty," she said, pushing back my hair from my forehead. "I can't believe how grown-up you look. When did you get here? Did you have any trouble? Oh, wait, don't talk right now. Are you hungry? Thirsty? Let me get you something."

I followed her through the small living room into a narrow kitchen, then sat down at a tiny, battered table to eat the bread and juice she set before me. I took a few bites as Aunt Liesel continued to pepper me with questions, then started yawning. I felt suddenly so exhausted, so drained, that I couldn't eat or talk any longer.

"Let's get you settled, you poor thing," said Aunt Liesel. She opened a closet in the living room and pulled out a rolled-up canvas cot, which she unfolded and placed against the wall. I flopped my sore body onto the cot, pulled a blanket around me, closed my eyes, and almost instantly fell asleep, a sensation of peace and contentment filling me as once again the words sang in my mind: *I'm free.*

I woke up all at once, sitting so abruptly my cot nearly tipped over. The room was dimly lit and for a few seconds, I couldn't think where I was. Then I remembered: the train ride, Willi, the trek through the hills, the potato wagon, Kassel.

"Aunt Liesel?"

The kitchen door swung open. Aunt Liesel came out, wiping her hands on her apron. "Well, well. Good morning! I was afraid I'd have to leave before you woke up."

"It's morning already?"

"You've been sleeping for hours, right through supper and all through the night without a sound. Come in the kitchen—we're just finishing breakfast."

I stood up stiffly, then walked gingerly across the wooden floor, each step burning because of blisters on the bottoms of my feet.

Inside the kitchen, a dark-haired man I didn't recognize was sitting at the table. Aunt Liesel was standing behind him, looking over his shoulder at the map he was reading.

"Tilli, I'd like you to meet Fritz Baumann," she said. "He lives with us. He's my business partner. Remember last night I told you I had a business, selling processed wool to farmers? Well, Fritz runs it with me."

"Hello, Tilli," said Fritz, who was about thirty. His eyes swept over my wrinkled dress and wild hair and I suddenly felt embarrassed.

"Hello, Herr Baumann," I said softly.

"Call me Fritz. After all, we're going to be living together now." Fritz smiled at me.

"Tilli, would you like some coffee?" Aunt Liesel asked, turning to the stove, where a pot was brewing. "It's not real coffee, just that barley stuff. Real coffee costs a fortune. How about some bread and syrup to go with that?"

"Yes, please." I sat down while Aunt Liesel served me breakfast. I tried to eat slowly and not inhale the food like some kind of wild animal, but I couldn't help myself. I was starving.

Aunt Liesel folded the map. "We've got a lot of ground to cover today. Tilli, I'm sorry, but I've got to work all day. Paul's already at work. So's Peter—our boarder, remember I told you about him yesterday?"

I didn't remember much about what Aunt Liesel had said yesterday, but I nodded anyway.

"They should be home around suppertime. Fritz and I might be a little late. I was wondering if you could do something for me? Would you mind going to the grocer? It's right across the street. You can't miss it."

"Sure," I said. Aunt Liesel handed me some money and her grocery list. Then she and Fritz rushed out the door.

I sat numbly for a minute. Everything felt so unreal, as if I'd been dropped down into the middle of another planet, a million miles from the farm life I was used to. Then a glorious shiver ran through me: this was my first day of my new life, my new free life.

I spent the morning exploring Aunt Liesel's apartment, cleaning up and then grocery shopping. The apartment was small, with just a kitchen, living room, two bedrooms, and a bathroom, plus front and back balconies. I found out later that Uncle Paul and Fritz shared the larger bedroom, the boarder Peter had the smaller one, and Aunt Liesel slept every night on the sofa. All the rooms had

Aunt Liesel's touches: faded lace doilies on the tables, flowers in cracked vases, curtains in patterns that brought together the orange and green colors of the mismatched furniture. No matter how poor she was, Aunt Liesel knew how to make a place feel cozy.

Aunt Liesel's bathroom wasn't anywhere near as nice as Victoria's, but it still put our outhouse to shame. She had a real toilet and a sink, running water, and a bar of soft pink soap that smelled like roses. I loved its gentle feel on my skin, so different from the harsh, stinging lye soap we used at home. I even rubbed it on my wet hair, trying to clean out the remnants of straw and branches and mud that clung in matted clumps.

I walked across the street to the grocery store, which was busy and crowded. I had to wait for a long time at the end of a line of impatient-looking people. I didn't mind, though. It was so interesting to see what everybody was buying. There were so many foods here that I hadn't seen before, that we never got in Doelitz or Gnoien, such as oranges and bananas. I wished I had enough money to buy an orange; I was so curious to see what one tasted like. But I didn't have a single coin to my name and oranges weren't on Aunt Liesel's list.

When it was my turn, I said hello to the grocer and handed him the list. The grocer was fat and balding, with three chins disappearing into the collar of his sweat-stained shirt. His lips were wide, his nose bulged, and his eyes were like two black buttons buried in the pink flesh of his round, pig-like face.

"You're new here," he announced, looking me over intently.

I nodded, feeling awkward and uncomfortable. There was something odd about his stare. Maybe there were still pieces of straw in my hair. Why else was he looking at me so strangely?

"So who are you? Where are you staying?" he asked as he filled my order. He smiled, showing his thick pink tongue.

"I'm across the street, but I'm only here for a few days," I said quickly, then rushed out of the store. I didn't know why, but the grocer made me nervous.

"Come see me again," the grocer called, as I hurried out the door.

Once back at the apartment, I washed my dress and hung it on the clothesline strung across the back balcony, which overlooked a small dirt yard. It was warm and breezy outside; I hoped my dress would dry by suppertime, or else I would have nothing to wear.

Suddenly I heard heavy footsteps thumping up the stairs. They stopped in front of the apartment door. I heard rustling sounds and, dressed only in my underwear, I ran into the bedroom to hide. Who was here? Had they tracked me down already?

A spray of letters shot through a metal slot in the door and slid across the wooden floor. The footsteps continued on. I came out of the bedroom laughing at myself. I had been spooked by the mailman. When would I get over my fears? How long would it take for the sound of loud boots to stop scaring me?

I gathered the letters, which were addressed to Liesel and Paul and Fritz and Peter, and felt a stab of loneliness. I wished I could be getting mail, but of course, that was silly, since nobody knew I was here.

Hoping Aunt Liesel wouldn't mind, I took a sheet of paper from her desk and wrote a quick letter home. "Dear everybody. I made it! I'm here at Aunt Liesel's! How's Willi? What happened to Willi?"

I stopped. What if they didn't know? What if Willi never came back from Wernigerode? The Russians were capable of making people disappear. I didn't want to think about what this would do to Paula if Willi were one of the disappeared ones.

After my letter was finished, I sat down on the sofa to wait. The minutes, the hours, ticked by, with nothing to do. I should have been so happy not to have any chores stealing my time, to be able to do whatever I wanted, to nap and daydream in peace. Instead, I found myself thinking of home, of what each member of my family would be doing right then. I wondered if they missed me as much as I missed them.

Although I didn't find any books or magazines in the apartment, there was a radio in the living room. I found a station playing American dance music. I held out my arms to the air, to my imaginary American dance partner, and floated around the little apartment. Soon I would be there, dancing in America.

Late in the day, I changed into my own dress again, which had dried outside and now smelled of brown coal. At home, clothes dried on the line smelled of fresh air and flowers.

Footsteps creaked up the stairs, a kick rattled in the lock, the door opened. I fought the urge to run as a man entered the apartment.

"Hello," he said, smiling. I recognized my Uncle Paul from photographs. He was thin and faded-looking, with pale skin and sparse brown hair.

"Hello, Uncle Paul," I said. "Remember me? Tilli?"

"Of course, of course. Welcome to Kassel."

The front door opened again and another man walked in. He was young, about twenty. He nodded shyly at me.

"Tilli, this is Peter, our boarder," said Uncle Paul. "His father owns the wool factory here."

"Hello," I said. "Pleased to meet you."

"Hello." Peter spoke in a soft, high-pitched voice, his eyes on his hands and not on me.

We sat on the sofa, not knowing what to say to each other. "Did you have a nice day?" Uncle Paul finally asked me. "Fine, thank-you," I replied.

A few minutes later, Liesel and Fritz came in. They were somber, their shoulders slumped, their feet dragging. Liesel brightened when she saw me. She gave me a hug. "How did it go today?"

"Just fine."

"Did you get the groceries? Good. Can you help me in the kitchen?"

Aunt Liesel took a white package out of her purse. "We'll have supper ready soon," she called out to the men. Then I followed her into the kitchen, where she put on an apron, spooned some grease into a fry pan, and lit the stove, all the while talking non-stop about her busy day in the countryside, trying to sell wool.

"Guess what?" she said, unwrapping the white package. "We got some horsemeat sausage today while we were out. I thought we'd have that for supper."

Horsemeat? I hadn't heard of people eating horses before. I thought of Max, Moritz, Astra. How could I eat a horse? The thought took my appetite away.

"Tomorrow, we'll have potato pancakes," Aunt Liesel said, tossing the horsemeat sausage into the frying pan. "That sound okay?"

"Sure," I said. At least it wasn't fried potatoes, which I had had every single night for as long as I could remember.

"Good. There are potatoes in the pantry. Tomorrow while I'm gone you can get them started."

Great, I thought. I was back to peeling potatoes already. At least it wouldn't be for long.

Aunt Liesel had me set the table, then handed me her spatula. I poked uncertainly at the hunks of sausage, browning and sizzling in the grease.

"You do know how to cook, don't you?" Aunt Liesel asked, taking off her apron.

"No, not really."

Something passed over Aunt Liesel's face, a shadow that looked like disappointment. I couldn't tell, because the next thing I knew, she was smiling reassuringly. "Don't worry. I'll teach you. I'm surprised Regina didn't. Your mother is such a good cook."

"Paula and Mami always do the cooking. I've never been good at things like that." I didn't tell Aunt Liesel that I hated to cook, just as I hated all kitchen chores.

Aunt Liesel then asked me to serve the food to her and the men. I brought the meal out on a chipped ceramic tray, concentrating as hard as I could on not tipping everything over. It felt strange setting food on everyone's plates while they talked to each other and ignored me; I felt like a servant.

"Thank you, Tilli," Aunt Liesel said, when I was finished. I sat down at my place. "You're welcome," I murmured, confused about my place in this new household of mine. Was I there as family, as a guest, or as an employee?

The horsemeat sausage tasted just like regular sausage, but I could still manage just one small bite. I filled up on bread and lettuce instead. When the men were finished eating, they moved to the living room, leaving their plates behind. They sat on the sofa and smoked.

Aunt Liesel asked me to help her clear the table. "And would you mind doing the dishes? The floor could use sweeping, too. The broom is in the closet."

Aunt Liesel then went to sit with the men. I did the chores she'd assigned as best as I could, though by then the blisters on my feet were sore again and I was very tired. When I was finished, I went to the living room and sat beside Aunt Liesel on the sofa.

"All done?" she said, putting her arm around me. I nodded, trying to stifle a yawn. "Thanks for your help, Tilli. How would you like a treat, to celebrate your first day in Kassel?"

Aunt Liesel went into the bedroom, then reappeared, holding something in her hand. She stood in front of me. Resting in her palm were several dark-brown squares that looked like pieces of smooth mud.

"Take one," she said.

I picked up one of the squares. It was soft and smelled unusual, like no scent I had ever encountered before. I nibbled at the edges of the square and found that it tasted heavenly: sweet, but not too sweet, with a melting quality that made my mouth tingle. I wanted more, but Aunt Liesel's palm was empty. She and Uncle Paul and Fritz and Peter had eaten the rest.

"There's nothing like good chocolate, is there, Tilli?" said Aunt Liesel.

So that was chocolate. I remembered how Fraulein Meyer had talked about the delicious chocolate desserts in America and now I had another reason for wanting to get there as quickly as possible.

I curled up in the corner of the sofa, the chocolate taste lingering in my mouth. I tried to stay awake as Aunt Liesel and the men talked about the wool business and the government and cars and on and on. Despite my efforts, I fell asleep, right there on the sofa.

The next day, I went to the courthouse to register as a new resident. Aunt Liesel gave me directions; she couldn't come with me herself because she had to go on another business trip with Fritz. The courthouse was several miles from Aunt Liesel's apartment; the road to it led through the downtown shopping districts, where I lingered for a few moments, ogling the things in the store windows, the fruits and sweets and beautiful clothes and fine-looking shoes. Since I didn't have any money, I couldn't have any of these things.

I trudged on to the courthouse, where I found a long line snaking out the door. I settled in to wait. Time passed slowly. A little boy started to cry; an old man rolled and smoked cigarette after cigarette; a family shared a loaf of bread.

At last I found myself in a dim, dusty office, in front of a tall wooden counter. A tired-looking woman was standing behind it.

"Good afternoon," I said, smiling.

The woman looked at me coldly, as if my cheerfulness annoyed her. Rows of papers were lined up on either side of her like columns of soldiers. On the desk behind her were even more papers, a regular army of work waiting for her.

"I'm reporting here to live," I told the woman, handing her my identification paper. "I'm moving here from Doelitz to Kassel."

The woman looked at my paper, then handed it back to me. "Oh no you're not," she said.

"Excuse me?"

The woman tapped my paper. "This is Russian. Where is your western passport?"

"I don't have one," I said, confused. Couldn't I simply trade in my Russian identification card for a new, western one? "I just arrived. I escaped."

"You certainly don't belong here, then. You need to go to the refugee processing center." The woman looked to the line behind me. "Next!"

"Wait," I said. "I am not a fugitive. I'm staying with my family, with Liesel and Paul Schmidt. They're citizens."

"Doesn't matter," said the woman, drumming her fingers on the countertop. "You belong at Uelzen, not Kassel. That's the law. Now step aside. Next?"

A heavyset woman behind me pushed forward to the counter. I moved away, holding my useless identification card.

Over the next few weeks, Aunt Liesel did some checking with various officials. All of them told her the same thing: that I had to go to Uelzen.

"What's Uelzen?" I asked. "Is it so bad?"

"Yes, it is so bad," said Aunt Liesel. "It's a refugee camp, with tents and all kinds of people all over the place, some of them dangerous, some of them criminals. There are diseases and people are hungry and it takes forever to get out, to get processed. You can't go there."

Aunt Liesel asked a neighbor, Herr Hofer, who was a lawyer, what we should do.

"Until this is settled," said Herr Hofer, "you are legally considered a fugitive. That means you can't emigrate. Nor can you legally work here."

"How long will it take to straighten this all out?" asked Aunt Liesel.

"I have no idea," said Herr Hofer, patting my hand. I could tell he felt sorry for me, which frightened me. I would rather he would be confident and laugh off my problem as a silly mix-up that would be easy to resolve. But he didn't; he puckered his brow and pulled at his chin and gave me a pitying look. "Don't worry, my dear," he said. "I'll let you know as soon as I hear anything."

But I did worry. As I tried to sleep that night, fear circled my mind and whispered in my ear. Maybe, it said, maybe you have left one prison only to become trapped in another.

Trapped, trapped, trapped. The word beat in time with my heart and I fell asleep to the sound of it, the freedom song forgotten.

31

Once again, I was caught in a state of perpetual waiting, a kind of non-being existence. I was a fugitive, caught in a foreign, gray land, far from my family and the things that I loved, waiting for faceless authorities to rule on my fate. Just as in the attic, I had to try to create meaning out of day after day of nothingness. Although I didn't live in mortal fear of soldiers bursting through the door, I did worry that somehow the Russians would be able to make a claim on me, to reach out beyond the western border to drag me back. My other fear was that the officials in Kassel would force me into the camp at Uelzen, which sounded suspiciously similar to a concentration camp.

If I had had more to do or if there had been people for me to be with, especially young people my own age, the time might have passed more easily. As it was, Aunt Liesel was gone almost every day with Fritz. In the mornings, before she left, she would tell me what to buy for supper and what chores she expected me to do that day. Washing walls, wiping out cupboards, scrubbing floors, ironing the men's shirts so their collars were nice and stiff—I did all these things and more, but still was left with hours of spare time.

At first, I wrote a lot of letters to my friends and family. But then Aunt Liesel said she couldn't afford to keep paying all that postage. I couldn't listen to the radio, either, because she said the electricity was too expensive. When I was finished with my chores, all I had to do was pace around the apartment, read the newspapers, and eat. I began putting on weight for the first time in my life.

The only two people I saw during the day were two old ladies who lived in the apartment across the street. They stepped out onto their balcony every morning to shake their just-washed underwear out to dry. They would flap their dingy damp panties vigorously, pin them to the clothesline, then go back inside. Watching them do this was sometimes the most entertainment I had all day.

At least Sundays were a break from the boredom. Aunt Liesel and Uncle Paul didn't go to church—this made me feel guilty, as if I were doing something wrong that God would surely punish me for. We had always gone to church in

Boddin, every Sunday without fail. Aunt Liesel and Uncle Paul and Fritz, on the other hand, spent Sundays eating and driving. First, Aunt Liesel would make a big dinner, usually Hungarian goulash, sometimes pot roast. When the wool had been selling well, she would splurge on oranges for dessert. I loved oranges from the first bite, even more than I'd loved chocolate. After dinner, Fritz would take us for drives through Kassel and the countryside in his rusty green car, which sounded like it was going to fall apart any moment.

I also visited Dora and Ingrid a couple of times a month. They lived about a half-hour walk away in another part of Kassel. To get to their house, I would pass the big black bomb shelter, which was still standing. I didn't know what, if anything, it was being used for. It gave me a chill to see it and think of all that Dora and Ingrid and Liesel and everyone else in Kassel had endured.

It was good to see Dora, now that I knew she was my sister. Since the war, she'd had a son, Hans Joachim, who was two, ran around all the time, and, because of his joy in living, was fun to watch. Dora, though, was another story. She was pale and jittery, her hands constantly twisting her skirt or a napkin or a strand of hair. She jumped at the smallest sounds, like the door shutting, and her eyes periodically filled with tears, for no apparent reason. Aunt Liesel said Dora still hadn't gotten over the bombings.

Ingrid was twelve and quite little-girlish: she played with dolls and was small for her age and liked to giggle and run around. Even though I was only four years older, it felt like there was a decade's difference between us. I had hoped that maybe we could be friends, but I felt more like her aunt than her cousin. We didn't have anything to talk about.

Although I couldn't write letters home very often, I could receive as many as people cared to send me. The first letter I got was from my mother, who had terrific news: Willi was safely back with them; the Russians had kept him overnight, then released him the next morning.

I also liked hearing from Aunt Bertha. "Don't worry about the delays," she would write. "You are meant to be here. I know it."

Aunt Bertha sent Liesel and me shoes and dresses and other things, such as peanut butter, that weren't available in Germany. One time she sent a clear plastic bag filled with puffy-looking white squares. On the bag was written an English word I didn't know: Marshmallows. Aunt Liesel didn't know what they were either. She tore open the bag and handed me one of the puffy things, which was light and airy and smelled somewhat sugary.

"They're food of some sort," I said.

"I wonder how we should cook them?" asked Aunt Liesel. "Are you sure there aren't any directions on the bag?"

"I'm sure."

"They seem too light to fry. Maybe we should boil them?"

Aunt Liesel filled a pan with water, then emptied the marshmallows into it. They floated together on the surface. As the water heated, the marshmallows began slinking down into the pan. "I think they're forming a sauce," said Aunt Liesel, stirring away. The water turned a pale, milky color, then boiled. After a few minutes, the marshmallows were gone.

"I don't think we were supposed to boil them, after all," I said.

"I think you're right," said Aunt Liesel, frowning. "Oh, dear. I hope they weren't too expensive, because I think I ruined them."

Every week or so, I went to see Herr and Frau Hofer upstairs, to check on the progress of my case. Unfortunately, nothing seemed to be happening. But at least I got to get out of Aunt Liesel's apartment, and I liked talking to Frau Hofer, a tall woman with straight black hair cut in a sharp angle that I found very fashionable. The Hofers' son was in America studying at a university. Frau Hofer showed me his picture and talked about him and asked me questions about my life back home. She actually seemed interested in my answers.

My mother offered to pay the postage for me to write home more often, since Aunt Liesel had said she couldn't afford it. All I had to do was send all the letters I had written to my friends to my mother, and she would mail them for me. After that, I felt like my lifeline had been reestablished. I wrote to everybody I could think of: all my girlfriends, Fraulein Meyer, our pastor, other schoolteachers I had liked. Unfortunately, I really didn't have much to write about. Every day was the same for me. What was there to tell people? I went to the grocer, who still eyed me funny and made me nervous; I watched the Underwear Ladies shake out their wet drawers; I did Aunt Liesel's housework. I made dinner, I served dinner, I cleaned up after dinner. I listened to Aunt Liesel and Fritz and Peter and Uncle Paul talk. I went to sleep.

The months passed, winter into spring, with no change and no word from the government. Every day was the same. All I did was work in Aunt Liesel's apartment, or at least that's what it felt like to me. The euphoria of my escape was a distant memory.

As the days went on and on and on with no news, no hope, no friends of my own to talk to, only cooking and cleaning and chore after chore, I started to resent Aunt Liesel. I know I was wrong to feel this way; she was, after all, providing me with free room and board, and she had very little money to spare. My work around her apartment was the only way I could pay her back. Still, it felt to me sometimes like Aunt Liesel had worked out a great deal. She had gained a maid, a cook, a servant—a slave, I thought bitterly—at very little cost to herself.

One day, I came down with a toothache that wouldn't go away. For the first time in my life, I went to see the dentist, Aunt Liesel's dentist, an old, white-haired man who lived in the next apartment building and had his office right next to his apartment, with his wife working as his office manager and receptionist. For three visits, the dentist dug at my tooth with his age-spotted hands and I learned the meaning of the word pain.

At the end of the last visit, with his wife in the next room, the dentist tried to climb on top of me, right there in the dental chair, squeezing and grabbing at my breasts and kissing my neck with his dry old lips. I didn't know if this was how he expected me to pay for his services, but I screamed and fought him off and ran back to Aunt Liesel's apartment sobbing. When she got home from work, though, I couldn't tell her what had happened. I was sure I had done something wrong. I had said something, or looked at him a certain way, and he must have been able to tell something about me, something that I was trying so hard to forget.

After that, my depression worsened. I began having nightmares again, about that day in October, with the men on the road. I started eating even more, whatever I could find. Lard sandwiches were my favorite. Once I ate an entire crock of plums Aunt Liesel was saving for jam. My clothes grew so tight they were hard to button, but I couldn't stop eating. It was my only pleasure. And it made me numb.

Not long after my seventeenth birthday, Herr Hofer came to visit. My heart leaped when I saw him at the door. But he didn't have good news. My application had been rejected, yet again.

"The big stumbling block is proving who you are," he said. "The government says your identification card from Doelitz is worthless, since they don't trust anything issued by the Russians. Because we can't prove you're you, they won't authorize your citizenship."

"But I am me, and there are people back home who know that," I said. "What about my schoolteachers or my pastor, who has known me my whole life?"

"It's worth a try," said Herr Hofer. "Let me see what I can do."

Herr Hofer left, promising to write to all my old teachers and Herr Pastor Scharnweber, to see if they could send letters to the government on my behalf.

In May, Aunt Liesel decided to have the apartment painted. The painter came one day when she and Fritz were gone. The wool business had failed, but she and

Fritz had started another venture, a car-rental agency. Aunt Liesel took care of the bookkeeping from the apartment, so she was home a lot more, but still she and Fritz had to drive around on business, buying new cars and trying to retrieve old ones that had broken down at the side of the road.

I was alone in the apartment with the painter, a stoop-shouldered man of about fifty, who alternately slapped yellow paint on the walls, wheezed, and smoked cigarettes. I was working in the kitchen, boiling milk, when the painter came to see me.

"I need a break," he said, coming to the stove and looking over my shoulder at the pan of milk. The hair on the back of my neck rose; suddenly his paint-splattered hands closed around my waist. "How about joining me?" he whispered in my ear. "We'll have a good time, you'll see."

I was trapped, the painter behind me, pressing himself against me. The hot stove in front of me.

"Please don't," I said, feeling myself start to tremble, feeling the nightmares that I kept penned away so deep inside start to stir to life. "Please. No."

The painter pressed harder against me, squeezed more tightly.

"No!" I screamed. I pushed back from the stove and stomped his foot, then ran as fast as I could for the front door. I stumbled down the stairs and outside, onto the dirty gray street.

I spent the rest of the afternoon wandering through Kassel. Just as with the dentist, I didn't tell Aunt Liesel what had happened. When she asked why supper was late and why the ironing hadn't been done, I told her I had to leave because the paint fumes had made me feel sick.

At the end of the month, I got a letter from my mother announcing important news: Heinz and his girlfriend, a girl from the village named Gisela, were getting married. My favorite brother, getting married. How much had happened in less than a year!

"We all wish you could be here," my mother wrote. "We will be thinking of you. We miss you so much."

I was going to miss Heinz's wedding, I realized, my joy at his good news turning to sharp sorrow. It wasn't fair. It wasn't right.

I wanted more than anything at that moment to be home. I wasn't that far away, if you looked at miles. If it weren't for the Russians and their borders, I could just hop on a train and be there by the next day. If it weren't for the Russians, I would still be living at home.

After hearing about Heinz's wedding, each day seemed darker than the last. I walked with Ingrid and Hans-Joachim and Dora through Kassel's park and barely noticed how lovely things had become in that little island of green, with the sun bringing the lilies and other bright flowers to vibrant life. It didn't matter to me any longer. I was ruining my life, suffocating in that dirty city, with its dirty, evil men, all for the sake of a foolish daydream. I belonged with my family and friends. I was meant to be there, not in Kassel. Not in America.

I wanted to escape again—to escape back home. Could I do it? Would it be possible? I still had my Russian identification card, after all. I could try to find my way through the mountains again. Maybe Herr Burger would take pity on me and would hide me again in the bottom of his potato wagon, even though I didn't have any money with which to pay him.

Although I didn't tell Aunt Liesel what was in my mind, she sensed my despair. She kept shooing me outside, a concerned look on her face. "Tilli, go take a walk," she would say. "You need to get out. Go ahead, I'll manage here."

I did what she said, but it didn't help. There was nothing new to see. I had seen it all already: Kassel's factories, with their smoke and grit; the stores, filled with forbidden treasures. What was the point?

The day before Heinz's wedding, I woke up too weak to lift myself off my cot. I stared at the ceiling, picturing the wedding. The neighbors would be at Gisela's house, laughing and drinking and smashing old dishes for her and Heinz to clean up. I knew Gisela—she hadn't lived too far from us—and I liked her; she was quiet but good-natured, a fitting match for Heinz. I imagined Heinz and Gisela riding a flower-covered wagon to church. Later everyone would dance and the couples would parade through the village behind them, all without me.

Tears slid down my cheeks. I was too tired to brush them away. They cooled my face, which was so hot. I was terribly thirsty, too, but I didn't have the energy to get a drink.

"Tilli, what's the matter?" Aunt Liesel was standing over me. She seemed to be floating, just her face—no neck, no body—in front of mine. Such a strange expression she had. Alarmed. As if she were staring at a dead person.

I wondered what it was like to be dead. I almost died when I had typhoid. I wondered if I had typhoid again? Was that possible, to get it twice?

"You are burning up, just burning up! Why didn't you tell me?" Cool silky things were touching my face. Aunt Liesel's hands, I saw, as she pulled them away.

Her hands were like birds. Pink birds, fluttering up to the window, then soaring off into the sky.

I wish I were a bird. I know what it's like to fly. I am flying now. Can you see me, Aunt Liesel? I am flying over the mountains. My apron is falling to the ground and I am in the clouds now, high above the Russians and their guns, so high they can't reach me, no one can reach me, no evil men can touch me. Over cities and villages and meadows and fields, I fly. Flying to a family, to my family, that's what I'm doing. I'm looking through the clouds for a one-hundred-year-old stone house with the most beautiful flower garden you will ever see. That's where I will land, once I can figure out how.

"There's nothing wrong with her," a man's voice was saying.

"That's ridiculous." It was a woman, someone whose voice I recognized. "She has a fever. She hasn't moved in two days. She's delirious. How can you tell me nothing is wrong with her? What kind of a doctor are you?"

"She has no signs of any disease," the man said angrily. "What more can I say? Keep her cool and get her to drink something."

On the other side of my closed eyelids was bright light. I could sense it and I was afraid to open my eyes to it because it might hurt me. My head was throbbing and I was boiling and I was chilled down to my trembling bones.

"She's my sister's child and I have to take care of her. I can't let anything happen to her." The woman's voice was begging. "Don't you understand?"

"I'm sorry. Good day."

Footsteps and the door shuts and more footsteps, lighter ones, coming towards me, and then the cool silk on my face again.

I'm sorry, but I don't want to be here, Aunt Liesel. I keep trying to leave, as hard as I can, and I keep waking up and finding myself still in my body, still in your house, and I want to scream at the injustice of it all, but instead I go to sleep and once more I am a bird, soaring through the skies to my blessed freedom, even though my freedom can only be found in a prison, guarded by Russian soldiers.

32

Nobody ever knew what had been wrong with me; no one else in the house got sick, and after a few days I was fine again. I secretly believed I had been so severely homesick that I became physically ill. It scared me to think that I could wish myself into such a state. I wondered whether a person could actually will himself to die. How close had I come? At least I knew that I had turned back, that there was something deep inside me that wanted to live, to survive no matter how miserable the day might be. If living with Aunt Liesel in Kassel was the only life I could have, then I was going to have to figure out a way to endure it.

One morning in early September, I was writing my mother a letter when I heard the familiar tromp of the mailman's feet, then the clank and swish of letters dropping through the slot. I gathered the scattered envelopes. One for Aunt Liesel. Three for Fritz.

And one, a heavy one, addressed to me. My name was typed on it. Nobody I knew had a typewriter. I ripped the envelope open.

"Dear Fraulein Horn, your work permit has been approved—"

I screamed. No one was home to hear me, to share my news. I had been approved to live and work in western Germany.

I had to tell somebody, so I ran to the Hofers' apartment, waving the letter before me like a flag. "Thank you, thank you," I said to Herr Hofer. "I wish I could pay you, or do something for you. You don't know what this means to me."

"I think I do," said Herr Hofer, smiling. "And that's payment enough for me."

That afternoon, I walked as fast as I could to the courthouse. The long lines didn't bother me. The hours flew by, now that I had a future. I felt as though I had been granted permission to dream again. I brushed the dust off my old fantasies of freedom; I added sparkle and shine to them and took them out for a drive, traveling all over the America of my mind, which had never looked more spectacular.

"Don't get your hopes up, Tilli," Aunt Liesel warned.

We were eating a quick breakfast before I went to apply for my first job. It was the day after my papers had arrived. A restaurant called Schimcke's had advertised in the newspaper that it had an opening for a secretary. Aunt Liesel said that Schimcke's was well-known and popular and probably would attract a lot of other applicants. But I didn't care. My luck had turned; I knew it.

"Your aunt is right," said Fritz. "There are probably five hundred people to each vacant job these days, people with years and years of experience."

"I can still try," I said, determined not to let Fritz or Liesel ruin my mood.

I will get a job today, I kept telling myself as I walked downtown to Schimcke's. I kept repeating the words—*I will get a job today*—even as I turned the corner and saw a throng of people, at least two hundred women, snaking in a huge line outside the restaurant.

"Are you here for the secretarial job?" I asked a woman at the end of the line. She shrugged indifferently, her face cold. I was competition; I was unwelcome.

I didn't care. I stepped in line behind her.

A few minutes later, another woman stood behind me. Within an hour, there were about twenty people after me in a line that hadn't budged an inch. I hadn't even seen the doorway to the restaurant yet.

An hour passed. Two.

Maybe Fritz had been right. I wouldn't get this job after all. All these people probably had much more experience than I did. All I had was my secretarial training in Rostock, and no way to prove I had even done that. I would simply have to keep trying other jobs, when they opened up.

If they opened up.

I refused to leave the line, even as the hours kept passing. I tried to banish my black thoughts, to think positively—I will get a job today—but the worries kept whispering in the back of my mind: What if I couldn't find work at all? Look how long it had taken simply to get permission to hold a job. What if nobody wanted to hire me and I had to spend all my days in Aunt Liesel's apartment, hours and hours of nothingness, alone, gray, empty. I couldn't go through that again.

Discouraged women began dropping out of the line, dead leaves falling from a tree branch. The line began to creep, ever so slightly, forward.

Then a man called out the door: "The job's been filled."

The line collapsed. People scattered, their faces sad and drawn. A few of us remained. "Maybe they have something else," muttered the woman in front of me. I followed several other women through the doorway of the restaurant, down a little hall to an office with a glass door. A man was inside, sitting at a desk, going over a huge stack of papers.

One by one, the women went into the office, then left, stony-eyed.

It was my turn. I went in, my hands clasped in front of me, my fingernails digging into my sweaty palms. "Hello, I'm—"

The man didn't look up from his papers. "The job's been filled. Didn't you hear?" His voice was curt.

I couldn't move. All the bad experiences, all the frustrations and disappointments, everything that had gone wrong in Kassel during the past year overwhelmed me. I felt like the candlelight had blown out, the door was slamming shut, I was back in my gray cave once more. Before I knew what I was doing, before I could at least make an attempt at controlling myself, I was crying. The thought of leaving, of going back to the apartment with nothing, made me cry harder. The fact that I was crying like that in front of a perfect stranger was worse yet.

The man looked up, alarmed. He was Uncle Paul's age, with wiry hair and a mustache. He stood and reached across his desk to pat my arm. "Are you all right?"

"I'm sorry," I choked out. "I'm sorry."

We stood like that for a minute.

"You know," said the man slowly. "I might have something else. The secretarial position was filled, but if you wouldn't mind waitress work, if you'd be—"

"I'll do anything," I said. "I just want to work."

"Well then," the man said, sitting down, businesslike now. He took my papers and made some notes. "Well then, Tilli Horn. When can you start?"

My job was to run the cake buffet. I stood behind a pastry display and asked customers which piece of cake they preferred. They pointed to what they wanted; I gave them a number, then put a matching number on the plate with the cake they wanted. The waitress would then bring them their cake. I was not allowed to actually serve anybody anything, since I hadn't been formally trained as a waitress.

For this, I made a modest salary—125 marks a month, plus meals. It was low-paying compared to most other jobs, but I didn't care. It was my money—even though I gave most of it to Aunt Liesel as soon as I was paid.

I worked at Schimcke's from 11 a.m. until about 8 p.m., when the last customers were finished. Sometimes, when the restaurant was slow, I was allowed to leave early. I didn't really like to leave early, because I wanted to avoid dinner duties at the apartment. It was so wonderful not having to shop, cook, serve, and clean up dinner every night.

With my first paycheck, I gave Aunt Liesel everything except enough money to buy a pair of shoes, the first new pair of shoes I had had since my escape. They were black and matched my black uniform, which had a starched collar and frilly white apron. They were the cheapest pair I could find: they had a cardboard lining which got so wet with sweat during my long hours on my feet that often they were still wet the next day.

After my first week at Schimcke's, I wrote to the American consulate in Frankfurt, telling them that I wanted to emigrate to America, which I could now do since I was officially a west German citizen. Herr Hofer warned me not to expect an answer right away. "It's the bureaucracy, you know," he said. "In Germany, we have the best bureaucracy in the world. It will probably take months before you hear a word."

I didn't mind waiting, though. My depression had lifted. Getting out of the house every day, making my own money and being around other people had helped me immensely. I found myself singing bits of songs that I remembered from home, folk songs from harvest parties, church songs that were my mother's favorites. Songs that I hadn't sung since arriving in Kassel.

A couple of months after starting work at the restaurant, Herr Schuhmacher, the man who hired me, switched me from the cake buffet to the bar, and put the woman who had been working in the bar—Frau Steinke, who was nearly sixty—in charge of the cake buffet. "I think the guys in the bar will like seeing a younger girl like you," said Herr Schuhmacher. "Maybe they will stay longer and buy more." Frau Steinke was angry about the switch and felt like she'd been demoted. She grew cold to me, where once she had been friendly, almost grandmotherly. I tried not to let it bother me.

Working in the bar was more fun than standing behind the cake counter. I got to talk to a lot more people. Sometimes American soldiers came in and I got to practice my English with them. There were very few obnoxious men, and Herr Schuhmacher knew how to handle them if they came around.

One night a familiar-looking man perched his large bulk on a barstool next to the beer tap and stared at me expectantly. It took a few seconds to recognize him. I associated this man so much with his store, with his white apron. It was the grocer. As always when I saw him, I shuddered.

"Hello, fraulein," he said. "Your aunt told me you were working here now. I wondered where you'd disappeared to."

"Can I get you a beer?" I asked.

"I'd rather just talk for a minute. I've come up with an idea." The grocer leaned across the counter and grabbed my hand, pulling me close to him. "I know you're in need of certain things, fraulein. Well, so am I."

I yanked back my hand and stepped back. "I don't need anything."

"That's not what I hear. You walk here, all by yourself at night, instead of taking the streetcar. Your aunt is poor, too. You want to repay her, I'm sure. I can help. I can get you food, the best things at the market. I have connections. I can get you clothes, jewelry. I can help you a great deal. If you help me."

He reached for me again. "I know you want me."

"No!" I shouted. Heads turned at the other end of the bar. "I'm not interested," I said more quietly. "Please leave."

"How can you say that?" said the grocer, looking hurt. "I know the way you've looked at me."

I shook my head in disgust. The grocer's face reddened; his eyes disappeared into his angry frown. "I hope you know what you're doing," he snapped, pulling his hand back. "You won't get another opportunity."

"No," I whispered.

The grocer's lips pressed together stiffly. He stalked out of the bar. I pressed my hands to my face, their coolness a relief to my burning cheeks.

Not long after that, Aunt Liesel took a weekend trip to Berlin to visit friends and do some shopping. The rental business had made some money and Aunt Liesel wanted to buy material and new dishes for Christmas.

On Sunday morning, Fritz sat down next to me on the sofa, where I was flipping through a magazine Aunt Bertha had sent, looking at pictures of the latest American fashions.

"Tilli, I have an idea," Fritz said. "I was wondering if you'd like to learn to drive. Today would be a perfect day to try it out."

"Drive? Me? A car?"

"Sure, why not? Everybody should know how to drive."

"But don't you have to be eighteen to drive? And get a certificate from a school and a license from the government?"

"Oh, who cares? Nobody cares. Come on. It'll be fun."

I had nothing better to do. "Sure," I said, following Fritz to his latest car, which wasn't any better than his previous car. It roared and bucked and shimmied down the road, with what sounded like gunshots coming out of the back end.

"I know it makes a lot of noise, but it's really quite reliable," said Fritz, turning the steering wheel with one finger, the other arm stretched out across the back of the seat, almost reaching to my shoulder. Now and then he pulled it back to shift gears, brushing my arm as he did so.

Soon, we reached an area of deserted streets near the park, with few people around. "Watch me first," Fritz said. "You know that this is the steering wheel. This is the gearshift. That's the brake and the clutch and the gas."

He drove up and down the quiet street, showing me how the car worked. I watched his legs and hands carefully, thinking that I could never do these things so easily, so automatically.

After a few minutes, Fritz stopped the car, shut off the engine, and got out. I slid over to the driver's side and he moved in next to me, pressing close so that he could guide my hand on the gearshift. "Let's just sit here and practice," he said.

I twisted the wheel, pushing at the pedals with my feet. Fritz's hand pressed harder on mine, atop the shiny black knob of the gearshift. "Stop," Fritz whispered. He put his hand on my cheek and turned my face towards his. Then he was kissing me, his lips dry and hot against mine, his body pressing against mine.

I squealed and pushed him back. Then I jumped out of the car and stood there, in the stillness. I couldn't believe this had happened yet again. What was wrong with me?

Fritz climbed out and stood next to me. "I'm sorry," he mumbled. "Please don't be mad. Please don't tell Liesel."

"Just take me home," I said. "I don't want any more driving lessons."

"So you won't tell Liesel? Promise?"

I shrugged, puzzled at his concern over Aunt Liesel. Why did he care what she thought? Did he think Liesel would quit being partners with him because he had made a pass at me? That didn't seem too likely.

We rode back to the apartment in stiff silence. I sat as far from Fritz on the front seat as I could, thinking how much I hated men. All men were disgusting.

On New Year's Eve, a private party rented Schmicke's for the night. I had to work later than usual, until 1 a.m. Aunt Liesel and Uncle Paul and Fritz were going out together and weren't sure whether they would be home by then or not.

The evening passed quickly. The private party arrived around 9 p.m., a group of men and women decked out in flashy evening clothes, about thirty of them, completely filling the bar, ordering beer after beer. I could barely keep up.

Shortly before midnight, there was a loud thumping on the front door. Herr Schuhmacher went to the door and called out: "We're closed! Private party only!" He turned to me, shaking his head. "I put up a sign, but I guess some people can't read."

"Let me in!" a woman's voice cried. The raps on the door continued. "You can't keep us out! Let us in!"

Herr Schumacher sighed and pulled open the door. To my horror, Aunt Liesel was standing in the doorway, swaying. Her hair was wild, her lipstick smeared, her coat buttoned crookedly. She clung to Fritz, grinning. Uncle Paul stood behind her, his arms crossed, a scowl on his face.

"Tilli, dear!" Aunt Liesel shrieked, waving at me.

I had never seen her drunk like this before. Sometimes she and her friends got tipsy, but never smashed.

"I'm sorry, madam, but we are closed," Herr Schumacher said. "You will have to leave."

"But you can't do this to me!" Aunt Liesel roared. "That's my niece you've got working there! My niece! If you don't let us in, I won't let her work here anymore!"

"I'm sorry, madam, but you will have to leave." Herr Schumacher pushed the door shut. Aunt Liesel screamed and pounded the door some more. "Tilli! Tilli!" she cried.

I was mortified. "Herr Schumacher, I'm so sorry," I said. What if he fired me? Then what would I do? I couldn't lose this job. "Please don't listen to her. She isn't herself."

"Don't worry, Tilli. I understand," he said. "Why don't you take off early tonight and go home with your aunt?"

"Are you sure?"

He nodded. "It's almost midnight. We're almost done. Go ahead, go."

"Thank you. Thank you so much."

I grabbed my coat and hurried outside. Aunt Liesel was drinking from a clear glass bottle. She saw me and rushed over to me, sweeping me into a hug, smelling of cigarettes and perfume and alcohol. "Tilli, Tilli," she said, her words slurred. "Let's forget this stuffy old place. Come home with us."

Aunt Liesel and Paul and Fritz began walking toward the apartment. I followed slightly behind them, angry and embarrassed. How could my aunt humiliate me like this?

We left the busy restaurant district. The streets were quiet, our shoes on the pavement the only sound. Uncle Paul tossed the flaming end of his cigarette onto the ground, where it sizzled in the snow. He was stalking more than walking, his arms folded tightly. Fritz and Aunt Liesel were shoulder to shoulder, slightly swaying into each other. I got the feeling that I had stepped into the middle of something unfinished between the three of them.

Halfway to the apartment, Uncle Paul suddenly spoke up. "You think you're fooling me, don't you?" he said loudly, glaring at Liesel and Fritz, who stopped and stared at him in amazement. "Well, I know what I know. This is going to end, one way or the other. You're not going to keep making a fool out of me."

"Oh, Paul," said Aunt Liesel. "You're wrong."

"Be quiet, Paul," Fritz said, his voice low and even.

Paul stared at him, lit another cigarette, then stomped ahead, his shoulders hunched. We went inside the apartment. I saw from the clock on the wall that 1952 had arrived. It was 12:30 a.m.

Paul started pacing across the living room. Aunt Liesel and Fritz sat on the sofa. "Happy New Year!" cried Aunt Liesel.

"Shut up!" Paul glared at her. "I know the truth. You're having an affair. You and Fritz."

"No, Paul, no," said Aunt Liesel. "Don't be silly. You're drunk. Sit down."

"Fritz, I trusted you," said Uncle Paul. "I brought you into my home. And now you're sleeping with my wife. Aren't you! Aren't you!"

"Paul, you're crazy. You're drunk. Of course not," said Fritz, his eyes darting from Paul to Liesel to me. "Here, have a drink and let's forget about this, all right?"

"You're lying. I know the truth!" Paul yelled.

My throat closed. This was all too familiar: yelling, ugliness, hatred, destroyed love. This was my parents all over again. I couldn't stand it, what people, what men and women, did to each other.

Paul went into the bedroom. I heard drawers opening and closing. Liesel and Fritz looked at each other in alarm. "Do something," Liesel hissed. Fritz got up and went to the bedroom door. "Hey, Paul, come on," he said. "Don't do this."

Uncle Paul came back into the living room, holding a suitcase. He pushed Fritz hard. Fritz fell back, almost to the floor, but caught himself. Paul stalked to the door. "Happy New Year," he snarled. Then he left.

"Paul!" cried Aunt Liesel. She looked at Fritz. "Don't just stand there! Go after him!"

Fritz left. I could hear his footsteps on the stairs, his voice calling after Paul. I didn't hear any sound from Uncle Paul. Aunt Liesel was crying, her shoulders shaking, her head bowed.

"Aunt Liesel," I said finally. "I don't understand any of this."

She sniffed and wiped her eyes. "I know, Tilli. I'm sorry." Then she started to sob again. I patted her back. I didn't know what to do or say. Aunt Liesel was practically old enough to be Fritz's mother.

"How can Uncle Paul possibly think you're having an affair with Fritz? I mean, after all, you're seventeen years older than he is."

"Only sixteen and a half," Aunt Liesel said quickly. Then she started crying again.

I stood up, confused. I got my cot and my blanket and changed into my nightgown, all the while trying not to think what I was thinking.

The next day, Aunt Liesel woke up sick. I gave her some tea and she tried to keep down some bread. She walked around numbly, her eyes puffed and swollen. She wouldn't look at Fritz, and he ignored her as well, although I got the feeling it was all strictly for my benefit. Peter was gone for the holiday, so I was the only audience Fritz and Liesel had.

I went to work. At least Herr Schuhmacher didn't seem to hold what had happened with Aunt Liesel against me. I was grateful and tried to work even harder than usual to show my appreciation.

Uncle Paul never came back to the apartment. Aunt Liesel and Fritz continued to keep a tense, uncomfortable distance from each other whenever I was around. I ignored them, happy when it was time to leave for work and I could get away from that apartment filled with ugliness and illusions.

I told Dora what had happened. "I think Uncle Paul has left Aunt Liesel, maybe for good," I said.

Dora's eyebrow lifted, but she didn't look surprised. "Really? Why?"

"He thinks Aunt Liesel and Fritz are having an affair."

"So he finally wised up. Good for him," said Dora.

"You mean it's true?"

"Of course it is. Didn't you know? They've been having an affair since before you got here. Paul brought Fritz to live with them a few years ago. Fritz was Paul's friend. For a long time, Paul tried not to see it happening. But I knew about it. A lot of people knew."

"I didn't," I said quietly.

I suddenly felt like crying. What was it about this city, this eternally gray, crumbling, agony-strewn city, that was causing all these people to behave shabbily, from the clutching old dentist to the painter to the grocer to Fritz and now Liesel? Was there something about the city, or was it an after-effect of the war, which made people want to grab for pleasure, any kind of pleasure, to hide the memories of all the pain and terror they had endured?

Or maybe this was just how adults acted, how men were, no matter where in the world they lived, no matter whether they had been through a war or not.

Maybe America would be the same, and not the shining happy perfect place of my dreams.

Maybe I was growing up and learning how adults really were, behind the smiles they gave to children to fool them.

My head spun with the mystery of it all. The only thing I knew for certain was that I was never, ever going to get married. It was not worth the pain.

33

"Tilli, some mail came for you today. I think it's from the consulate."

It was late May, nine months since I had written to the American consulate, asking for permission to emigrate.

I hurried to Aunt Liesel and tore the long white envelope open. "Dear Fraulein Horn: In response to your recent inquiry, please appear at our office in Frankfurt for an interview and to make formal application for emigration—"

I held the letter in front of me. I couldn't have read it right. It couldn't be real.

Aunt Liesel grabbed me in a spin. "You see? It's all going to work out."

Fritz drove Aunt Liesel and me to Frankfurt on the day of my appointment. I filled out forms and answered questions and showed my western papers. The man handling my file told me that everything appeared promising. My sponsors were Aunt Bertha and Aunt Anna, and they had checked out. Although the Americans allowed only so many Germans into their country each year, I was within that limit. He asked me to come back in six weeks for a physical examination and immunizations.

I spent the next six weeks trying not to get too excited. Nobody at work knew yet that I might be leaving; something could still go wrong, and I didn't want to jeopardize my job.

When it came time to return to the consulate, Fritz no longer had a working car. I had to make the three-hour trip on the back of his motorcycle. By the time we got there, my face was black with soot and I looked horrible. Nobody at the consulate seemed to care, though. A doctor looked me over and gave me two shots. They hurt a little bit, but I didn't mind, especially after the man in charge of my file told me that everything had been approved. I was free to leave for America.

I barely noticed the trip back to Kassel. My mind, my heart, my spirit were all soaring with the wind, flying to the clouds and beyond. My dream was coming true. It was actually happening.

The next day, I gave notice at work. "I'm so happy for you," said Herr Schuhmacher, and I could tell he meant it. "If there is anything we can do to help you, let me know. And you can keep working here for as long as you want."

"Thank you," I said. "I appreciate everything you've already done, starting with giving me this job."

The news spread quickly through the restaurant. Soon, everybody was congratulating me. Two American soldiers who were regular customers and with whom I had often practiced speaking English were so thrilled that they offered to take me to their PX for some real American food.

"A Coke and a burger, that's what you need," said Bob, a chubby red-haired man from a place called Wisconsin.

A few days later, I rode the streetcar with Bob and James, a black man from Mississippi, to their Army base. We sat at a long counter inside a metal building. Bob ordered three hamburgers, three Cokes, and three orders of French fries.

"I can't believe you've never had a hamburger before," said Bob. "I live on burgers. A lot of Americans do. And hot dogs. I suppose you've never had a hot dog, either? Or apple pie?"

A soldier wearing an apron slid our plates in front of us. I stared at mine, at the thick brown circle of meat, resting on a white bun, with red sauce on it and another white bun sitting beside it. I started to cut the mean with my knife and fork.

"No, no," said James, laughing.

"Like this," said Bob, putting the top bun on the hamburger, then picking it up and stuffing it into his mouth.

I tried it. Doughy, tasteless bread and bland, greasy meat filled my mouth. It couldn't begin to compare with my mother's ham or sausages or roasts.

"Well?" said Bob. He and James watched me eagerly.

"It's good," I lied. "Really good."

"You see?" said Bob proudly. "You can't beat American burgers. Now try the Coke."

I took a sip and felt like spitting out the bubbly, soapy-tasting brown water. Again I tried to act delighted. "Wonderful!"

As Bob and James grinned at me, I wondered what other American treats would disappoint me. What if the whole country fell flat, after all the build-up I had given it in my mind? What if I couldn't stand living there?

I pushed my fears from my mind and took another sip of Coke. It really wasn't that bad, after all; just different. It would take some getting used to, that's all.

As soon as Aunt Bertha found out that I had been approved to leave Germany, she sent me a box of clothes for the trip: a silky black dress with a red cloth rose pinned to the front; another dress, all red, which was less fancy than the black one; and a wool suit, with a jacket and skirt.

Tucked among the clothes were a ticket and some American money.

Aunt Bertha had booked me on a ship called the *Italia*, which was owned by a famous rich man named Aristotle Onassis. She hadn't been able to get me a tourist-class ticket—they were sold out for months. So she had splurged and bought a first-class ticket instead. The dress was so that I would have something fancy to wear, so I could fit in with the other first-class ticket holders.

The date on my ticket was Sept. 12, 1952.

In less than one month, I would be leaving. Unless something else went wrong.

◆   ◆   ◆

I spent my last days in Kassel inside a giddy cloud, floating down to earth only when necessary.

The tension between Aunt Liesel and Fritz no longer touched me. I didn't look at the grocer when I picked up our milk. I didn't see the dirty gray buildings all around me or smell the air, bitter with brown smoke.

Again and again I ran my hands along the fabric of my new dresses, which hung in Aunt Liesel's closet, waiting for me. Besides the clothes Aunt Bertha had sent, Aunt Liesel had given me another dress, one made from shiny maroon material by a seamstress in our building. It was amazing to me to have so many clothes.

The trips to the consulate in Frankfurt had taken most of my savings. I'd had to pay some fees, plus the cost of gas and meals. With the little money that I had left, I bought dress shoes, which were black and looked like they were made out of alligator skin. Unfortunately, they were really made out of cardboard, which would melt if they ever got wet. But they had been all I could afford.

When I wasn't working or daydreaming, I wrote letters to just about everybody I had ever met. Friends, relatives, schoolteachers: all heard my exciting news, that in a few short weeks I would be leaving Germany. At least twice a week I wrote to my mother, feeling as though we had to hold onto each other even more fiercely than before, because soon I would be an ocean away.

Aunt Liesel, Fritz, and I took a weekend trip to see my mother's side of the family, who lived in a little town in Hessen. Many of the women looked just like my mother, which made me wish all the more that it could be my mother I was hugging and saying my good-byes to. If only I could have seen her just one more time. Then everything would have been perfect.

My friends at Schimcke's threw me a going-away party. Some of the regular customers, like Bob and James, also came. I would miss so many of my new friends.

The *Italia* was due to sail out of Hamburg. Aunt Liesel made arrangements with friends of hers in Cuxhaven, which was a small harbor town outside of Hamburg, to put us up the night before the voyage, so that I could be on the ship first thing in the morning. Fritz, who had a working car again, agreed to drive Aunt Liesel, myself and Ingrid to Cuxhaven.

The morning we left Kassel it was overcast. How typical, I thought. Gray skies yet again. Fritz and Liesel rode in front; Ingrid and I sat in back. I stared out the windows as we drove away, not looking back even once.

Down the street we went, past the building where the Underwear Ladies lived, past the grocer, the dilapidated factories, the downtown shops, the old, scarred bomb shelter.

Good-bye to it all. I wouldn't miss any of it.

Fritz pushed harder on the gas as we left the city and headed into the country-side. The clouds opened and rain began to pour down, along with a cool wind that blew through me like pure joy.

"This is it," said Aunt Liesel, turning to me. "Tilli, you are on your way."

In the middle of the afternoon, we arrived at Cuxhaven, a small town lined with modest houses, the air sharp with the tang of the nearby sea. Fritz pulled up in front of a small house with white shutters. A young woman opened the door and came to greet us. A girl of about seven followed behind her.

"Hello, hello," said Aunt Liesel. She introduced us to the woman, Frau Broder, and her daughter, Arianna, who showed Ingrid and I upstairs. I set down my suitcase and looked out the window to the street. The elation of my leave-taking had been ebbing away as the hours on the road had passed, and now I felt chilled and almost dizzy.

After supper, which I picked at, Herr Broder asked us if we wanted to see Hamburg. We squeezed into Fritz's car, Arianna on her father's lap, and made the half-hour drive, leaving Cuxhaven and traveling into the city of Hamburg, which was almost as big as Berlin, with huge buildings looming on either side of the busy downtown roads.

We turned into the harbor and my mouth dropped open. I had lived for nine months in Rostock, which had a small harbor, with tug boats and freighters. But that was nothing compared to this. Ships, dozens of them, as far as I could see. Ships as tall as office buildings, ships like white whales, so many ships, and so many people scurrying about, even though it was evening, with the moon casting its calm glow on the silver-black water.

Fritz parked and we walked along the dock, which swayed beneath our feet. Seagulls screamed and dove at the water. A brisk breeze whipped my hair. I shivered and pressed my arms around myself, trying to get rid of the chill settling in my bones.

"It's going to be cold on the ocean," Frau Broder said, putting her arm on my shoulders. "I hope you brought something warm to wear."

I nodded numbly, concentrating on putting one foot in front of the other.

"Look, Tilli, look!" cried Aunt Liesel, pointing to a white ship that wasn't quite as big as the hugest liners, but was still one of the tallest boats there. Painted on its side, in curving black letters, was the word *Italia*.

"That's your ship, isn't it? It's already here."

We walked alongside it. Men in white uniforms were carrying trunks onto it. Others were mopping and washing and waxing the top deck and the railings. The ship bobbed gently in the water, which slapped its sides.

I stared at the *Italia*, trying to comprehend the fact that the next morning I would be climbing those polished stairs, that in less than twenty-four hours I would be sailing away, forever.

34

The ceiling in Arianna's bedroom slants at a steep angle, following the line of the pitched roof. I am lying next to her, closest to the wall, where the ceiling reaches down into the room, and in this dim light it is just like it was in the attic. I fight panic, the overwhelming feeling of being trapped, of walls pressing in on me, ceiling in my face, air so thick, nowhere to turn, my heart a caged bird, fluttering and flapping its restless wings, my stomach a snake, twisting and squeezing until I can't breathe.

I roll back and forth, trying not to bump against Arianna, who looks dead, she is so still. So does Ingrid, on the other side of Arianna. How can they both sleep like that, so calmly? I guess because their lives aren't about to change forever, like mine is.

A shudder of panic surges through me again. I can't go through with it. I can't get on that ship. I know it. It's so clear to me, how wrong I've been, how impossible this is. When morning comes, I will tell them. Then I will go back to—to—what?

I can't go back. I have no choice. I have left the castle and crossed the bridge and the bridge has fallen away, there's nothing but the moat behind me. I have to go forward. There is no other way.

I close my eyes and I see my mother's face. She is gazing at me so lovingly. I would give anything to hold her again. I haven't seen her, haven't touched her, in two years.

Mami, help me. Please help me.

And then she is turned from me, she is in the kitchen, she is looking at the floor. Go then, go, she says, her voice empty, hollow, and then she is gone and I can no longer picture her face.

I am alone.

So alone.

◆   ◆   ◆

When it is finally morning, I don't feel any better, any calmer. I feel like throwing up.

Arianna's mother and father are walking around downstairs. I hear Fritz's laugh and then Aunt Liesel's voice and then she is laughing, too. How can they be so cheerful?

I walk downstairs, my legs shaky. "Good morning," says Aunt Liesel. She looks at me sharply. "How are you doing?"

"Fine," I mutter.

"Are you sure? You look pale."

"I'm fine."

"If you say so. Can you wake up Ingrid and Arianna? Then we'll have some breakfast and then we'll go. Isn't this exciting?"

I go through the motions, waking the girls, brushing my hair, putting on lipstick. But inside, I'm paralyzed.

After breakfast—again I don't eat—we go to the harbor. Even more ships are there, even more people. Herr Broder, who has a camera, insists on taking pictures of us and poses us in various groupings. I want to scream for him to stop. Doesn't he realize that I can't concentrate on smiling for the camera? I am on one side of the greatest chasm I have ever seen, getting myself ready to jump.

And then it is time. A line of people is forming in front of the *Italia*. The Broders hug me good-bye. Aunt Liesel and Fritz and Ingrid are going to board the ship with me and say good-bye there. Then they will get off the ship and meet back up with the Broders at the dock. They will ride back to Cuxhaven Harbor and wait for the *Italia* to pass by on its way out to sea. "We'll be able to see you again from the harbor, so be sure to look for us," says Frau Broder.

With Aunt Liesel and Fritz and Ingrid trailing behind me, I walk slowly up the ship's wooden stairs, noticing the shine of the white paint.

The world has become unreal. I feel like I am in a soap bubble, watching everything happening through a filmy glaze. I am watching myself, too, as if I were in a movie.

Suddenly, somehow, I am on deck. A vast deck, like a dozen ballrooms with no ceilings or walls. Hundreds of people milling about, some moving quickly, purposefully, others standing still. I am one of the frozen ones.

"Now, isn't this just something?" says Aunt Liesel.

"I can't wait to tell my friends about this," Ingrid chatters. "I've never ever seen a boat so big and beautiful. Can we see your room? Aren't you happy?"

A group of men in white uniforms is standing at a table, examining tickets, and directing people to their cabins. I walk across the deck and take my place in line. When it's my turn, I show my ticket. A man in a suit so white it glows points to some chairs leading to the bottom of the shop and, in flawless German, tells me how to get to my cabin.

"Guests of the passengers can remain for one-half hour," he says as he hands me my ticket back. I notice that his fingernails are shiny and perfectly manicured. I'm not used to men with hands like this.

I follow the man's directions and find myself in a maze of narrow passageways. Then I see my cabin. The door is open. It's a tiny room, barely large enough for the three bunks and three nightstands crammed in it. There is a porthole and a bathroom and some shelves.

"Look at these beautiful flowers," says Aunt Liesel, admiring a bouquet of heather on one of the nightstands. "Look at the card—these are for you, Tilli!"

"That can't be," I say.

She pulls the card from the bouquet and hands it to me. "Best wishes on your new life," says the card, which is signed by the Höpfners, friends of mine from Gnoien, who sometimes let me stay at their house during snowstorms. How in the world had they managed to get a bouquet onto the ship?

Two women came into the cabin, older women with hair in buns and fox stoles wrapped around their necks. "Hello," one says stiffly.

"Hello," I say.

"Who is traveling?" the woman asks Aunt Liesel.

"I am," I say. "I am Tilli Horn."

"You're traveling by yourself?" The woman looks at me skeptically. I nod. "How about that. Well, I am Frau Sturm and this is my sister, Frau Hammer." Frau Hammer nods to me, a polite smile on her face, disapproval in her eyes.

I set my suitcase on a shelf. The sisters pull their luggage into the cabin: huge leather trunks on rollers that dwarf my tiny cardboard suitcase.

We leave the sisters to their unpacking and take a quick tour of the ship, which is like a miniature city, with a beauty parlor and a laundry and a swimming pool and a gift shop and a library and two dining rooms and a bar and two ballrooms, one for tourist class and one for first class.

Chimes sound and everyone around us begins going upstairs, back to the deck. A man is announcing in a loud voice: "It is now time for all visitors to leave the ship! It is now time for all visitors to leave the ship!"

We follow the crowd back to the upper deck, where people are streaming off, waving good-byes, wiping tears from their eyes.

My mouth is so dry I can't swallow. Mami, help me. I can feel my knees trembling. Liesel puts her arm around me. Ingrid grabs my waist. "Oh, Tilli," she says, whimpering.

Liesel's eyes are full. "I can't believe it," she says.

"I know," I say shakily.

"Good luck to you, dear." She gives me a long, hard hug. "I love you, Tilli."

"Thank you for everything," I say. "Without you, this couldn't be happening."

She turns away, her hand over her eyes. Fritz pats my shoulder, keeping his distance. Then he and Liesel take Ingrid's hand and walk toward the stairs.

"Remember to look for us at Cuxhaven!" Aunt Liesel calls over her shoulder.

They join the crowd filing off the ship, taking slow steps down the ladder, stopping now and then to look back and wave. I stand against the metal railing, feeling its coldness. The windows of the big buildings that line the shore look like hundreds of eyes, staring at me, wondering, accusing.

I want to move, to run after Aunt Liesel. But I don't. A crewman calls out the last warning and the men pull the stairway away from the dock. The ship's engines growl and hiss, then settle into a loud, roaring hum.

A band begins playing. It is a song I know, a song we all know. I join with the other passengers in singing it as we pull away from shore. We sing louder, even as we cry, united in this moment, united in our hearts.

Good-bye, my dear homeland, good-bye
How you laugh, with your sky so blue
Good-bye, my dear homeland, good-bye
How your fields and your meadows smile at me
Good-bye, my dear homeland, good-bye
God knows that while I will always keep you in my heart
I'm being pulled in a different direction
Good-bye, my dear homeland, good-bye.
I stand the last time,
I stand the last time and say,
Dear homeland, good-bye.

35

After the band finishes playing, the *Italia* blasts its whistle and begins chugging faster, smoke spewing from its tall chimney. Half the passengers go below deck, their good-byes said. A young man standing behind me takes pictures of the shore.

A bell clangs. "I think it's lunchtime," the man says. I follow him downstairs to the first-class dining room, which is a grand place indeed, with massive golden chandeliers hanging from a painted ceiling, and candles on every table, all of which are set so elegantly, with white cloths and china with gleaming gold rims and sparkling crystal goblets and centerpieces overflowing with orchids.

A man in a white uniform, holding a clipboard, stands at the doorway, giving our table assignments. I am seated at a table next to the captain's table. The young man with the camera also is assigned to my table. I find out that his name is Herbert and he's leaving Germany for a job in the United States making prosthetic devices. Also at my table is the ship's doctor, an older man with silver hair to match his uniform; a married American couple returning to New Mexico; a mother and daughter from California, who have been visiting German relatives; and a young Greek man named Stavros, who has slicked-back hair and dark-rimmed glasses and works for Aristotle Onassis, owner of the *Italia*.

Almost immediately, waiters began carrying out platters of fruit on silver trays, resting on top of white towels draped over their arms. Next come breads and pastries, then soups and platters of meats and vegetables and cookies and sherbets.

"Now don't eat too much," says the ship's doctor. "Dinner is going to be pretty good tonight. This is just a snack." He laughs at our surprised expressions.

The knot inside my stomach has finally relaxed. I eat some wonderful green soup—I have no idea what's in it—and a delicious sweet orange and a soft, hot roll with thick slabs of butter melting on it and a piece of chocolate cake four inches high.

After lunch, I go back on deck to watch for Cuxhaven. So does Herbert. He stands behind me, his camera in his hands. So far, there is no land, only the grayish-green, silvery water, flashing beneath us.

About a half-hour later, buildings and trees begin to appear on the horizon and we float into a narrow channel. Then I see Cuxhaven.

"Aunt Liesel, Aunt Liesel," I call softly, cupping my hands over my eyes to keep out the low sun that is breaking through the clouds. The ship moves quite close to the docks. I keep looking and looking and finally I spot Herr Broder with his camera, taking my picture, and then I see Ingrid and Arianna hopping up and down. Liesel and Fritz are beside them, waving and shouting. I can't make out what they are saying, but I shout back anyway: "Aunt Liesel! Aunt Liesel!"

The boat continues on, rounding the edge of the harbor and turning out to sea. Soon there are no more buildings, no more than the barest suggestion of something against the edge of the water, and then there is nothing but water.

I sigh, my emotions swirling as wildly as the foam under the prow of the ship.

Back in my cabin, I'm surprised to find, next to the heather bouquet, a stack of envelopes: letters from Henni and Klara and Ilse and my mother. I take them to the library, where I sit at a polished wooden desk and read them, then write back: "I'm here! I'm really here! And it's like a dream, like a fairy tale, only better than I could ever have imagined."

After an hour of writing, I walk back on deck. The waves are bigger now, with more white foam at the tops. We are surrounded by water. We are an island, an island on the move.

I find the gift shop, where I spot a gold necklace and bracelet that would go nicely with my formal dresses. The price tag says $10. I only have the money Aunt Bertha gave me: $17—not much, but enough for the jewelry. I almost walk out of the shop, then change my mind. Why not? I pay for the set, hoping the cashier is giving me correct change. Then I go back to my cabin. This time, my cabinmates are there.

"What do you think so far?" Frau Sturm asks politely.

"It's wonderful," I reply, trying not to sound as excited as I feel. "Look—I even got mail. Isn't that amazing?"

There's a rap on the door and a man carrying towels comes in, bowing. "Good afternoon, ladies. I'm Albert, your cabin attendant. Here are some warm towels. Is there anything else you need right now?"

"We're fine," says Frau Sturm. "Thank you, Albert."

Albert sets the towels in the bathroom, then goes to the door and bows again. "Dinner is in one hour. You may leave your shoes out in the hallway tonight to be cleaned. If you have any questions about anything, please let me know."

Albert leaves. Frau Sturm stretches out on her bunk and puts her arm over her eyes. "I'm going to try to get in a nap before dinner. I'm exhausted." Frau Hammer lies down, too.

I open the door to the bathroom, trying to find a private place to change clothes. Inside are a toilet and a shower. At least, that's what I think it is, from pictures I've seen of showers in American magazines.

My first shower. Why not do this, too, on my day of firsts? I lock the door, take off my clothes, and climb into the shower stall. I look around for a faucet or chain or some way to turn on the water. But I can't find anything.

I wrap myself in one of the fluffy warm towels Albert brought and step back into the cabin. Frau Sturm is snoring. Frau Hammer is lying with her eyes closed, but it doesn't look like she's asleep.

"Frau Hammer?" I whisper.

She doesn't move.

"Frau Hammer?" I say more loudly. Too loudly.

"What?" Frau Sturm yells, sitting up abruptly and looking like she doesn't know where she is. Frau Hammer sits up, too. "What is it? What's wrong?"

"I—I need help," I stammer, my cheeks hot. "The shower doesn't work."

Frau Hammer, frowning, follows me back into the bathroom. Frau Sturm sits up heavily and then she, too, comes in to see what the trouble is. Frau Hammer reaches into the shower and turns a knob that I hadn't noticed before. Water streams out of the nozzle. "What's the problem with it?" she asks.

"I couldn't get it adjusted," I say.

"You just turn here for hot and here for cold. Just like a regular shower," says Frau Hammer.

"Thanks," I say. "I'm sorry."

Frau Hammer and Frau Sturm exchange looks. They must think me the stupidest hick they've ever seen. I don't care, though. I lock the door again and climb under the streaming water, which is almost hot enough to burn, but not quite. Steam rises around me. Water hits and splashes me, all at once, tingling gloriously, unlike the little-bit-here, little-bit-there method of washing myself from a pail of water, which is what I've done all my life, even at Aunt Liesel's.

Afterward, I dress in the smooth, silky black dress from America. The gold necklace looks perfect with it. I fluff and pat my hair, put on lipstick, and feeling pretty and glamorous, go into the dining room, which is filled with women in sequin gowns and fur wraps and diamonds, with men in white and black tuxedoes, hair slicked back, shoes gleaming. Even though I'm not as grand as they are, I am one of them, at least for tonight.

The dining room for dinner is even lovelier than it had been for lunch. A table with ice sculptures in the shapes of swans sits at one end, covered with platters of fruit and pastries. A man plays a large white piano; other men with violins stand in the corners, their bows arched and ready. Bouquets of roses adorn each table and at each of our places rests a printed menu: "Premiere Dinner." Inside is a list of the courses we will be served, foods I've never heard of before: turtle soup and oysters and rack of lamb and goose pate and caviar.

"Ginger ale, fraulein?" asks a waiter, who has appeared at my elbow.

I take my first glass of ginger ale. It is golden and bubbly and tastes so much finer than the Coke I had in Kassel. It instantly becomes my favorite drink.

Along with the main courses, I sample crunchy purple grapes and slabs of juicy pineapple and two big oranges. I've never had grapes and pineapple before. Now there are trays in front of me with as many as I want, whenever I want them.

"I hope you have enjoyed your dinner," announces the captain. "There will be dancing in the ballroom until 2 a.m."

The captain leaves. Herbert and the daughter from California leave arm-in-arm for the ballroom, as does the married couple from New Mexico.

I follow, but pause at the entrance, watching the gilded scene before me, feeling far away, like a spy peeking through the window. This is too much. I don't belong here. These people waltzing and spinning and floating in their gowns and glitter aren't real.

I leave, looking for something that is a little more familiar. I find it in fast dance music blasting from the tourist-class hall. Here are people who look like me, in clothes that are not too fancy or probably even too new. There are no diamonds and furs in this room. Just a lot of laughter and cheers and, instead of champagne and caviar, beer and hot dogs.

Around 1 a.m., I finally leave the party. The air is chilly on the way back to my cabin, but I don't feel cold. The stiff frozen fear that filled me last night is gone. I am so relaxed, so warm, so happy that I barely feel my feet touching the ground.

I only wish my mother were here to share this with me.

The *Italia* stops twice, in South Hampton, England, and, the next day, in Le Havre, France, to pick up supplies and new passengers—and more mail for me. I catch glimpses of these foreign cities from the deck of the ship. We are not allowed to get off. From the harbor, the two countries look just like Germany. Big buildings and big ships and piers.

After leaving France, we encounter no more land. No more buildings or trees, no other people or even other boats, just the great nothingness that is the ocean, so dark and mysterious and beautiful. Its colors change constantly, depending on the light, on the waves, on what it chooses to reveal of itself. And it goes on forever. There is nothing else to see, except for the sky, and at certain times of day the ocean even claims the sky, the edges of blue fading into silver, melting along the horizon into the water until the entire world is nothing but a great shimmering vastness. Occasionally the sun or the moon or the stars break through to guide us, but it doesn't matter; even in darkness, we go on, on and on, the ship's engines a constant pulse of power, pushing us across the timeless, solitary sea.

In the afternoons, after lunch, I watch the crew toss our garbage into the ocean. When the unwanted pieces of lamb and chicken and veal hit the foamy tips of the waves, the sharks waiting just beneath the surface make their move. They rise, their black fins like the hilts of knives, their jaws already open, their yellow teeth flashing.

Some of the other passengers don't like watching the sharks, but I do. I don't fear them; I know that I am safe. I'm above them now, protected, unassailable. They can't hurt me. Nothing can hurt me any more.

Many people get seasick during the first few days at sea, as the ocean waters get choppier and the ship jumps and pitches. The dining rooms empty out; some days only Herbert and I and the ship's doctor are at our table. People throw up over the railings and walk around with peculiar greenish-yellow casts to their faces.

I don't get sick, though. Far from it. I don't think I've ever been this happy. All we are supposed to do on this ship, all that is required of us, our only task, is to enjoy ourselves. I've never had days like this before, days of pampering and ease and independence. I can sleep as late as I like, stay out as late as I like, eat whatever I want, not make my bed or do a single chore, all in the midst of a luxury and wealth that continues to amaze me.

I try to explain it to my mother in the letters I write her every day. I spend most afternoons in the library, writing. In the mornings, I sleep until 9 or 10 before taking a shower, then head to the dining room for breakfast. I've never slept this late in my life. Nor have I stayed up so late, either. I've been out every night until at least 2 in the morning, sometimes later, dancing and drinking, singing and chatting and laughing, with my new friends in tourist class. They aren't allowed to come into the first-class areas where I am staying, but I am free to go to tourist class—which is a good thing, because that is where I truly feel at home.

A few days after the trip begins, Stavros leans close to me at the dinner table. "I need to ask you something," he says haltingly. "Are you married?"

Oh, no. Not another one. "No."

"Do you have a boyfriend in America?"

"No."

Stavros smiles. I steel myself. I have no interest in him that way, or in any man.

"Good," he says. "Because Herbert wanted me to find out for him. He thought you were traveling to meet a boyfriend or husband in America and he didn't want to bother you if you were taken."

"Oh," I say. Herbert isn't at the table yet. He's a pleasant man and nice-looking, but I'm not interested in getting involved with anyone, especially not now. I've never had a boyfriend in my life; I've always been focused on getting to America. And now that I am almost there, a boyfriend truly is the last thing I need.

Not to mention the fact that I still don't trust men.

"Herbert likes you, you know," Stavros says, winking at me.

The next night, Herbert switches seats with Stavros, so that he can sit next to me. He asks me where I'm from, where I'm going. He tries to joke with me, to draw me out. He takes pictures of me at the table and promises to send copies of them to me after we get to America, if I give him my address.

I don't dislike Herbert. In fact, I kind of like him and I find his interest flattering. But I act as coolly as I can to him, while still being polite. Eventually he picks up on it and then he leaves me alone. He turns his attention to the many beautiful young women on the ship and I go back to my friends in tourist class, where Herbert never goes.

Every night at dinner, the captain announces our current time and the time it is in America. When we left Germany, we were six hours ahead of New York City. Every couple of days we cross a new time zone; every couple of days, we are an hour closer to America.

If it weren't for this brief mention of clocks and watches and the real world, I think it would be easy to forget that time even existed. In some ways, we are in a bubble, sealed off in our own private fantasy world. I feel as if I have always been here and always will be here, dancing and nibbling grapes and sipping ginger ale.

And then, before I know it, the trip is almost over.

"It's six o'clock," the captain announces. "And in New York, it is also six o'clock. This is our second-to-last dinner together. Enjoy!"

I try to do as he says, but the fizz is going out of my excitement. Fear, like fog, is creeping in around the edges.

The next morning, it hits me full-force. I wake up early, my heart racing. The sisters, as usual, are gone, their bunks already made. Everything is the same as yesterday and the day before and the day before that. The same rocking ship, the same soothing engine hums, the same faint sounds of people walking and talking and laughing.

But I'm not the same. The joy is gone. My stomach twists so sharply I bring my legs up. And then I am in the bathroom, getting sick. How can I get seasick now, when everybody else is back to normal? I skip breakfast, staying in the cabin, trying to breathe slowly and will my stomach into calmness. It doesn't work.

The sisters come back to wash up before lunch. They see me still in my bunk. "Are you all right?" asks Frau Sturm.

I shake my head. I can't talk.

After lunch, the ship's doctor comes to see me. He feels my forehead and my stomach. "How are we doing?" he asks gently.

"I don't know," I say. "What's wrong with me?"

"Nothing too terrible," he says, smiling. "Just some nerves causing some indigestion, I think. I'm ordering you some peppermint tea. That'll settle your stomach. Then you need to get up and start moving around."

He leaves and Albert brings me tea, which does help me feel a little better, though not well enough to think of eating anything. The thought of all the rich and foreign foods laid out in the dining room makes me queasy.

At lunch, I sip consomme and nibble crackers, not saying anything.

"You're awfully quiet today," says Herbert. "Is everything all right?"

"An upset stomach," I tell him. "How about you? Are you ready to land?"

Herbert folds his arm across his chest and frowns. "I don't know. I wish my English were better."

"Someone is meeting you, right?"

"My new boss. I've never seen him before. How about you?"

"My aunt." I don't want to talk about this, about landing.

The ship's doctor leans across the table and catches my eye. "Feeling better?"

"Yes, thank you."

"Good. You don't want to miss dinner tonight. The farewell dinners on the *Italia* are always the best."

Farewell. Good-bye. The last. The end.

I excuse myself and walk along the deck. So far, there is only the water, as far as I can see. There is no sign of America.

America, the land I've longed for all my life. Why am I so frightened now of finally arriving? It's true, though. I'm utterly terrified. I wish the ship would make a wrong turn and this dreamlike existence could go on forever. But it is time for real life to begin once again.

On my plate at dinner is an even fancier menu than usual. "Farewell Dinner," it says.

"This is it," sighs the woman from California. "Tomorrow we'll be in New York and then on a train to our home. It's been a good summer but I can't wait to get home."

"Me either," says the married woman from New Mexico.

Herbert and I look at each other. We are the only ones at our table who have left our homes.

"Will you be visiting America, too, Stavros?" I ask.

"No, I'm not allowed off the ship," he says. "I stay on and see how the ship is cleaned and refueled. Then I sail back again to Europe."

The waiters begin delivering the course, most of which I don't' touch, some of which I pick at. Beluga caviar, California fruit cocktail with cordial, soup a la Reine Hortense, green turtle soup with sherry, supreme of sole marguery, filet mignon with bearnaise sauce, roast turkey with liver stuffing, asparagus, demi-tasse.

I'd rather have my mother's fried sausage and potatoes than any of these foods. Actually, I'd rather have my mother beside me than anything else right now.

The plates appear, disappear. New plates, new courses, silverware clinking against the fine china, the murmurs of conversation floating across the room in accompaniment to the achingly sweet strains of the violinists.

The captain calls a final toast. "To the *Italia*," he says. We clink our glasses together around the room. "To America," he says. Another clink, like icicles breaking and falling to the ground.

"And to Germany. Never forget her."

"Hear, hear," some men call. I see a few women dab their eyes with their napkins and I remember how it was when the band played "Good-bye, Homeland, Good-bye" when we left Germany. I hope they don't play that song again. I don't think I could take it.

After the plates are cleared, I stay for a little while in first class, signing the backs of my tablemates' menus. They also sign mine, writing down their addresses so that we can keep in touch with each other.

"Honor your new fatherland but always love your own," writes the ship's doctor.

I hug the California mother and daughter good-bye and shake hands with Herbert and Stavros and the married couple from New Mexico.

Then I go to tourist class, where there is another hot-dog party in full swing. I try, but I can't seem to get into the jolly spirit of the place. I go on deck. The air tonight isn't as cold as it had been in the middle of the Atlantic. A few couples are strolling, arm in arm, but most people are still below deck, dancing.

I need to be by myself. I find a deserted spot at the end of the ship and stand for a long time, watching the stars in the sky and their reflection in the dark water.

36

When I wake up, Frau Sturm and Frau Hammer are rushing around, packing last-minute items and double-checking to be sure they haven't forgotten anything.

I sit up in a panic. I can't believe this day is finally here and I have overslept.

"I'm going to leave our tips in these envelopes on my nightstand," Frau Sturm tells Frau Hammer, as she slips paper money into some envelopes that she is carrying.

"All right," says Frau Hammer, who is putting a sweater into her large suitcase.

"Good morning, Tilli," Frau Sturm says. "My goodness, you slept late. Aren't you going to get ready? And by the way, where are you leaving your tips?"

"Tips?"

"You know, what you're giving the waiters and cabin attendants and everybody who has served us. You do know about tips, don't you?"

"No," I say in a small voice. "What are we supposed to leave?"

"Altogether, about ten percent of the fare," says Frau Sturm. She stands up. "Do we have everything?" Frau Hammer closes her suitcase. "We're all set."

"Good-bye, then, Tilli," says Frau Sturm, giving me a quick, polite hug. Frau Hammer follows. "Good luck to you, dear." Then the two women roll their suitcases outside the door for the porter and leave for the deck.

I don't know what to do about leaving a tip. I don't have any extra money. My ticket cost Aunt Bertha an enormous sum, 1,200 marks, or $400, which I plan to pay her back as soon as I can, as soon as I get a job. Ten percent of the fare is $40, but all I have is $3, which isn't enough for even one person's tip. To leave this would be an insult. And I don't want to step into a foreign country with absolutely no money in my pocket.

Frau Sturm's tip envelopes glare at me reproachfully. I look away. There's nothing I can do; I can't leave anybody anything. They will just have to understand.

261

I take a final quick shower, put on the wool suit, pack the rest of my dresses in my suitcase, lock it, and set it on my bunk. I hear shouts from the deck and run quickly upstairs. People are crowded along one side, yelling and pointing. I turn my head to see what they are looking at.

It is her: the Statue of Liberty, just like in the pictures. A great greenish-gray stone lady, with a crown that looks like the thorns on Jesus' head, in robes like the ones the Greek goddesses are wearing in the pictures on the *Italia*'s walls.

So many thousands upon thousands of people have come here before me, have traveled across the ocean like this, just so that they could redeem this statue's promise, this country's pledge. Freedom. This is the land of freedom. No Russians. No secret police or concentration camps. No spies and whispers, no doors kicked open, no terror in the night. No more of that for me.

People around me are crying and hugging each other and pointing. The wind has picked up and the tears on my cheeks feel frozen in place.

Closer and closer we get to the statue. She smiles gently. I spot Herbert in the crowd, snapping pictures. Behind the statue I see a skyline, a faint row of buildings taller than the clouds. Slowly the *Italia* approaches, almost drifting in the water, the engines louder now. Clusters of birds swoop in the sky and then we are in a harbor, turning slowly in the shallow water, making our way to the end of a long dock.

The ship jerks. The engine quiets. We are here.

Passengers crowd toward the stairs. One of the crew members starts yelling instructions. I can see other crew members climbing down from the ship and scurrying around the dock with ropes, tying things up.

"First class leaves first. Tourist class, you have to wait," the crewman calls out.

I push my way through the crowd down the stairs to my cabin, grab my suitcase, then go down the walkway to the edge of the dock.

I am in America.

Aunt Bertha, where are you? I look and look. There are people everywhere, but not the person I most want to see, most need to see. Aunt Bertha, where are you? Fear grips me. What if something has happened to her? What if she was in a terrible accident and can't meet me here?

What if I am alone?

A big sign says Customs. "Over here, over here!" a crewman from our ship is yelling, waving his arms to direct the crowd surging off the *Italia*. I follow the group and find myself in a line. Aunt Bertha?

"What's happening?" I ask a man in front of me, who is carrying two huge suitcases and pushing a third on wheels.

"Customs," he says shortly, checking his watch. "Shouldn't be long."

"What's Customs?" I ask.

"You have to declare what you bought in Germany, what you're bringing in of value."

"But I don't have anything," I say.

"Doesn't matter."

The line inches ahead. I can't believe I have come to America only to stand in more lines. But it's true and I do. Finally it's my turn. Two stern men in dark blue uniforms motion me forward.

"Passport?" one says to me in English. I hand it to him. He motions to my suitcase. "Open it."

"I have nothing," I say.

"Open it or you can't clear Customs."

I set the suitcase on the table and realize with horror that it is locked and I don't have the key.

"Open it," the man says impatiently. I can feel the crowd pressing against me.

"I don't have the key," I say. "It's on the ship. I have to go back and get it."

The man looks at me suspiciously. He turns to the other blue-uniformed man. They whisper together. Aunt Bertha, I need you. "All right," says the man. "We'll keep your bag here."

I turn around and fight my way against the stream of passengers, trying to make my way back to the stairway. At the foot of the stairs someone from the ship is directing traffic. "Please, I have to go back," I tell him. He looks at me skeptically. "Please, I was just on your ship and I forgot something."

"Name?" he says, looking at a list he is carrying. I tell him my name and he nods. "All right, but hurry. We're about to release tourist class."

I climb the stairs again. Hundreds of people—the entire tourist class—are still on deck, waiting, looking worried and impatient. I wave to a few of the people I've come to know from the dances and parties. Some of them wave back. Others ignore me.

I hurry to my cabin. Please be there. Please be there.

Inside my nightstand drawer is my wallet. In my wallet is my key. I sigh with relief, clutch my wallet to my chest and rush back up the stairs, out the ship, and down through the crowds to Customs. I find the official who has my suitcase, wait again until it is my turn, then produce my key, smiling.

He doesn't smile back. I guess it is his job not to smile. "Open it," he says.

I do. He lifts my clothes gently, sifting through my things. Then he closes the lid, takes my passport, stamps it and hands it back to me, along with my suitcase. "All right," he says. "Next!"

I take my suitcase and cross under the Customs sign, scanning the crowd, the endless crowd of people pushing their way along the docks. In the distance are huge buildings and I can smell the city, a smell of cars and heat and people and food and fish, all rolling up to greet me.

Aunt Bertha, please God be here.

Then I see her. At the same moment, she sees me.

"Tilli!" Aunt Bertha yells, waving. She starts moving toward me, fighting through the throngs of people, her arms reaching out to me.

"Aunt Bertha!"

We find each other in the crowd. Everything else melts away as she holds me. Then we turn, arm in arm, and step away from the docks, toward the city, toward my new life.

Epilogue

In America, I was reborn. That's how it has always seemed to me. I did not come fully alive, I did not find my true self, until I came to America.

After leaving the *Italia*, Aunt Bertha and I spent three days in New York, going to the top of the Empire State Building, Radio City Music Hall, Central Park. I didn't really like New York, though. There was so much poverty, which I had not expected, not in the land I'd always believed to be so wealthy. Everywhere we turned, there were men in rags, lying on the ground, begging for money. I hadn't realized that this, too, was the face of America.

We took a train to Canton, Ohio, to stay for a few days with a friend of Aunt Bertha's who lived in a lovely, flower-filled little house encircled with a white picket fence, just as I had pictured an American house would look. One day we visited the Hoover mansion, home to the Hoovers of vacuum-cleaner fame. Aunt Bertha had once worked at that mansion, which was even more magnificent than Victoria's castle back in east Germany.

Then we went to Chicago, where Aunt Bertha lived in a small house with Aunt Anna and Uncle Hans. I got a job right away, working in a television factory. That lasted only a few months, until Christmas, when the factory closed. After that, I got a better job at the A.C. Nielsen Co., doing secretarial work. As soon as I could afford it, Aunt Bertha and I moved into our own apartment.

My days were busy and happy. Every weekend, Aunt Bertha showed me a new part of Chicago. We visited every museum and, it seemed, every restaurant and shop as well. I joined the German-American Youth Choir and on weekends went to dances and parties at German clubs in Chicago. I also began taking English and typing lessons.

During my first year in Chicago, I learned who I was and, in a way, experienced the childhood I'd never had. I realized that I was a person who likes to laugh, to dance, to be with people. I liked to be silly. I'd never had much chance to be silly before. Now I reveled in it.

Shortly after settling in Chicago, I wrote to Herbert Schulze to ask him for copies of the pictures he had taken of me while we were on the ship. I had only been able to buy a couple from the ship's photographer, since I had so little money. I wasn't sure if Herbert would write back to me. The last time I had seen him was on the docks, after I had been reunited with Aunt Bertha. Herbert had walked past me, looking pale and nervous, his eyes scanning the crowds. "Can I help you?" I asked him, knowing his English was weaker than mine. But Herbert ignored me and brushed past me without speaking. I shrugged, a little hurt, but figuring that was the way things were on ships. Some friends were trip-friends only. Herbert must have been like that.

Still, he had promised me the pictures, and I did want to have them. So I wrote to him. Herbert wrote back that he would send me one picture in each letter. To get more pictures, I had to agree to write him back. That was his deal.

As our letters back and forth continued, they became longer and more intimate and suddenly I found that they were the thing I looked forward to most in my life. After about six months of this, in May 1953, Herbert came to Chicago for a visit. We got engaged the next month; a year later, on May 1, 1954, we were married.

The first man that I met on the *Italia*, the one that I am standing next to in the picture that Herr Broder took from the shores of Cuxhaven as I left Germany, was Herbert. He likes to tell me that we were destined to be together. I think he is right.

Herbert and I settled in the Midwest and raised two children. I live now in a comfortable house in the country, with a flower garden all along the back wall, surrounding a brick patio, where I like to sit in the evenings and watch for the family of wild turkeys that sometimes walks beneath the linden tree I planted at the edge of our yard to remind me of Doelitz. I have a peaceful life and yet still, when I am outside and a crop-dusting plane buzzes overhead, I jump, my heart pounding, and wonder when the fear will ever leave me.

In many ways, my life in America has been better than I dreamed. Of course, the country isn't as perfect, as ideal, as I had imagined it to be. I've had rough times and I've encountered prejudice. When I began working at the Nielsen Co., a woman there seemed to hate me and would tell me that I didn't belong there. I didn't understand why she didn't like me. My boss explained that she was Jewish. By then I had learned more about what the Nazis had done to the Jews—we were told very little in Germany, even after the war ended. I could understand why she would hate Nazis. But I couldn't understand why she was blaming me for their actions. I was a victim of the Nazis, too.

Later, when Herbert and I moved to various houses in small towns and suburbs, I was called Nazi. Mostly it was children: young boys, screaming the word and throwing rocks at my house; although sometimes adults called me this, too. Once, my daughter came home from school and told me she couldn't wear her beautiful dirndl dress from Germany any more. "The boys call it my Nazi dress," she said, puzzled and hurt. I figured all of them—the adults and the children—were ignorant and I tried not to let their words, their blind hatred, bother me.

I also didn't let their hatred of Germany poison my feelings toward my homeland. I tried to model myself after Aunt Bertha, sending what I could to my relatives still living there and helping those who wanted to come to America.

I wanted to bring Aunt Liesel to America right after Herbert and I were married, but we didn't have enough money to sponsor her, so Aunt Bertha did. Aunt Liesel and Fritz—who by then had gotten married—came to Chicago, where they stayed for the next seventeen years, before returning to Germany.

A few years after Aunt Liesel came, Herbert and I brought my brother Hugo over. He got a job in Chicago as an orthopedic shoemaker and eventually moved to California.

The only other person from my family who came to America is Ingrid, who emigrated in 1959, married an American, and moved to Florida.

Aunt Bertha stayed in Evanston until she retired. Then she moved back to West Germany, though she returned to America for visits several times. She developed Alzheimer's disease and died in the early 1970s.

My mother visited me a couple of times, but refused to leave Germany, even after all her land was taken away from her in 1956. The Communists said there should be no private land ownership, so they took away the farms of all of the seventy-eight farmers who had settled Doelitz. My mother was devastated. She had been so proud of being able to make something of herself and she truly loved her land. After that, she moved to a small apartment in Gnoien. Heinz and his wife, Gisela, and their children stayed in our old family home. When my mother was sixty-five and eligible for senior citizens' aid, the Communists finally gave her permission to leave. I think they didn't want to have to pay for her care. She went to stay with Helmut in West Germany.

Helmut had had a rough life. A few years after I left Doelitz, he was working on the farm and saw a man with a gun, which was a forbidden thing. Helmut took the gun away and tossed it in a nearby creek. Someone saw him and reported him to the Communists, who threw him in jail for a year. When he got out, he bought some gas that turned out to be stolen and got in trouble with the Communists again. Finally he escaped to West Germany.

I visited Helmut during the mid-1970s and couldn't believe the change in him. He looked broken, somehow; the wild, joyful spirit he had always possessed was gone. He never came to America, even for a visit. He died of esophageal cancer in 1981.

Willi and Heinz also both died of esophageal cancer, and I can't help but wonder if their deaths were linked to the chemical fertilizers the three of them used to spread, without gloves or masks, when they all worked together on our farm. I'll never know the answer to that.

Paula stayed in East Germany, even after Willi's death, living alone. She doesn't want to move to America. She visits me from time to time, bringing her knitting with her, helping out in the garden, cooking special yeast cakes for us. Her hands are always busy. She reminds me so much of my mother.

In November 1989, the Berlin Wall fell, finally freeing Doelitz and the rest of eastern Germany. In 1991, I traveled to Doelitz for my first visit since my escape forty years earlier. I stayed for a week, walking around, visiting my old school and the cemetery and the park, seeing my old friends and neighbors—the few who were still alive. I was amazed and saddened by the changes in the village, at how dirty everything had become. The air no longer was crisp, the sky no longer blue; the dirty coal that they had burned since the war had left a thick brownish haze over everything. Many people had gotten cancer or become alcoholics.

It was so odd to see my old house, which was so much smaller and darker than I had remembered. The brown air seemed to have slunk into the stone walls and left its stain everywhere. The upstairs had been remodeled; my bedroom was gone, the smokehouse room was gone. I didn't ask if the secret attic was still there. I didn't want to see it.

While I was in Doelitz, I stayed with Henni, who had married a farmer and had five children. One of her sons had refused to join the Red Army and been imprisoned for years; Henni didn't want to talk about this. She had had a botched hysterectomy and had lost an arm, a leg, part of another leg and most of the fingers on her remaining hand. Even more than the disfigurement of her body, what shocked me was the crippling of her spirit. She was so frightened by the fall of Communism, by the downing of the Berlin Wall. She didn't know what was going to happen to her without the Communists to run things and take care of everybody. Her freedom terrified her.

I saw Klara briefly; she had moved to Gnoien where she was living with her second husband. I didn't see Ilse, who had become a doctor. She had married another doctor, an orthopedic surgeon, and they began to practice in East Germany. But doctors were watched carefully by the Communists, who feared and distrusted them. Her husband couldn't stand it and defected. The Communists made Ilse stay in East Germany for years, until she fell ill. Then they allowed her to rejoin her husband in the West.

When my mother was in her seventies, she saw Robert—her first love, the man who had fathered Dora. He gave my mother a ring. They talked about how their lives had gone wrong, about how things might have been if they had been allowed to marry.

"Are you going to see him again?" I asked her.

"No," she said. "It's too late. Robert's married to someone else. That's all right. It's God's will."

My mother never saw Robert again. She died in 1979.

Every year on July 10, her birthday, I cut three of the most beautiful roses from my garden and put them in a vase beside my best picture of her. I close my eyes and imagine her next to me, and sometimes I can feel her presence, and always I can hear her singing.

My thoughts are free, who can guess them?
They fly by, like nightly shadows.
No one can guess them, no one can shoot them.
It's a fact, my thoughts are free.

0-595-66504-7

Printed in the United States
21215LVS00002BD/1-24